# MOO'S LAW™

## AN INVESTOR'S GUIDE TO THE NEW AGRARIAN REVOLUTION

# BY JIM MELLON

*Foreword by Bruce Friedrich*

**Fruitful**
PUBLICATIONS

This first edition first published in 2020

© 2020 Jim Mellon

Fruitful Publications Limited (t/a Fruitful Publications), English company number 09314658.

For customer service and for information about how to apply for permission to use any copyright material in this book (including permission to reproduce extracts in other published works) please email orders@fruitfulpublications.com or see www.mooslawbook.com

Cover design: Billie Argent  www.billieargent.co.uk

Internal design: Studio Kaioti  www.studiokaioti.com

**Animals have done us no harm and they have no power of resistance. There is something so very dreadful in tormenting those who have never harmed us, who cannot defend themselves, who are utterly in our power.**

Saint John Henry Newman

(1801-1890)

**J**IM MELLON IS A VISIONARY BRITISH ENTREPRENEUR, INVESTOR, AUTHOR, AND PHILANTHROPIST, WITH INTERESTS IN A NUMBER OF SECTORS. HE HAS SUBSTANTIAL REAL ESTATE ASSETS IN GERMANY AND THE ISLE OF MAN, AS WELL AS HOLDINGS IN PRIVATE AND PUBLIC COMPANIES THROUGH THE BURNBRAE GROUP, HIS PRIVATE INVESTMENT COMPANY.

After leaving Oriel College, Oxford, where he studied Philosophy, Politics and Economics, he worked in Asia and the United States in two fund management companies, GT Management and Thornton Management (Asia) Limited, before founding Regent Pacific Group Limited in 1991, subsequently quoted on the Hong Kong Stock Exchange.

Jim spends most of his time investigating and working on startup ideas, inspired by his ability to identify technologies and companies that will reshape people's lives, before they start trending. His investment philosophy of focussing on these hyper-innovative technologies and novel companies has led him to be recognised as one of the most successful investors of his generation. His monthly "Mellon on the Markets" column in *Master Investor Magazine*, where he updates his readers on his latest trading and investing activities, has gained him a cult status among investors.

6

He is the co-author of six books, all written with a view to identifying emerging thematic trends leading to early stage investment opportunities. Notably, in his book *Wake Up! Survive and Prosper in the Coming Economic Turmoil (2005)*, he forecasted the global financial crisis of 2008-2009. He followed this with *The Top 10 Investments for the Next 10 Years (2008)*, *Cracking the Code (2012)*, and *Fast Forward (2014)*. His last book *Juvenescence: Investing in the Age of Longevity (2017)* played a role in bringing ageing research into the mainstream. It led to the formation of the company of which he is co-founder and chairman, Juvenescence – which develops therapies that will enable people worldwide to live longer, healthier lives. They actively look for scientific founders probing exciting areas of ageing biology, and work with leading research institutions to create joint ventures combining their IP and Juvenescence's resources.

Like many of the founders featured in this book, Jim is deeply passionate about the fight against animal cruelty. He is a pescatarian and a dog-lover and has set his eye on the alternative proteins space having come to realise the alarming levels of food scarcity in the world and the environmental damage industrial farming has done to our planet. He views the alternative protein trend as a money fountain which will rapidly revolutionise global consumption habits. He is co-founder and director of Agronomics, a London-listed investment company which is building a portfolio of investments in the most promising cultivated protein companies in the field of cellular agriculture.

Mr Mellon is a non-executive director of Condor Gold plc and the executive chairman of the board of Manx Financial Group plc, which are listed on the Alternative Investment Market of the London Stock Exchange.

Jim is a co-founder and trustee of The Longevity Forum. He is on the Board of Trustees of the Buck Institute for Aging Research in California and of the American Federation for Aging (AFAR). He is also a trustee of the Biogerontology Research Foundation as well as The Lifeboat Foundation and sits on the Advisory Board for the Milken Institute's Centre for the Future of Aging. He is also a Fellow of Oriel College, Oxford, and the Chairman of the college Funding Campaign.

*This book is dedicated to*

HORATIO 2006-2020

# CONTENTS

# MOO'S LAW

# Contents

# Contents

# Contents

# TOWARDS THE NEW AGRARIAN REVOLUTION

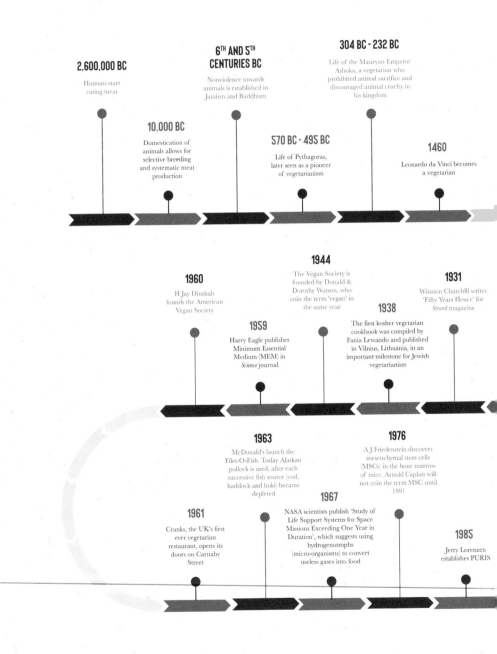

**2,600,000 BC**

Humans start eating meat

**6ᵀᴴ AND 5ᵀᴴ CENTURIES BC**

Nonviolence towards animals is established in Jainism and Buddhism

**304 BC - 232 BC**

Life of the Mauryan Emperor Ashoka, a vegetarian who prohibited animal sacrifice and discouraged animal cruelty in his kingdom

**10,000 BC**

Domestication of animals allows for selective breeding and systematic meat production

**570 BC - 495 BC**

Life of Pythagoras, later seen as a pioneer of vegetarianism

**1460**

Leonardo da Vinci becomes a vegetarian

**1960**

H Jay Dinshah founds the American Vegan Society

**1944**

The Vegan Society is founded by Donald & Dorothy Watson, who coin the term 'vegan' in the same year

**1931**

Winston Churchill writes 'Fifty Years Hence' for *Strand* magazine

**1959**

Harry Eagle publishes Minimum Essential Medium (MEM) in *Science* journal

**1938**

The first kosher vegetarian cookbook was compiled by Fania Lewando and published in Vilnius, Lithuania, in an important milestone for Jewish vegetarianism

**1963**

McDonald's launch the Filet-O-Fish. Today Alaskan pollock is used, after each successive fish source (cod, haddock and hoki) became depleted

**1976**

A J Friedenstein discovers mesenchymal stem cells (MSCs) in the bone marrow of mice. Arnold Caplan will not coin the term MSC until 1991

**1961**

Cranks, the UK's first ever vegetarian restaurant, opens its doors on Carnaby Street

**1967**

NASA scientists publish 'Study of Life Support Systems for Space Missions Exceeding One Year in Duration', which suggests using hydrogenotrophs (micro-organisms) to convert useless gases into food

**1985**

Jerry Lorenzen establishes PURIS

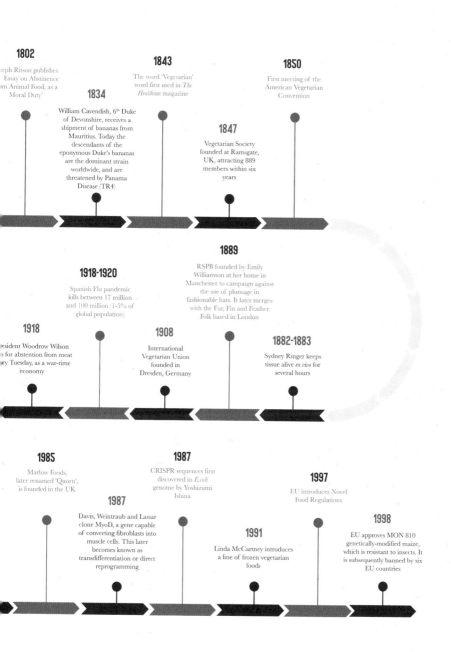

**1802**
...eph Ritson publishes Essay on Abstinence ...m Animal Food, as a Moral Duty'

**1834**
William Cavendish, 6ᵗʰ Duke of Devonshire, receives a shipment of bananas from Mauritius. Today the descendants of the eponymous Duke's bananas are the dominant strain worldwide, and are threatened by Panama Disease (TR4)

**1843**
The word 'Vegetarian' word first used in *The Healthian* magazine

**1847**
Vegetarian Society founded at Ramsgate, UK, attracting 889 members within six years

**1850**
First meeting of the American Vegetarian Convention

**1918-1920**
Spanish Flu pandemic kills between 17 million and 100 million (1-5% of global population)

**1889**
RSPB founded by Emily Williamson at her home in Manchester to campaign against the use of plumage in fashionable hats. It later merges with the Fur, Fin and Feather Folk based in London

**1918**
...esident Woodrow Wilson ...s for abstention from meat ...ry Tuesday, as a war-time economy

**1908**
International Vegetarian Union founded in Dresden, Germany

**1882-1883**
Sydney Ringer keeps tissue alive *ex vivo* for several hours

**1985**
Marlow Foods, later renamed 'Quorn', is founded in the UK

**1987**
CRISPR sequences first discovered in *E.coli* genome by Yoshizumi Ishina

**1987**
Davis, Weintraub and Lassar clone MyoD, a gene capable of converting fibroblasts into muscle cells. This later becomes known as transdifferentiation or direct reprogramming

**1991**
Linda McCartney introduces a line of frozen vegetarian foods

**1997**
EU introduces Novel Food Regulations

**1998**
EU approves MON 810 genetically-modified maize, which is resistant to insects. It is subsequently banned by six EU countries

17

# TOWARDS THE NEW AGRARIAN REVOLUTION

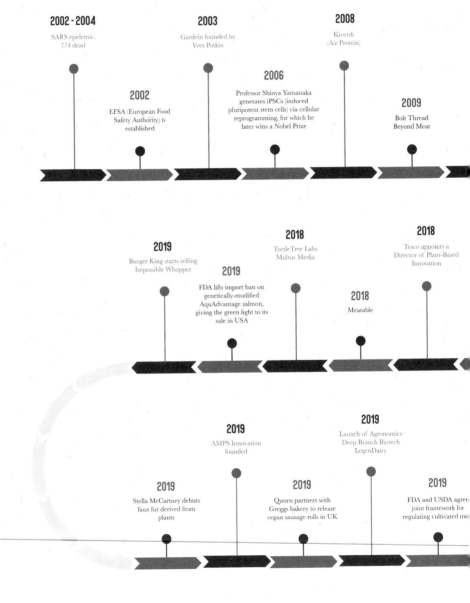

**2002 - 2004**
SARS epidemic.
774 dead

**2003**
Gardein founded by
Yves Potkin

**2008**
Kiverdi
(Air Protein)

**2002**
EFSA (European Food
Safety Authority) is
established

**2006**
Professor Shinya Yamanaka
generates iPSCs (induced
pluripotent stem cells) via cellular
reprogramming, for which he
later wins a Nobel Prize

**2009**
Bolt Thread
Beyond Meat

**2019**
Burger King starts selling
Impossible Whopper

**2018**
TurtleTree Labs
Multus Media

**2018**
Tesco appoints a
Director of Plant-Based
Innovation

**2019**
FDA lifts import ban on
genetically-modified
AquAdvantage salmon,
giving the green light to its
sale in USA

**2018**
Meatable

**2019**
AMPS Innovation
founded

**2019**
Launch of Agronomics
Deep Branch Biotech
LegenDairy

**2019**
Stella McCartney debuts
faux fur derived from
plants

**2019**
Quorn partners with
Greggs bakery to release
vegan sausage rolls in UK

**2019**
FDA and USDA agree
joint framework for
regulating cultivated me[...]

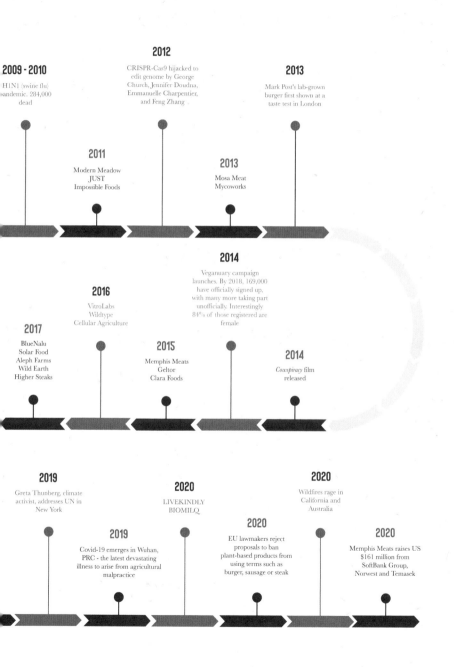

**2009 - 2010**

H1N1 (swine flu) pandemic. 284,000 dead

**2012**

CRISPR-Cas9 hijacked to edit genome by George Church, Jennifer Doudna, Emmanuelle Charpentier, and Feng Zhang

**2013**

Mark Post's lab-grown burger first shown at a taste test in London

**2011**

Modern Meadow
JUST
Impossible Foods

**2013**

Mosa Meat
Mycoworks

**2014**

Veganuary campaign launches. By 2018, 169,000 have officially signed up, with many more taking part unofficially. Interestingly 84% of those registered are female

**2016**

VitroLabs
Wildtype
Cellular Agriculture

**2017**

BlueNalu
Solar Food
Aleph Farms
Wild Earth
Higher Steaks

**2015**

Memphis Meats
Geltor
Clara Foods

**2014**

*Cowspiracy* film released

**2019**

Greta Thunberg, climate activist, addresses UN in New York

**2020**

LIVEKINDLY
BIOMILQ

**2020**

Wildfires rage in California and Australia

**2019**

Covid-19 emerges in Wuhan, PRC - the latest devastating illness to arise from agricultural malpractice

**2020**

EU lawmakers reject proposals to ban plant-based products from using terms such as burger, sausage or steak

**2020**

Memphis Meats raises US $161 million from SoftBank Group, Norwest and Temasek

19

# FOREWORD: THE NEXT AGRICULTURAL REVOLUTION

—

## BRUCE FRIEDRICH
## THE GOOD FOOD INSTITUTE

**T**HIS BOOK COULD NOT HAVE BEEN WRITTEN AT A MORE OPPORTUNE TIME. AS I SIT DOWN TO WRITE THIS FOREWORD, THE WALL STREET JOURNAL'S FRONT PAGE IS ANNOUNCING RECORD CLOSURES OF RETAIL STORES DUE TO COVID-19'S IMPACT ON SHOPPING. FURTHER INTO THE PAPER, WE LEARN THAT DISNEY AND THE AIRLINES ARE LAYING OFF TENS OF THOUSANDS OF WORKERS. THREE US STATES ARE ON FIRE. AND FOR THE FIRST TIME IN DECADES, EXTREME POVERTY IS GETTING WORSE. IT FEELS A LOT LIKE THE END TIMES.

This book is a vote in favour of a hopeful future. *Moo's Law*$^{TM}$ is about solutions and optimism and the ability of human innovation to radically transform something we thought we understood – the nature of food and farming.

I started thinking about the impact of agriculture in the mid-1980s during the famine in Ethiopia. That horrible event killed more than one million people and displaced millions more. I learned a few years later while studying resource economics at the LSE that while the famine in Ethiopia was a particularly stark example of a broken global food system, tens of millions of people globally were dying every year from famine-related causes.

However, because of the efforts of many highly dedicated people, humanity has made tremendous progress on famine since the 1980s. As Steven Pinker lays out admirably in Bill Gates' favorite book of all time, *Enlightenment Now*, famine and hunger are way down, and life expectancies are way up. By nearly every measure, there has never been a better time to be alive than today.

But it may not always feel like it. Eight hundred million people still live in extreme poverty and two billion are drinking water contaminated with faeces. After decades of progress, Covid-19 is increasing the number of people in poverty, and global warming is increasing hunger and displacement. The challenges are not going to get easier.

We need to figure this out. This is, by far, the wealthiest humanity has ever been, and it just keeps getting wealthier. We need to use this abundance to ensure that the whole world has its basic necessities met. We have to figure out how to feed 10 billion people by 2050. We're going to have to figure out what to do about wildfires in Australia, Brazil, the United States, and other countries around the world. We're going to have to figure out what to do about desertification and melting glaciers. We have to figure out what to do about the high likelihood of another pandemic, perhaps of a virus even more lethal or even more transmissible than Covid-19. Or both.

This book represents a great step forward in figuring out humanity's answer to those questions: We need to fundamentally change our food system. We need to make meat better.

In short, funneling crops through animals so that we can eat meat from those animals is vastly and inherently inefficient. According to the World Resources Institute, it takes nine kilojoules of energy fed to a chicken to produce one kilojoule in the form of chicken meat. That represents 800% food waste. And chickens are the most efficient animals at turning crops into meat. Similarly, one kilojoule of protein from chicken meat, the least climate-change inducing animal, causes 40 times as much climate change as one kilojoule of protein from legumes like peas and soya. All told, meat production causes more climate change than all the planes, lorries, cars, and other forms of transport combined.

And the list of other external costs of our current method of making meat goes on and on, including antimicrobial resistance, decimated oceans, biodiversity loss, food poisoning, and more.

Perhaps the most salient concern right now is the likelihood that our present method of farming animals will cause another pandemic. The UN Environment Programme has enumerated the seven most likely causes of the next pandemic, and number one is the farming of animals for protein, and number two is the intensive farming of animals.

But make no mistake: simply telling as many people as possible about the problem will not solve it. More and more articles will not solve it. At the end of the day, food choices are not made in our rational brain. For the vast majority of people, if they can afford to eat meat, they will eat meat. And the more they can afford, the more they will eat. That's what we've learned over the past 50 years as meat consumption has gone up and up and up.

So it's no surprise that the UN says we're going to need to produce 50 to 100 percent more meat by 2050 if we stay on our current trajectory. Honestly, we need a global solution, and it's not going to be some sort of educational campaign. That's been tried, and it hasn't worked, even in the US and Europe, where the external costs of meat production are very well-understood.

We need a new plan, and that's what this book is about: Giving consumers everything they love about meat – the taste, the texture, and the entire experience – but made in a way that both allows all to be fed and that does not jeopardize the future of life on this planet.

Right now, if you want to grow a chicken breast, you have to plan years in advance; you have to breed and grow breeder birds, incubate the eggs, and wait six or seven weeks from the time the animal hatches to the time she is sent to the abattoir. With plant-based meat, you can instantly turn crops into meat in a factory. With cultivated meat (meat grown directly from cells), you can grow that chicken breast in a few days.

Because these products are more efficient, as the production scales up, they will cost less. That means there is a lot of money to be made in this transformation. Just like cell phones and Zoom and Google Meet have replaced how we communicate, making meat from plants and growing it directly from cells will radically transform how we think about meat. In a generation or two, we will have divorced the concept of meat from the need for live animals, just like photography does not require film and phones do not require cords.

This new way of making meat will be better for farmers. The current culture of 'get big or get out' is destroying small farmers in both developed and developing economies. Plant-based meat will create an incentive and a market for high value crops. Similarly, the worst jobs in developed economies involve working on factory farms and in abattoirs. Production of plant-based and cultivated meat will create excellent manufacturing jobs that don't involve the unsafe and unhealthful conditions of massive animal factories and the slaughter of live animals.

This book is the story of the happy and optimistic food heroes who are leading the charge to the next agricultural revolution. I hope you enjoy their stories as much as I have.

# BRUCE FRIEDRICH

*Founder and executive director, The Good Food Institute*

# INTRODUCTION

—

**W**HEN I WAS A YOUNG FUND MANAGER, MORE THAN THIRTY YEARS AGO, I VISITED TAIPEI ON BUSINESS, AND MORE RELEVANTLY ITS FAMED SNAKE ALLEY. THERE, IN THE MIDST OF A LESS THAN SALUBRIOUS DISTRICT, RESTAURANTS AND STALLS PEDDLED SNAKE BLOOD MIXED WITH STRONG SPIRIT, AND OTHERS SOLD SNAKE MEAT.

All those restaurants and stalls have now closed, and the market, formerly boisterous and exotic, is a sad shadow of its former self.

Taiwan is one of the few countries to have handled the coronavirus in an exemplary and disciplined fashion, with few cases and relatively few deaths.

However, on the mainland, in the People's Republic of China, exotic markets (so called 'wet markets' because animals are slaughtered in front of customers), still persisted right until the recent worldwide pandemic swept them away, at least we hope so. These types of markets, or in particular, the infamous Wuhan Wet Market, were the most likely source of the coronavirus that has killed many thousands and crashed the world economy.

Whatever the truth of the matter, it is certain that the coronavirus was caused by animal to human transmission, so-called 'zoonosis' – probably via bats – of a virulent disease for which humans were ill prepared.

Similarly, all the other respiratory diseases of recent history – SARS, MERS, H1N1 swine flu – are the direct result of animal to human infection, and all relate to methods of farming and the misuse of animals.

There is no doubt in my mind that this transmission route, which has caused the greatest health emergency since the Spanish Flu of 1918 to 1920 is an immediate consequence of these unsound farming and husbandry practices.

It is for imperative human health reasons, along with others encompassing the environment, animal cruelty, land and water usage, and food security, that I have written this book.

Farming MUST change, attitudes to food HAVE to change, we MUST change.

And we have the means to do it. Today. Plant-based proteins are already being sold widely, including the well-known burger substitutes such as The Beyond Burger, and cell cultured meats are going to be sold at scale in the relatively near future. These meats, grown in labs, and encompassing most of the species widely eaten across the world, represent a singular advance in farming methods that will sweep the world, and render inhumane and, frankly, dangerous farming practices obsolete. In my opinion, there is no humane way of farming animals.

Along with longevity and climate change initiatives, farming forms part of the 'Holy Trinity' of investment opportunities in the next 50 years.

This book covers the key areas in the new field, the potential winners (and losers), the makers of products, both meat and animal by-products, as well as the engineering and biotech skills needed to make this revolution happen.

*Moo's Law*™ touches on the reasons why this must and will occur and deals with the ethical and regulatory issues surrounding the nascent industry.

As in all new industries, there will be failures, disappointments and hurdles to be overcome – and so selection of companies based on management, intellectual property and commercial savvy is a prerequisite to success. Here I attempt to triage the best of them for my readers' consideration.

It is early days yet, but the time to make the investments is NOW and I present readers with possible opportunities for their portfolios at the back of the book.

I have deliberately kept this book stripped down, with the science explained at a high level and the detail of the companies presented in a bare-bones fashion.

But I have also included a substantial bibliography, links to useful research tools, and reflections on my access as an investor and early adopter of the industry to the best minds and people in the field.

My thanks go to everyone who has helped me: Anthony Chow, my long-standing colleague who is running Agronomics, the leading investment company in the field; Trish Wilson, Luke Sheridan and Ben Goddard of my office for putting the book together, and Laura Turner of Agronomics, who has helped massively with the research, as well as Dafina Grapci who has taken the time to thoughtfully review and edit large swathes of the book.

And of course, Bruce Friedrich of the Good Food Institute, the world leader in advocacy for clean food, and a prescient promoter of this vital and fast-growing industry. I am grateful for his insights along with those of the rest of his team who reviewed this text for

*Snake meat at Tomohon Beriman Market, North Sulawesi, Indonesia.*

its accuracy. The scientists at the GFI who have reviewed this book include David Welch, Liz Specht, and Erin Rees Clayton.

I find it interesting that the leaders of the clean food movement are in some ways like the leaders of the longevity revolution that I described in my last book, *Juvenescence*. These people are uniformly collaborative and committed to a mission beyond pure entrepreneurship. I interviewed many key players in this industry over the course of researching this book. It was a pleasure talking with them, and I really enjoyed hearing what motivated them, what they were developing and how they were bringing their products to market.

## JIM MELLON
*November 2020*

# THE IMPERATIVE
# OF AGRICULTURAL
# CHANGE

———

**THE NEW AGRARIAN REVOLUTION IS JUST GETTING UNDERWAY, AND PERFECTLY TICKS ALL THE BOXES FOR TODAY'S ZEITGEIST. AT THE HEART OF THIS CHANGE IS AN AWAKENING TO THE ENVIRONMENTAL DAMAGE CAUSED BY OUR FOOD SUPPLY AND CONCERNS AROUND OUR HEALTH AND FUTURE FOOD SECURITY. A NEW AND GROWING GENERATION OF CONSUMERS HAS BEEN PITTED AGAINST THE OLD GUARD OF THOSE STILL ENGAGED IN OBSOLETE FARMING PRACTICES AND THEIR ILL-INFORMED ALLIES.**

Unsurprisingly, these groups are particularly powerful in places where industrial animal farming is highly concentrated – the US, China, Brazil, Denmark, France and Holland – and it is fair to say that they are today's version of the Luddites.

Their support is weakening, thanks to societal shifts in attitudes to food supplies, the environment, animal cruelty and human health. But they represent a real obstacle to the swift adoption of the innovations that are necessary to effect radical change, and thereby to the protection of the environment, the reduction in cruelty to animals, the safeguarding of food supplies and most importantly, the promotion of human health. Yuval Noah Harari, the celebrated Israeli historian and author of the book *Homo Deus*, has written that animal farming is 'the worst crime in history'. And yet it persists; at any time there are about 100 billion farmed animals alive on the planet, about 13 times the number of humans. Americans alone each eat an average of 21,000 entire animals in their lifespans, according to the excellent Jonathan Safran Foer.

The Agro-Luddites, generally representing a small but vocal percentage of countries' populations, have several weapons at their disposal. They can – and they do – advance the narrative of the 'need to preserve jobs and the old way of life', but then so did horse carriage drivers in the 1890s, when the automobile came along. They can lobby regulators to slow the progress of cultured foods to the market. They can engender fear in consumers by suggesting that cultivated proteins are somehow 'Franken-engineered', and they can mobilise support for anti-progress candidates in the political arena. They can also – as they have been seen to do – impugn the rapidly growing plant-based alternative meat and dairy product sector by suggesting that it represents 'fakeness', when it is nothing of the sort.

The intellectual arguments, however, rest with the good guys. Here I will group those arguments into seven key reasons for advancing the New Agrarian Revolution.

**First**, we live in a world where human health is directly threatened by current farming and livestock rearing methods. The Covid-19 pandemic is just the latest and most severe iteration of a lethal zoonotic disease. These animal-to-human transmissions of disease, both viral and bacterial, will continue to pose a real threat to global health unless we significantly change the way that proteins enter the food supply.

**Second**, there can be no doubt that climate change is a reality, and that outdated agricultural practices, specifically the rearing of farm animals are a major contributor to the Earth's warming. A huge reduction in harmful greenhouse gas emissions would occur if farming practices were to change radically. This fact alone should be enough to convince people of the merits of new ways of producing protein.

**Third**, the industrial farming of animals and their products (e.g. chicken's eggs or cow's milk) is almost always cruel at best and abhorrent at worst. Many people are unaware that the food they eat is quite often the result of practices that would disgust them if they were better informed. To this end, clean meat companies, such as Aleph Farms, which has recently opened a visitor centre, have made transparency a focus of the new industry. There will no longer be the need to disassociate the meat product from the actual animal using clever marketing tricks and misshapen designs (such as nuggets and drummers). The majority of people will, for the first time, have a good answer to the question: 'do you truly know where the meat you eat comes from?'

**Fourth**, the damage to land used in existing agriculture, which contributes to 80 per cent of global deforestation, and the extent of land use, can and will be reversed by the new production methods that are coming down the line. About 99 per cent of land currently used to rear animals could be released back for other use, making space for housing, rewilding or recreation.

**Fifth**, water use for animal production is enormous – as shown in the table to the right. In a world where the viability of entire countries' is threatened by the absence of reliable water supply, the New Agrarian Revolution will dramatically reduce the consumption of our most important but finite resource.

**Sixth**, the 'clean' quality of protein production, and the introduction of healthy supplementation into it, will vastly improve nutritional standards and reduce unwanted and harmful by-products of current food production. This includes faecal matter in many meats; microplastics, mercury and cadmium in fish; and waste such as viscera, bones and tails.

**Seventh**, the high-tech factories and laboratories of the coming revolution will need workers to turn out clean foods and other products. The vast sectors of employment thus created will more than compensate for the jobs inevitably lost on traditional farms.

| | | | |
|---|---|---|---|
| 🐂 | Beef | 1kg | 15,415 litres |
| 🐑 | Sheep Meat | 1kg | 10,412 litres |
| 🐖 | Pork | 1kg | 5,988 litres |
| 🐓 | Poultry | 1kg | 4,325 litres |

*Water used to produce one kilogram of meat from livestock. Source: Institute of Mechanical Engineers.*

In any case, existing jobs in the supply chain will likely remain, and vegetables, cereals and plants will continue to be grown (although in varying amounts), so farms will persist; just in different forms.

The bucolic narrative that the Agro-Luddite lobby promotes is an unrealistic marketing ploy which falsely romanticises contemporary farming. Two myths in particular need debunking. First, far from being dominated by small animal farms, the industry has seen huge consolidation, and therefore concentration, of animal production in the hands of a small number of large businesses. In 1967 there were 9,627 slaughterhouses in the US, compared with just 1,100 today. According to Bloomberg, of those, just 215 supply the US with 85 per cent of its meat. Agriculture is already big business, and rallying against innovation of the type that clean meat offers won't change that. Second, the same businesses that rail against the use of new science as 'unnatural' use a huge amount of science in their current agricultural practices. The 'natural', 'living off the fat of the land' narrative advanced by the traditional meat industry could not be further from the truth.

These *seven virtues* (a Harvard study suggests that there are 90 such reasons, but I am sticking with the biblical allegory) are of such potency that they represent, alongside healthcare and climate change, one of the key pillars of the new economy that will define our decade, and therefore the most important investment opportunities of our time.

In later pages in this book, I will outline those opportunities, but for now I turn to the reasons why we must, as a species, fully embrace the change that is coming, nurture it and shift our consumption patterns. We will end up healthier, the world will be healthier and safer, and future generations will applaud us.

# MOO'S LAW

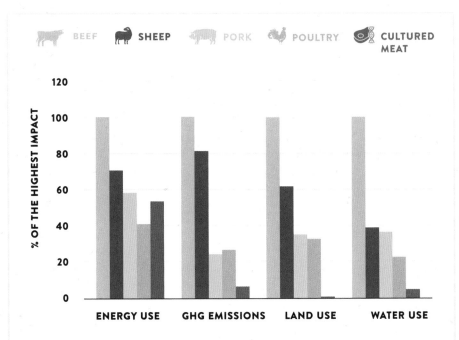

BEEF    **SHEEP**    PORK    POULTRY    **CULTURED MEAT**

Comparison use of primary energy imput, greenhouse gas (GHG) emissions, land use, and water use of cultured meat production with conventionally produced European beef, sheep, pork and poultry per 1000kg edible meat as a percent of the impacts of the product with the highest impact in each category.

*Graph reproduced from Tuomisto and Mattos, 'Environmental impacts of cultured meat production' (2011) 45:14 Environmental Science & Technology, courtesy of the American Chemical Society.*

# PUBLIC HEALTH WILL IMPROVE IN AN AGE OF EXPANDED LONGEVITY

It is thought that humans, first as hunter-gatherers, and then as farmers, have been eating meat for 2.6 million years. Latterly, the process of farming animals and plants has become industrialised, and this evolution into 'mass production' methods of farming animals has had direct consequences on human health.

There are multiple reasons to cheer on the New Agrarian Revolution in respect of human health. The most obvious and immediate one relates to the zoonotic diseases that have ravaged the world, including the most recent and current Covid-19 crisis, which is believed to have originated in a wet market in Wuhan, China. The transmission of novel disease as a result of unsafe farming and wildlife consumption in developing nations has been shown to be disastrous for the health and economies of almost all nations.

Closing these types of markets, banning the consumption of exotic wildlife and better monitoring intensive farming methods in countries including China, and many others besides, would be a step in the right direction. This might be achievable given the reach, for instance, of the Chinese state, and the horrors that these cultural habits have imposed on us all, but it would merely be one step.

It takes only one person, from any part of the world, to eat an infected bat or pangolin; just one farm to harbor a swine fever; just a single flight to bring infected people from one geography to another, and we would have the basis of another pandemic.

There is currently no *safe* way to commercially farm or husband animals, but *safety* can be and is engineered into plant and cell-based products. With health safety and food safety key concerns for today's generation of consumers, clean food will not be a niche food category. It is projected to represent the bulk of protein consumption within 30 years. Cows, pigs, sheep and chickens will still exist, but they will, in my opinion, be 'hobby' animals, and only eaten by an affluent few.

Engineered plant and cellular foods, ranging from all the principal meat categories to fish, dairy and possibly novel proteins, will have replaced 'traditional' sources of food, and they will come to be cheaper within the next fifteen years.

From a health perspective, this shift towards clean foods will represent a huge leap forward from current methods.

Clean foods will radically reduce the incidence of harmful viruses entering the human population. The way we currently farm swine, for example, creates the conditions for incredibly deadly avian flus to enter the human population. Pigs become the perfect incubator for the genetic exchange to take place between human and avian flus which would otherwise find the leap into humans difficult. Keeping chickens and pigs in proximity is therefore a ticking time bomb. In fact, this is most likely what happened with the Spanish Flu of 1918-1920 which probably originated on a farm in Arkansas.

Antibiotic and hormone use in animals will be *eliminated*. Antibiotic use in farmed animals is estimated to be four times that of human consumption. If this usage is not curbed, there is a significant risk that the next pandemic could be microbial in nature, rather than viral, and that the death toll caused by a new superbug could be even worse than Covid-19. By eliminating antibiotic and hormone use we will *eliminate* swine fever, along with all other zoonotic diseases.

The incidence of *E. coli* and botulism will be *eliminated* in the animal food chain due to lack of faecal contamination. Furthermore, animal diseases caused by mistreatment and transmitted to humans, such as Creutzfeldt-Jakob (a human variant of mad cow disease), will be *eliminated*.

Engineered food products, both those that are here now and those that are coming down the pike, can be made to taste better, have zero impurities, generate no waste, can be supplemented to achieve superior nutrition, have cholesterol removed, and will have longer shelf lives than traditional meat and fish products. Additionally, because production of fish products can and likely will be inland, the constant threat posed by flooding, natural disasters and contamination from, for instance, oil spills to fishing grounds, will also be eliminated.

## BACTERIAL GROWTH AFTER 48 HOURS

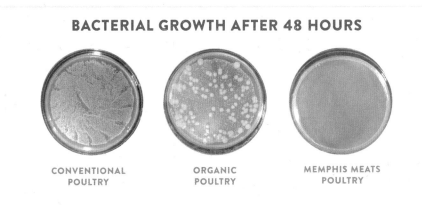

| CONVENTIONAL POULTRY | ORGANIC POULTRY | MEMPHIS MEATS POULTRY |

*Cultured poultry meat experiences negligible bacterial growth after 48 hours, compared to conventional and organic poultry. Reproduced courtesy of Memphis Meats.*

The risk of famine will likely be significantly reduced, if not eliminated. The vagaries of the weather, the effect of climate change and the need to produce vast amounts of crops to feed animals – which are inefficient convertors of protein into meat, producing only thirty calories for every hundred a person would get if they ate the crop directly – will be vastly lessened in their negative effects.

Cultivated meat, insofar as it is concerned with the hyper specialised scientific control of optimal conditions for growing food is in this respect, a successor to innovations like hydroponic farming. The amount of science in use in our agriculture industries is already significant; the New Agrarian Revolution simply marks the introduction of radically better science. Science which can improve food security while solving the problems created by our increased demand for animal proteins.

One such example is in the area of food processing. New science can eliminate substances used in meat processing (nitrites etc.) and with that the release of harmful compounds when cooking 'traditional' red meats at high temperatures. This in turn, could reduce the incidence of colon cancer and heart disease by a significant amount. It is established that excess consumption of red meat in its current form contributes to shorter lives. This effect can be *eliminated* by the consumption of *engineered proteins*.

# ENVIRONMENTAL BENEFITS ARE ENORMOUS

The adoption of new agricultural practices will be of tremendous assistance in reducing the impact of man- and animal-made emissions on the environment. There can be no one alive who is not aware of, and does not have a view on, the fact that global warming is a direct result of these polluting emissions.

Global warming is helped along its path by the growth of intensive farming and the rise in the world population. This is coupled with the insatiable demand of developing nations such as China, India and African countries to consume more proteins, particularly animal proteins, where they are seen as a sign of affluence. At the same time the affluent in developed countries are reversing their consumer habits.

About one third of all emissions which are now known to be causing global warming arise directly from animal husbandry. This could be reduced by three quarters if modern agricultural practices were adopted.

It is estimated that by 2030 over 5 billion tonnes of animal waste will be produced by global livestock annually. This leads to contamination of both land and water. Smithfield, the large US meat company, slaughters more pigs every year than the combined sum of the inhabitants of the fifteen largest US cities: over 30 million. These pigs are big producers of waste, each producing three times as much faeces as a human. In *Eating Animals*, Safran Foer explains that just the Smithfield pigs on their own produce as much faecal waste as the humans in California and Texas combined! Jeff Tietz of *Rolling Stone* magazine detailed some of the components of the waste produced by factory-farmed animals: 'ammonia, methane, hydrogen sulfide, cyanide, phosphorous, nitrates and heavy metals and more than a hundred microbial pathogens that can sicken human beings'. This travels into waterways and is often sprayed on fields, or even into the atmosphere, where it can cause humans serious harm.

The Smithfield experience is replicated on a vast scale all around the world.

# PIGS SLAUGHTERED FOR FOOD

 = *30 million*

## 1995 - CHINA 406,403,450

🐷🐷🐷🐷🐷🐷🐷🐷🐷🐷
🐷🐷🐷

### US 94,591,921

🐷🐷🐷

## 2005 - CHINA 551,859,157

🐷🐷🐷🐷🐷🐷🐷🐷🐷🐷
🐷🐷🐷🐷🐷🐷🐷🐷

### US 98,859,704

🐷🐷🐷

## 2014 - CHINA 735,100,000

🐷🐷🐷🐷🐷🐷🐷🐷🐷🐷
🐷🐷🐷🐷🐷🐷🐷🐷🐷
🐷🐷🐷🐷

### US 106,957,700

🐷🐷🐷🐷

*Data from the FAO, USDA, Reuters and the BBC.*

Furthermore, because animals consume about two thirds of all the crops produced in the world, their cultivation leads to substantial deforestation, which in itself is a direct contributor to global warming. New agriculture would no longer require the destruction of forests to produce, say, soy beans for animal feed, and this would have huge environmental benefits.

The farming of animals also uses a lot of land. It is estimated that about 80 per cent of land currently used in the cultivation of animals and fish (yes, buildings and plants are needed!) could be liberated for other uses (housing, recreation etc.), if cellular meat cultivation were to substantially take over from traditional methods of producing meat. Similarly, water usage, which is enormous in the meat and dairy production process, would be vastly lower if new agricultural practices were widely adopted. In many countries, water is in short supply, and drought is a regular feature.

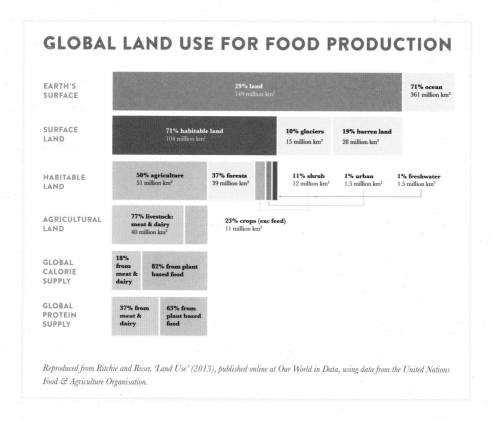

Reproduced from Ritchie and Roser, 'Land Use' (2013), published online at Our World in Data, using data from the United Nations Food & Agriculture Organisation.

These water shortages could in large part be *eliminated* in the context of clean agriculture, which is estimated to use only one twentieth of the water used in conventional meat production.

In addition, if fish is produced on land, plastic pollution of the oceans, which is a huge and growing problem, would be substantially reduced. It is estimated that about half of all plastic pollution in the oceans is caused by the fishing industry.

These plastics make their way through the food chain and into the human body as microplastics, resulting in an average human consumption of around 50,000 particles of plastic per year. According to WWF that amounts to one plastic credit card per week, per person.

Unregulated and criminal fishing is estimated to constitute almost half of the global catch. It deprives poor coastal communities of an estimated US $20 billion a year (*The Economist*), and means that about four fifths of fish species are under threat.

# CRUEL AND USUAL PUNISHMENT

It is a sad fact for people like me, who do not eat meat, that over *one trillion* animals are slaughtered worldwide to be consumed by humans on an annual basis. That is about 180 animals, per person, per year.

Most of these animals are reared more and more intensively, often confined to cramped pens in sunless sheds, never to experience the outdoors: their lives are nasty, brutish, and short. At the back of this book, there are links to disturbing films and articles about the mistreatment of farmed animals of all types. Most of us have some knowledge of the process whereby food gets from farm to fork, but in the same way that we tend to shun thoughts of our own mortality, we do not give much thought to how meat ends up on people's plates. We should, because the processes by which it does are *common* and *usual*, and it is a fact that animals feel much more pain, suffering and anxiety than most people give them credit for.

There is of course, a small subset of animal farming that engages in best practice, such as the three per cent of UK farms which are organic, with animals leading decent lives, reared outside in summer months, well-housed in winter and fed on natural substances, be it grass, hay, or better-quality grains. The majority, however, do not enjoy such luxuries. They are fed on mulch pumped with antibiotics and growth-promoting hormones, confined to such an extent that their whole bodies become distended and painful, and are then herded to their deaths, frightened and anxious. While the majority of us might remain in blissful ignorance about these abhorrent conditions, those who work in slaughterhouses are well known to often develop a form of post-traumatic stress disorder (PTSD) because of the harrowing experience of dispatching the poor and miserable beasts that pass through their portals of death.

The selective breeding of broiler chickens, for example, which has been used to make them grow larger and faster, means that they can now no longer stand. The average chicken today is four times larger than one in 1950, and the size of its breast has increased by 80 per cent. With legs that cannot support the weight of their bodies, these chickens become crippled and it is common for them to die from ascites, a disease arising from the inability of their hearts and lungs to keep pace with their rapid skeletal growth.

And there are, of course, the corporate scandals surrounding large chicken producers, particularly in the US, where the market for chickens is worth about US $65 billion a year. Pilgrim's Pride and Perdue, amongst others, have recently been indicted on charges of price collusion stretching back many years, and key executives have been arrested.

The process by which cow's milk is produced is hardly more humane. Dairy cows are

# SIZE COMPARISON OF EIGHT-WEEK-OLD COMMERCIAL BROILER CHICKENS OVER TIME

| 1957 | 1978 | 2005 |
|------|------|------|
| 905g | 1,808g | 4202g |

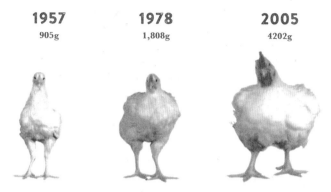

*This illustration originally appears in M J Zuidhof, et al., 'Growth, efficiency, and yield of commercial broilers from 1957, 1978, and 2005' (2014) 93:12 Poultry Science 2973, and is reproduced courtesy of Elsevier.*

typically milked several times a day and kept continuously pregnant, with calves ripped away from their mothers shortly after birth and very few kept alive. Most have severe health problems due to the weight and condition of their udders. They are mostly kept in "zero grazing" confinement, in pens with feeding troughs. Furthermore, they typically live very short lives compared to non-milked cows. On average, dairy cows live for five years, wither and are killed or die from exhaustion or disease, compared to 15 or 20 years for non-dairy cows. In addition, the key proteins in milk account for only 3.3 per cent of the total – the bulk being water. It is clear, then, that the highly processed and interventionist nature of current farming practices means that a revolution away from 'natural' farming has already occurred, but it is a cruel and a desperate one. The New Agrarian Revolution will further push the science of food production into a place of safety and humanity in a way that will be much more sustainable.

Almost every species of meat- or milk-producing animal is cruelly treated. The possible exceptions are sheep bred for wool, free range chickens that are genuinely free to roam, and a few lucky (for a while anyway) Japanese Wagyu cattle which are massaged daily and fed beer!

Fishing will also be radically altered by the scientists ability to create 'clean' fish and crustacean meats. The appalling conditions in which many fishermen live will be ameliorated; the bycatch of dolphins, corals and other endangered marine species will largely come to an end; and the filthy state and dubious food sources of the farmed fish industry, which accounts for around half of all seafood production worldwide, will be eliminated.

Indeed, the geopolitical strife and connected prevalence of slavery resulting from the depletion of fish stocks will be rectified. Overfishing, particularly around the Horn of Africa and Thailand, has generated economic pressures which fuel the use of slave labour and create the conditions for piracy. The diminishing returns experienced by local fishermen mean that vessels must stay at sea longer, and the exploitation of human trafficking networks is seen as the ready solution to man the boats and reduce costs. Violent intimidation, murder and the selling of children into slavery to bring cheap seafood to market could be immediately eliminated when fish can be grown in labs.

The development of cell-based and plant-derived alternatives which are healthier, more environmentally-friendly and cruelty-free means that there will be soon no legitimate reasons to stop their widespread adoption. As Moo's Law™ comes into play, rapidly reducing the cost of cultivating meat year on year, the price of cell/plant-based meat alternatives will only come down, not go up, unlike conventional meat. These meats and other products, superior in every way, will allow the gradual rundown of herds, flocks, and fisheries – and, most importantly, the replacement of barbarism with science and civilisation.

RethinkX, which seems somewhat optimistic, but on the right trajectory says that "the cost of proteins will be five times cheaper by 2030 and 10 times cheaper by 2035 than existing animal proteins, before ultimately approaching the cost of sugar. They will also be superior in every key attribute – more nutritious, healthier, better tasting, and more convenient, with almost unimaginable variety. At current prices, revenues of the US beef and dairy industry and their suppliers, which together exceed $400bn today, will decline by at least 50% by 2030, and by nearly 90% by 2035". **This is big!**

# THE CLEAN MEAT GRINDER

Clean meat will be good for the world economy. Meat and other proteins will now be producible near the point of consumption, avoiding long supply chains and ensuring food security. Countries which have traditionally imported most of their food – those in the Middle East, for example – will now be able to produce proteins domestically. The media, or 'food' that make up cell-based products to grow, will be manufactured almost anywhere, and the plants that go into plant-based protein alternatives will be growable using new cultivation techniques such as vertical farming, where crops are stacked in layers in climate-controlled conditions. Prices of foods will fall in real terms, boosting disposable incomes.

Indeed, there is a fair amount of money flowing into new forms of water-sparing greenhouses, some of which are enormous. For instance, AppHarvest, a developer and operator of giant greenhouse farms, has recently merged with Novus Capital, a so-called SPAC (special purpose acquisition company), to provide US $475 million. The entire operation has been valued at US $1 billion. AppHarvest has opened an indoor farm in Kentucky to produce, amongst other things, tomatoes from its 250,000 m² facility.

As the report from RethinkX explains: "large endowments of arable land and other natural resources are not required to lead the disruption, so the opportunity exists for any country to capture value associated with a global industry worth trillions of dollars that ultimately emerges over the course of this disruption. We will, in short, move from a system of scarcity to one of abundance. From a system of extraction to one of creation".

The release of land back to housing and recreation will have positive benefits for the quality of life as well as employment. New, higher skilled biotech jobs will replace those lost on the farm. In some respects, this is already happening. The number of farmers has been dwindling most of the world for many years. In the same way that, for instance, coal mining jobs in the developed world have been largely replaced by others, so it will be with farmers when the agrarian revolution is in full swing.

'New' types of food, with novel tastes and characteristics, will expand the palette and palate of foodstuffs humans currently enjoy; supplements will be specifically developed to add 'health' to modern foodstuffs, and entire new supply chains will develop. New industries, including ones producing the 'picks and shovels' for the Agrarian Revolution, will be developed.

Animal byproducts will be produced industrially. Leather is a good example: tanneries will become less toxic and it will be producible in formerly unimaginable batch sizes, as the material will no longer be limited by the size of a cow's hide. Dairy, already refashioned by new nut/plant-based versions, will be completely revolutionised by the production of cell- or fermentation-based milk products.

Farming practices have been exposed as injurious to human and environmental health, cruel in nature, inefficient in output and dangerous to participants; all these will be swept away, and the tide will bear great riches for the knowledgeable.

**This revolution is here and now, and it could not have come at a better time.**

# HOW, WHY AND WHEN CLEAN AGRICULTURE WILL TAKE OVER THE WORLD

—

# THE CONFLUENCE OF THE CORONAVIRUS PANDEMIC OF 2020, THE RAPID DEVELOPMENT OF NEW FOOD TECHNOLOGIES AND THE RISING GLOBAL DEMAND FOR PROTEIN MEAN THAT WE ARE ON THE CUSP OF A HUGE AND PROFITABLE INVESTMENT WAVE INTO NEW FORMS OF AGRICULTURE. THE GREATEST BENEFICIARIES OF THIS INVESTMENT WAVE WILL BE CULTURED AND PLANT-BASED FOODS.

The worldwide plant-based meat market, excluding dairy substitutes and other plant-based foods (such as tofu), is currently estimated to be worth about US $12 billion, with sales likely to reach US $28 billion by 2025. In the USA alone, the plant-based food market rose 29 per cent from US $3.9 billion to US $5 billion, between 2017 and 2019 with the plant-based meat market increasing from US $682 million to US $939 million. When considering that these figures do not include future cultured meat sales, which I expect to be underway in some smaller protein categories and geographies by then, the industry's cumulative potential over the next decade will be substantially higher than these projections.

At current consumption rates, and at current population growth projections, it is estimated that by 2050 the production of meat around the world will double, to over 500 billion kilograms per year. The world cannot sustain this level of production, when considering the scarce resources of land and water and the overuse of pesticides, fertilisers and antibiotics that such a level would necessitate. Nor can the planet afford an increase in greenhouse gas emissions, further deforestation, and the continual devastating loss of biodiversity.

When viewed against this backdrop, the production of alternative protein such as plant-based formulations and cell-based meat, as well as animal-free forms of producing materials, will be a key factor not only in meeting our future food needs, but, in doing so, saving our planet as well.

A key feature of plant-based and cultured foods is the transparency of the manufacturing process when compared to traditional animal-derived food production, as will be explained in more detail in this chapter.

This transparency will ultimately drive a move towards greater adoption of these products and, importantly for investors, will divert consumption dollars towards genuinely clean food.

Currently, most companies in the field are private, but increasing numbers are expected to go public in the next few years, offering investors the chance to participate in a major boom. In this book's later section on investment, I triage what I believe to be the best of them, covering the gamut of meats, both plant- and cell-based, as well as by-products, and the 'picks and shovels' that are making the revolution happen.

In this chapter, there follows a brief description of the range of technologies used in the creation of these new foods and products; an analysis of where, how and when the resulting products will be sold; and an estimate of their market and investment potential.

✱✱✱

Broadly speaking, the New Agrarian Revolution can be split into three main investment areas: plant-based, cellular agriculture, and enabling technologies and tools.

The plant-based food producers are already the subjects of heavy investor interest, and their products have been rapidly gaining market share. These plant-based foods include burgers – such as the famous *Beyond Burger* and *Impossible Burger* – but also many other meat substitutes, including chicken, pork, beef, and, of course, seafood. Included in the plant-based market are substitutes for cow's milk made from soy, almonds, rice, and oats. There are also many animal-free product lines in snacks, pet food and baby food. While undoubtedly successful in most cases, companies involved in this sector generally have more limited intellectual property than those in the cell-cultured space, and are more reliant on superior marketing and manufacturing skills to establish their brands.

The second investment area is a fast-developing, yet thus far largely under-the-radar, business of using biotechnology, typically cell culture, to replicate meats, seafoods, dairy products, leathers, and proteins. This industry has the potential to create novel 'engineered' foods which will not relate to any existing animal or fish species.

This sector is most interesting from an investor's point of view. It is at an earlier stage of development than the plant-based sector but has huge momentum behind it. In my view, its products are likely to be in wide dispersal within 10 years, if not sooner, with sales likely in the next 18 months at a small production launch.

The third investment area pertains to the tools-and-technologies industry that enables clean foods: namely machinery, feedstock ('growth media'), and other elements necessary to fuel the new food revolution. There are currently some investable companies in this area, but many of the means of production are held within large companies where the effect of increased sales in this area are diluted by size, which limits their investment potential.

When I embarked on this book, I had no idea that the processes involved in making the spectrum of clean foods were so complex, involving high science and research and development, particularly in cellular agriculture. I have tried to describe the salient features of these processes to reduce them to a simple, bite-sized (excuse the pun!) precis, giving readers some idea of how our food will be produced in future.

While there is a wide variety of new foods and therefore a wide variety of production methods, plant-based foods are generally produced by extrusion. Cell-based products are produced in bioreactors, where different cell lines are provided with nutrients. These include sugars, salts, vital amino acids and growth factors (hormones) that replicate the natural process of growing meat on the body of an animal, without the slaughter and other downsides of traditional animal husbandry.

There are, in addition, other forms of food made by biotech processes, including yeast-based foods and proteins made – literally – from thin air and electricity.

Cellular agriculture still lags behind in comparison to the production and commercialisation curves of the plant-based sector, but it is catching up rapidly, and offers the prospect of defensible IP, lower costs, and greater efficiencies in production. I estimate that in 10 years, products made in bioreactors will be sold at scale in most parts of the world.

This is the industry about which I hold the most optimistic viewpoint, and the one into which I would recommend the highest investment concentration, with portfolio additions from the plant-based foods industry, which is here and now with its products.

# PLANT-BASED FOODS

Plant-based foods, where analogues of meats are fashioned from plants, have been around for a very long time. Comprised of plant material, they are designed to be substitutes for traditional (i.e. derived from animals, including fish) proteins.

Vegans – a term coined in 1944 by Donald Watson, the English founder of the Vegan Society – only eat plants, and eschew all products related to animals. The WHO has recently affirmed that this diet is just as healthy as a balanced vegetarian diet. Vegetarians eat plant-based diets supplemented by eggs and dairy products. Pescatarians – such as I – add fish to the mix, and flexitarians combine a plant-based diet with occasional meat consumption.

The number of people worldwide in each of these categories has risen rapidly and driven the consumption of plant-based foods, which is now the fastest growing part of the food industry. In 2019, US consumption of plant-based foods was growing at eight times the rate of "regular" food. It is estimated that the European market for plant-based foods – the largest in the world, with the UK the largest European individual market – will grow by 60 per cent between 2019 and 2025. Even so, today plant-based meat alternatives are less than one per cent of the European total, hence the excitement about potential market size.

Although veganism and vegetarianism had some adherents as early as the 18th century (notably Scottish doctor George Cheyne, author of the 'Essay of Health and Long Life' (1724) and a strong advocate of a plant-based diet), it was really in Victorian times that vegan/vegetarian practices began to gain traction, and even then among only a small fraction of the British and European populations. The word 'vegetarian' seems to have been first used to describe a diet in a magazine called the *Healthian* in 1843; advised along with other such bracingly good things such as cold baths, celibacy and crack-of-dawn starts.

Only in the modern era, however, have plant-based diets moved out of the faddish and into the mainstream. The Vegan Society, for instance, estimates that as many as a quarter of the British population will be on a largely plant-based diet by 2025. Even though they are presumably talking their own book up, the speed at which food consumption patterns are likely to change makes this a possibility.

Every metric points to rapid growth of the industry: the market share of milk substitutes made with plants is now substantial in Europe as well as in the US. In addition, the new vegetarian burgers have appeared on the menus not just of specialist restaurants, but also of many fast-food outlets and supermarkets. Plant-based meat substitutes are now available for chicken, beef, sausages, seafood, turkey, and pork, and they are more realistic and tastier than could be envisioned just 10 years ago.

Chains such as A&W, Burger King and TGI Fridays are now selling Beyond Meat or Impossible Foods plant-based burgers. This has the dual effect of raising consumer awareness of the "clean meat" menu choices, but also of allowing plant-based meat companies to scale up, and thereby reduce costs.

Furthermore, scientists have recently found a way of using an annular slit die (a rounded opening) to improve throughput by about five times over conventional techniques. The newest, and currently best way to make these 'meats' is to use twin-screw extruders, which better align the fibres in plant-derived proteins to give the product a more authentic look and taste.

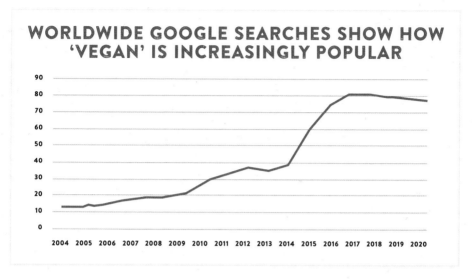

# WORLDWIDE GOOGLE SEARCHES SHOW HOW 'VEGAN' IS INCREASINGLY POPULAR

Plant-based meats differ in composition, but at present most are made with plant proteins, extracted from peas, wheat, or soy. The plant protein is mixed with fats, starches and fiber, binding ingredients, spices, and sometimes colourants from vegetable and fruit dyes. The objective in all cases is to mimic the texture and flavour of the relevant species and cut of meat. In future, it is expected that other proteins will become much more popular in the manufacturing process, including canola, chickpea and corn, as well as peanut and algae protein.

The addition of natural ingredients such as haem will likely improve the characteristics of plant-based foods even further. The key differentiator between the market leaders, Impossible Foods and Beyond Meat, is that Impossible Foods has a patented technology for producing its soy leghaemoglobin protein (which contains haem) using yeast fermentation, whereas Beyond Meat uses beetroot juice to recreate the "ooze" of blood that is characteristic of normal burgers.

Vegetarian foods were previously thought to be bland and flavourless, eaten by pasty-faced, sandal-wearing types, but that image has been dispelled in recent times, and the number of people describing themselves as vegan or vegetarian is growing rapidly. From Paul McCartney and Ariana Grande to Lewis Hamilton and Natalie Portman, veganism is becoming a far more visible and attractive choice. The numbers reflect this too. The bookshop Waterstones was stocking 9,030 book titles with the word 'vegan' as of December 2019, in contrast to the 944 in August 2018. More than a quarter of all evening meals in the UK are now vegan or vegetarian. Finder/Onepoll has estimated that in 2020, 6.9 million British people (about one in ten) are meat-free.

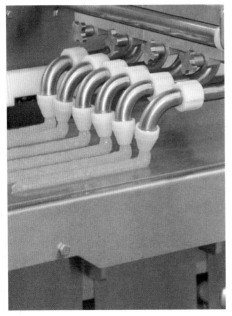

*Food extrusion machine.*              *Food processing machine extruding strips of food.*

It is clear, then, that both diets are becoming more widely adopted, and the public interest in them is becoming increasingly mainstream.

The modern plant-based food industry can in some ways be traced to the foundation of Garden Protein International, now Gardein, by chef Yves Potvin in 2003. Potvin developed the Gardein brand, which is now part of the massive Conagra Brands food empire. Gardein's product ingredients are all vegan and include fibres from carrots and beets as well as soy, pea, and wheat. Gardein's USP was to use the double extrusion process, making for more authentic products.

The leading work in developing the modern extrusion processes was done by engineers at General Mills, the US food conglomerate. It is worth noting that despite all the recent innovation, the biggest patent portfolios in food technologies today are held by behemoths such as Nestlé and DuPont.

But something important has been happening in the last few years which explains why the plant-based food market has been growing so quickly, and that is to look at the processes by which the two best-known plant-based burgers, which come from Beyond Meat and Impossible Foods, are made.

Trying to make plants into aggregated and solid foodstuffs has been going on for at least two millennia. Tofu provides a good example: it is essentially ground-up and heated soy, moulded into blocks, and the process was developed in China thousands of years ago.

Until the modern processes came along, however, it was impossible to make plants into something that really resembled or tasted like farmed meat. Animal meat is three-dimensional and fibrous; it is cohesive and has a firm 'feel' to it.

These characteristics were hard to recreate, until Gardein came along. It took some adept use of technology and a wide variety of combined ingredients (which are even now being tweaked continuously) to get it right or, at least, nearly right.

For example, the Beyond Burger is made up of 18 components, the principal one being pea protein. The pea protein is mixed with water and other ingredients to form a "dough", which is put through a high-moisture extrusion process. The temperature, pressure, and mechanical forces of the extrusion process denature the plant proteins and align them into fibres to create a meat-like texture.

Non-protein ingredients are important for making the final product as meaty-tasting and natural-looking as possible. Coconut oil replicates the marbled look of meat and has the benefit of melting in the mouth. Beetroot juice gives a bloody appearance to the product, especially as it creates a "browning effect" at high cooking temperatures.

The Impossible Burger, the other famous product in the burger substitute market, uses a somewhat different ingredient to produce its meaty colour and texture: soy leghaemoglobin. However, the overall burger production process is similar, with the creation of a plant-based protein "dough" that undergoes high-moisture extrusion to produce a fibrous texture. Fats, spices, flavours such as leghaemoglobin, and binding agents are included in the end-product formulation, but some of these components are added after the dough has cooled. This is to prevent the haem from turning the product brown before it has been cooked by the consumer.

The extrusion of ingredients – which leads to the creation of an aligned protein network – is crucial to the production of these (and most other) successful plant-based meats.

The extrusion process involves the use of mechanical and thermal stresses on the proteins to restructure them into fibrous forms. This is done by heating the barrel of the extruder, using internal screws to shear the proteins under high pressure, and then pushing the product through a cooled die to create the required consistency. The process of extruding can be altered to produce different types of products. The products are then chilled and moulded into patties, strips or whatever shape they will be sold as. Extruded products can be sold in frozen or chilled form as well as in shelf-stable pouches or in cans, depending on the ingredients and conditions used to manufacture the product.

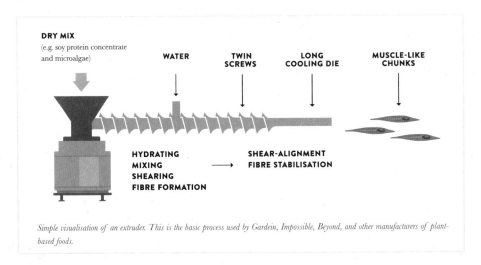

**DRY MIX**
(e.g. soy protein concentrate and microalgae)

WATER        TWIN        LONG        MUSCLE-LIKE
             SCREWS      COOLING DIE  CHUNKS

HYDRATING                SHEAR-ALIGNMENT
MIXING         ⟶         FIBRE STABILISATION
SHEARING
FIBRE FORMATION

*Simple visualisation of an extruder. This is the basic process used by Gardein, Impossible, Beyond, and other manufacturers of plant-based foods.*

Though extrusion is the most common manufacturing method for plant-based meat, new techniques are being developed. One such technology involves 'shear cells', which employ high temperatures and dual cylinders to create larger pieces (e.g. steak equivalents) of fibrous meat analogues. This technology is being developed at the University of Wageningen in Holland, along with Meyn Technology (manufacturers of the equipment), Unilever and Givaudan.

Plant-based foods come in many types, and over 300 companies around the world produce them. For the purposes of this book, however, the most important ones are the meat and seafood substitutes that have emerged in the past two decades.

Until relatively recently the best-known plant-based brand known to consumers was Quorn. This company is owned by Monde Nissin Corp, a Filipino manufacturer of biscuits and noodles, owned by Betty Ang and her family.

Quorn largely sells products to be cooked as burgers, mince, or nuggets, some of which contain eggs and milk and are therefore vegetarian, not vegan. In 2016, however, they did launch some vegan counterparts to their existing vegetarian range. The company, which is based in the UK, was originally formed in 1985 as Marlow Foods, a joint venture between Rank Hovis McDougall and Imperial Chemical Industries. After several owners it was sold to Monde Nissin (no relation to Japan's Nissin Foods) for £550 million in 2015. Quorn products, which have been advertised by Mo Farah, the British Olympian, use mycoprotein as their main ingredient.

Mycoprotein is a type of mould which is fungus-like but not derived from mushrooms. Instead it is a protein extracted from *in vivo*, which is fermented with glucose, oxygen, minerals and nitrogen via a highly-processed system to produce the food. It does so by converting wheat, as the base food, into alternative protein. This process is somewhat akin to the fermentation of beer. Mycoprotein is generally considered to be safe for human consumption, but in a small number of cases (five per cent of the population) it can cause an allergic reaction. For this reason, even though it is not a genetically-modified ingredient, it is not sold everywhere. Most notably, Quorn has not attempted to seek approval to sell its products in Canada.

Despite this drawback, Quorn has been a big success, and since inception has sold over three billion meals. Although a highly-processed food, it is low in calories and saturated fat, and high in protein and fibre. It also contains zero cholesterol.

Quorn is a private company, owned by another private company, and so its results are not published according to a stock market schedule. Nonetheless, we know that it is highly profitable. In 2018 the company made £27 million profit on sales of £220 million, those sales being up seven per cent on the previous year. In 2019, Quorn partnered with Greggs, a large UK bakery chain, to produce a widely acclaimed line of vegan sausage rolls. The same year, it started producing a fish substitute called Fishless Fillets.

At the end of 2018, Quorn opened a large facility of almost 100,000 square feet in Billingham, in the North of England. This doubled their output to 40,000 tonnes per annum and produced 1.3 million additional packs of meat substitutes a week, saving the equivalent of about 80,000 cows a year. In 2021 it will be the first company to roll out carbon labelling on its products, certified by the Carbon Trust, to enable consumers to better understand the environmental impact of their shopping.

Notwithstanding Quorn and Gardein's early successes in producing meat substitutes in the New Agrarian Era, they have been overtaken by the emerging US titans Impossible Foods and Beyond Meat. Both, coincidentally are led by individuals whose last name is Brown.

These companies, after trial and error – as well as significant capital infusions – currently produce a range of meat substitutes, but are best known for their burgers. Although the US market for meat is only 12 per cent of the world's total, it is characterised by a unique fact that 60% of beef sales are in the form of minced (ground) beef, which is largely used to make America's favourite: hamburgers.

This makes the US burger market the juiciest and most accessible of all, and it is where the greatest inroads have been made by plant-based meats.

Beyond Meat, a public company with a US $10.3 billion market capitalisation at the time of writing, is the leader in the plant-based meat substitute market. Impossible Foods, a private company, is not far behind, raising fresh funding in mid-2020 at a pre-money valuation of US $4 billion.

The Beyond Meat food range incorporates not just its burgers, but also sausages and a limited-time launch of its Beyond Fried Chicken at KFC, which has been tested in numerous US cities throughout 2020. All products are largely composed of pea protein isolates, coconut oils, beetroot juice to simulate the colour of "real" beef, as well as canola oil – and, of course, water, which is the principal ingredient of most prepared foods.

Impossible uses soy as its protein base, as well as potatoes, coconut oil, cultured dextrose, added minerals, vitamins and hydrocolloids. As explained above, it also uses fermentation-produced leghaemoglobin to add haem, the flavourful additive that gives it a beef-like mouth feel.

*Jaap Korteweg, aka the Vegetarian Butcher. Reproduced courtesy of William Rutten and the Vegetarian Butcher.*

The success of these two companies has brought some of the biggest food industry players to the party, using surprisingly similar names for some of their products to those of the upstarts. Nestlé sells the 'Awesome Burger' and 'Incredible Burger' (the latter for the restaurant trade), both made with pea protein. They are sold through Nestlé's recently acquired Sweet Earth subsidiary and alongside its Garden Gourmet plant-based range. The burgers are now sold both in the US and Europe, in direct competition to Beyond and Impossible's products.

Kraft Heinz was an early player, too, with its BOCA (Spanish for 'mouth') range of meatless products, including beef, turkey, and chicken, using soy proteins as the main ingredient. These products, both vegan and vegetarian, were among the most popular in America before Beyond and Impossible really took off.

In the seafood space, plant-based products are also gaining momentum, with Bumble Bee Foods, one of the largest seafood producers in the world (owned by FCF Limited of Taiwan but based in California), partnering with Good Catch Foods (a brand of Gathered Foods), a startup from Ohio. This startup was built by the famous chefs the Sarno brothers as well as industry guru Chris Kerr, whom I have interviewed for this book. Good Catch produces plant-based tuna made with legumes including pea, chickpea, soy, fava, and lentils. Real tuna is low in fat and high in protein and omega oils, and Good Catch claims the same for its analogue products.

New Wave Foods of San Francisco, California, has extended the seafood options among plant-based producers by producing a seaweed and soya-based alternative to shrimp, one which looks remarkably realistic.

Overall, there is now a wide range of companies producing plant-based foods around the world, but particularly in the US. Their products cover the entire gamut of meats, including seafoods, but also, of course, milk and eggs and other animal-derived products. And they need not even be for human consumption: Ananas Anam manufactures a leather substitute from pineapple leaves called Piñatex, developed in the UK but made in the Philippines and Spain.

Possibly one of the trendiest and best-known companies to have emerged from the Californian food tech scene is Eat JUST, Inc. (known as JUST). JUST has produced over 30 million egg substitutes from mung beans, which are sold as bottled liquid and used for scrambling and omelettes. Surprisingly, they taste very similar to the real, chicken-laid, thing. JUST now has over 100,000 distribution points for its products worldwide. It also has a cultured meat research division working on growing chicken cells to produce meat. This new venture was named Project Jake, after the late dog of Josh Tetrick, the company's co-founder and CEO.

JUST is reported to have raised large amounts of money to further its mission (perhaps a total of US $220 million, though this is not currently verifiable) on the premise that the company helps avoid the negative environmental impacts that result from intensive farming. It is worth noting here that JUST, formerly known as Hampton Creek, has had a chequered past, including hygiene problems with its JUST Mayo range and involvement in a buyback scandal, when it was allegedly buying its own products in stores to bolster investor interest.

JUST uses high throughput screening techniques to find plant combinations that suit different types of foods, and looks specifically for optimal thermal stability, protein yields, binding and browning ability, and taste factors. So, for instance, they used sorghum as the basis of their cookie dough substitutes and Canadian yellow pea for their JUST Mayo line. They claimed they would have a regulator-approved, commercial line of cultured chicken in 2019, but this is yet to happen. This is a somewhat controversial company, which has in the past over-promised and under-delivered – another reason why investors should do their research when looking to enter a relatively new but high-potential industry.

Having examined the processes by which plant-based foods are made, and sketched some of the most prominent companies in the sector, let us quickly look at the key sources of plant protein and other ingredients:

Soy, a legume, was until relatively recently the main protein source for vegans and vegetarians. It is a widely grown crop and has characteristics that make it suitable for both human and animal consumption. It is widely used in traditional farming, particularly as a supplement to grains fed to cows.

Soybeans are grown in many countries, but Brazil and the United States each account for around one third of the 330 million tonnes produced annually worldwide.

Humans consume soybeans in various forms, including soy milk and its derivative tofu. Soy sauce is made by fermenting soy, and many ingredients in meat and dairy replacements are made with soy. Soy vegetable oil is used in food processing.

Pulses are also used to produce plant-based foods. The most commonly used pulses include lentils, green peas, fava, chickpeas, and mung beans. There are companies working on chickpea protein, such as ChickP and Innovopro, which are currently scaling production.

Other sources of plant-based proteins include root vegetables (such as carrot and potato), leafy vegetables (such as broccoli and sprouts), seeds (such as sunflower, watermelon, almond and pumpkin), and coconut. Grains of all types are also used.

Water lentils, or duckweed, have an excellent growth profile and can double in mass every day. Parabel, a private company, produces high volumes of these leaf proteins under the trademarked name Lentein, which possesses a better amino acid composition than soybeans, a high protein content, significant levels of Vitamin B12, and are non-allergenic. They are grown hydroponically in Vero Beach, Florida, in a facility where all the water is recycled. The product is designed to be a food ingredient as well as a milk substitute, which is due for launch later in 2020.

Since seafood has a 'marine' taste, different types of proteins from plant-based inputs are used in its construction. Here, seaweed and microalgae are most commonly used, particularly microalgae, which contains much more protein than seaweed. Good Catch adds seaweed powder to its products.

Microalgae are abundant and come in a huge variety of species. They produce about half of all oxygen in the atmosphere and, along with bacteria, are the foundation of the entire food system on Earth.

Large meat producers, such as Tyson and Perdue in the US, have also taken to producing "blended" meat products that are a combination of traditional meats and plants. This strikes me as equivalent to an early 20th century company producing a half-horse, half-car means of transport.

# PROTEIN DERIVED FROM THE AIR AND FOODS DERIVED BY FERMENTATION

This concept dates back all the way to 1967, and NASA research into sustaining life on ultra-long space missions. NASA investigated using hydrogenotrophs, which are very common microbes generally resident in the human microbiome, to make protein from carbon dioxide.

More recently companies, including Solar Foods of Finland and Air Protein of the USA, have been using air and cleanly-generated electricity (at least in part) to produce single cell proteins that aggregate to form food with a high (70 per cent) protein content. The technique is a form of fermentation, comparable to the brewing of beer. Solar Foods' product, Solein, is higher in many of the amino acids essential to life than most other comparable foods, including beef, soy and mycoprotein. Furthermore, Solar Foods claims that Solein's production requires only one per cent of the water used in arable farming, and less than 0.25 per cent of the water used in cattle farming, and only a small fraction of the land used in conventional crop or livestock farming.

Solein is also highly efficient in terms of greenhouse gas emissions, compared to traditional farming, because of its energy-light manufacturing process. The company claims that their process also uses less than one per cent of the energy used to raise beef on average. Solar Foods, which based on my analysis is neck and neck with Air Protein, expects to launch commercially on a large scale in 2022, and to produce over US $1 billion in revenues in 2023, generated by the sale of over two billion meals. If they can pull it off, that would be quite remarkable.

Other foods created by precision fermentation include dairy products. The leader in this field is Perfect Day, another Bay Area company, which has raised over US $360 million in venture funding so far.

Perfect Day describes its products as "flora-based", and the company is creating a line of products centred around ice creams, feta, cream cheese and, in due course, milk. Although Perfect Day sells some consumer-facing products, including the Brave Robot brand, the bulk of its business is eventually expected to be with food service providers, who will use the company's dairy proteins as ingredients. Indeed, the company has recently contracted with agricultural giant Archer Daniel Midland to produce their whey proteins in bulk, scaling up to many thousands of tonnes of production by 2022.

In addition to Perfect Day, New Culture and LegenDairy Foods also utilise fermentation to produce animal-free dairy proteins, such as casein, the protein that gives dairy its distinctive taste and functionality. This will offer an alternative to using cow's milk to create delicious cheese.

All three companies use a process whereby the DNA sequences responsible for expressing key dairy milk proteins are identified and inserted into the genome of a fast-growing, highly-efficient host microorganism, such as yeast. The microorganism subsequently produces these proteins during fermentation in a bioreactor, where the microorganisms are fed essential nutrients in a medium to grow. The proteins can then be separated from the cells and purified. These proteins are then ready to be combined with other ingredients to form food products.

Since only the protein of interest is purified and used, it is different to the cellular agricultural techniques used to create meat and other cell-based products, described later in this chapter, where the cells are the product.

New Culture is yet another fermentation company based in San Francisco (although originally from New Zealand). It is a relief to know that there is at least one company based in Europe working on this fermentation approach: LegenDairy Foods, based in Berlin. I have spent time with its charismatic and energetic founder, Raffael Wohlgensinger, and find his vision to be very exciting. New Culture raised a seed round in September 2019 of US $3.5 million and LegenDairy Foods closed their seed round of EUR 4 million in December 2019.

TurtleTree Labs, based in Singapore, is attempting to replicate human breast milk by growing mammary gland cells to produce milk. The seasoned co-founders include a former CEO of a Silicon Valley tech company along with alumni from Google and Salesforce.

TurtleTree uses cellular technology, an alternative approach to fermentation, to culture human mammary cells *in vitro* and then induce these cells to produce the components of human milk, including human milk oligosaccharides (HMOs). TurtleTree Labs is unique in its strategy and targeted market: no other company in the sector is operating a B2B model to supply human breast milk for infant formula. TurtleTree's USP is clever. Particularly in Asia, there is a deep suspicion of certain types of infant formula milk; a replicant of mothers' milk, including the full range of oligosaccharides, carbohydrates and fats, without any nasty pathogens, hormones or antibiotics, would offer a powerful selling proposition.

The infant nutrition market is estimated to be worth US $50 billion worldwide and expected to more than double over the next decade or so. The infant global market size alone is expected to reach US $100 billion by 2027, according to Fortune Business Insights.

However to achieve a viable product, TurtleTree Labs must navigate through a complex process. The first is to extract viable cells from milk, and then to proliferate and grow them to a larger number. These cells are then put in an in-house lactation media to yield the resulting milk, which is then separated from the cell biomass via filtration. The cells that TurtleTree Labs are working with can potentially produce milk for an extended number of days. This separates them from other cell-based food tech solutions where cells are present in the product.

It is interesting to note that TurtleTree Labs is based in Singapore, a city-state with very limited food production capacity, but one that nonetheless has the stated goal of producing 30 per cent of its nutrition locally by 2030. This feat which is more attainable through the adoption of cellular agriculture. Shiok Meats, focussing on cultured shrimp, is another company based in Singapore and one that I will look at later in the book.

Motif FoodWorks is a company based in Boston, Massachusetts, headed up by food industry veterans and born out of the successful biotech company Ginkgo Bioworks (synthetic biology specialist valued at more than US $4 billion). It has raised US $90 million in a Series A in 2019 from top flight venture investors including Fonterra, Breakthrough Energy Ventures and Louis Dreyfus Company. It is focussed on the provision of fermentation-derived, animal-free ingredients to the food industry, and again sits between the plant-based and purely cell-based agricultural sectors.

# CELL CULTURED FOODS

Cell cultured foods represent the cutting edge of the New Agrarian Revolution and some of the companies gearing up to produce them are the most exciting investment opportunities in the food sector.

Foods made from cultured cells are generally meat or fish analogues, although it is very likely that entirely novel types of foods will be developed in the future using bioengineering.

The techniques employed in cultivated meat (and other animal by-products) production are mostly borrowed from the biotech industry, which has been using them for years to produce medicines. However, whereas the biotech industry can afford to pay for expensive inputs because of the high profit margins on its products, the cellular agriculture industry cannot afford these expensive growth hormones without pricing itself out of competition with farmed meat. The cost of production for cell-cultured foods therefore must fall significantly, as I explain later in this chapter with the concept of Griddle Parity™.

Cultivated meats are made by taking biopsies from the relevant animals whose meat is to be 'replicated'. From these biopsies, the relevant cells are identified, isolated, and converted to stable cell lines. The right cells (the 'seed train') have to be used to start the proliferation process, which takes place in a bioreactor. Together with the cells, the ideal mix of nutrients and growth factors, buffering solutions, temperature and sterilisation are necessary to encourage rapid growth within the bioreactor. Bioreactors may be large or small, single-use or reusable. After sufficient proliferation, the cells are then differentiated into muscle fibres that aggregate into a biomass material equivalent to meat. Depending on the desired end product, the cells can be arranged on scaffolds made from biologic or plant materials to produce structured, 3D muscle tissue. The process of multiplying the cells is one that takes approximately, varying by species, two to three weeks.

In practice, producing food from cells is even more fiendishly complicated than the brief explanation above, which is why cultivated meat and fish are only now becoming possible. The technology has progressed mightily in recent years, largely as a result of advances in the parallel biotech industry.

But possible it is, and of the approximately 50 companies in the world engaged in cellular agriculture, many have produced samples of a cell-derived product grown in a bioreactor – and conducted tastings of their prototypes.

The very first such product, initially a research project, but one which today forms the basis of Dutch company Mosa Meat, was presented by its inventor in 2013. In front of the world's press, Professor Mark Post unveiled his very expensive (and dry) burger, which reportedly cost US $300,000, with funding from Sergey Brin, co-founder of Google. I have heard that the cost was even higher than that but, for the purposes of showing the decline in the cost curve, this figure will suffice.

Since then, dramatic improvements have been realised in the technology, cost, and scale of production for cell-cultured food. Mosa Meat, for instance, claims that a single tissue biopsy from a cow can yield 20,000 burgers, and that the price of making one of its burgers, much improved since, has fallen to the low hundreds of dollars. It's still highly uncompetitive, but undoubtedly on a curve to equal the price of conventional burgers in the relatively near future.

The reason why this book is called Moo's Law™ (riffing on Moore's Law, which is so beloved in the semiconductor industry), is that the whole success of the cultured food industry will depend on its ability to scale up production and to lower costs.

The main, but not exclusive, emphasis of the cultured foods industry is to commercialise meat cultivated from cells, rather than grown in whole living animals. Whether this is successful will depend ultimately on whether these meats achieve what I call 'Griddle Parity'™ with conventionally-farmed meats. This Griddle Parity™ (another term made up by me, this time riffed from the clean energy business) will depend on the products reaching an equal or lower cost than existing meats, while retaining significant health and environmental benefits over conventional meat products in the long run.

There are already signs that plant-based meats are better for human health than conventional meats. In August 2020, the Stanford School of Medicine reported on a significant trial comparing plant-based meat to conventional meat, one that was highly favourable to plant-based meats. The 16-week randomised SWAP-MEAT study, published in the American Journal of Clinical Nutrition, compared Beyond Meat's chicken, beef, and pork to the consumption of organic, animal-based versions of the same products.

Participants in the SWAP-MEAT study consumed two or more servings of plant-based or animal-based meat every day for eight weeks each. The consumers of the plant-based meats had much lower 'bad' cholesterol than the conventional meat eaters at the end of the study and, significantly, weighed a kilo less on average.

It is likely that cell ag derived meat will display similar health benefits as well, without the antibiotics, contaminants and hormones found in much farmed meat.

Over the long term, the differentiating factors between plant-based meats and cell ag meats will be based in large part on intellectual property. There are multiple ways in which the production of meats and other products derived from animal cells differ. This is why individual companies own intellectual property that is generally more defensible than that of plant food producers, who rely more on trade secrets and savvy marketing.

This is also the reason some of the companies in the field may end up being more valuable than successful plant-based food companies. As Moo's Law™ kicks in, the price of cultivated meat and other products currently derived from animals will fall dramatically, making it possible for companies in the sector to price their wares at ever-cheaper levels while retaining the substantial advantage of a "clean food" designation.

But – and it is a big but – that point is a fair way away, and possibly not for another decade. That is why it is so important to choose the runners and riders in your cellular agriculture portfolio with great care, as there will be plenty of companies that will fall by the wayside in the race to get to mass scale for the production of bioreactor-grown foods.

Notwithstanding the technical differences in production processes that set companies apart from their peers, the basic process of creating cellular food is schematically similar.

## CELL LINE CHOICE

Choosing the cell lines used to produce the different types of meat or fish is of paramount importance to the success of the product.

There are two main classes of stem cells used in the cultivated meat industry: pluripotent stem cells (PSCs) and adult (somatic) stem cells (ASCs). Stem cells used for producible cultivated meat need to be able to be directed to differentiate into the cells that comprise

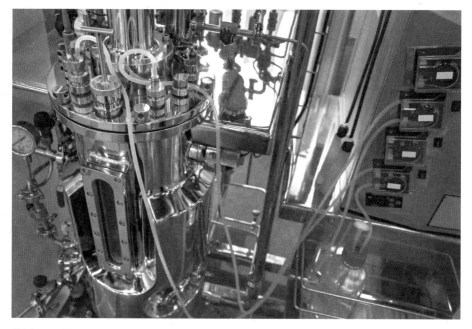

*This is a typical bioreactor. Cellular agriculture companies use vessels like this to proliferate and differentiate the desired cells.*

meat: myofibrils, fibroblasts, adipocytes, chondrocytes and endothelial cells.

ESCs, derived from embryos, are pluripotent, meaning they can self-renew and generate all three of the so-called germ layers, which are the ectoderm, mesoderm and endoderm. These primary layers are groups of cells that are formed at the early stages of embryonic development. They include some of the first multipotent stem cells, which are of a lower potency and differentiate to become specific types of cells, tissues or organs, such as neurons, red blood cells and skin. These primary germ layers are the building blocks to forming entire organisms, but of course cultivated meat companies do not need or want to do that.

ESCs are sourced from blastocysts (an early phase of mammalian embryonic development), typically after the embryo has matured to around 100 cells. Acquiring these ESCs is tricky, as they appear only briefly a few days after fertilisation. Stable embryonic stem cell lines are difficult to achieve as their pluripotency means they have a high potential to differentiate into the three germ layers described above. Unwanted cells are likely to form. In fact, the first ESC lines in mice were not derived until 1981, and it was only in 2018 that the first bovine (cow) ESCs were successfully isolated.

Because ESCs are so difficult to work with, induced pluripotent stem cells (iPSCs) are one of the favoured cell lines for researchers in the cellular agriculture sector. Since iPSCs are derived from adult cells, they are easier to source than ESCs. As their name implies, iPSCs are pluripotent and can give rise to all cell types in the body.

The existence of iPSCs are only possible due to cellular reprogramming, a revolutionary technology developed in 2006 by Professor Yamanaka of Japan that won him the Nobel Prize in Physiology or Medicine. Cellular reprogramming enables many adult somatic cell types in the body to be reprogrammed into a pluripotent state, including white blood cells and skin fibroblasts, both of which are easily obtained from non-slaughter biopsy samples.

To create iPSCs, Yamanaka overexpressed four specific genes (c-Myc, Oct4, Sox2 and Klf4 gene-encoding transcription factors, also known as the Yamanaka factors) in somatic cells, inducing the cells to reprogram to a pluripotent state. These factors are highly expressed in ESCs, and their effect on potency indicates that they regulate the development signalling network to reach this state. The Yamanaka factors are also highly conserved across mammalian species and so most agriculturally relevant species which will be cellularly cultivated have had iPSCs generated already. By contrast, generating iPSCs for fish remains a greater challenge.

Today, there are multiple routes scientists can take to reprogram cells, some of which are permanent genome-integration methods, such as the use of a lentivirus, or non-integration approaches, including using mRNA gene delivery, small molecules or proteins.

On the other hand, adult stem cells include mesenchymal stem cells, hematopoietic stem cells and tissue specific cells such as myosatellite cells and fibroblasts. They exist within living animals and humans to replenish dying cells and aid the regeneration of tissue that may have become damaged. A key distinguisher of adult stem cells, compared to ESCs and iPSCs, is that they are multipotent, meaning they have a limited differentiation capacity, and can only differentiate to certain types of cells. While iPSCs and ESCs can form cells in any of the three germ layers, adult stem cells cannot. Typically, adult stem cells derived from a particular germ layer can only differentiate into cells within the same germ layer. For instance, hematopoietic stem cells (blood stem cells) derived from the mesoderm can differentiate into specialised cells found in the blood such as lymphocytes, red blood cells and platelets.

Mesenchymal stem cells (MSCs) have the capacity to differentiate into mesodermal lineages such as adipocytes (fat), chondrocytes (cartilage), osteocytes (bone) and of course myocytes (muscle).

MSCs are most commonly sourced from bone marrow, but they can also be obtained from adipose tissue as well the umbilical cord tissue, and even human wisdom teeth. MSCs have shown great promise in regenerative medicine, playing a vital role in tissue engineering, gene therapy, and transplants for humans – they are even capable of differentiation into cardiomyocytes (heart muscle cells). Their potential applications have only been unlocked over the past three decades: MSCs were not discovered until 1976 (by A.J. Friedenstein, in the bone marrow of mice) and Arnold Caplan did not coin the name 'MSC' until 1991.

MSCs are easier to source than ESCs, given that a biopsy from human or animal bone marrow is a much simpler procedure than the aforementioned methods.

Myosatellite cells, also known as satellite cells, are another type of multipotent adult stem cell, and are even easier to source than MSCs. These cells can typically be isolated from muscle tissue in a biopsy of a human or animal at high cell populations. These are tissue-specific cells with directed lineage to form myoblasts and subsequently myocytes, which then become multinucleated myotubes and eventually myofibres.

However, the downside of multipotent stem cells is that they have a limited proliferation capacity, and are not immortal like ESCs or iPSCs. Unless manipulated, MSCs and myosatellite cells typically have the capacity to double up to 50 times.

Other possible adult stem cells to use for the process are fibroblasts, which are even easier to source than the cell types mentioned above. Fibroblasts' original function is to synthesise the extracellular matrix and collagen, which produces the structural body that makes up muscle tissue. The process of transdifferentiation, also known as direct

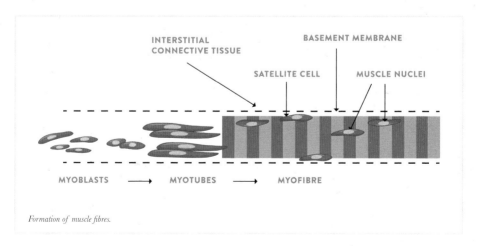

*Formation of muscle fibres.*

reprogramming, which was first achieved in 1987, allows for one somatic cell type to be directly converted to another without needing to enter a pluripotent state. Since the discovery of iPSCs, more research has been done to understand transdifferentiation and use it in regenerative medicine.

This technology opens up the possibility of using many other somatic cells, including fibroblasts as the initial cell source. Transdifferentiation can even allow somatic cells to differentiate to cells outside of their germ layer. Most companies in the space use their own proprietary cell lines, which is a key element of their IP.

No matter what cell lines are used to start the process of cultured meat production, they must be stable and free of pathogens. Stability of the cell lines is required to avoid genetic drift as the cells divide and replicate, which could cause efficiency and quality issues during the cultivated meat manufacturing process. This is why cell line development and cell banks, where stringently vetted cell lines are cryopreserved, are important to the industry. Currently, most cultivated meat companies keep their cell banks in-house. This allows them to have master and working cell banks to provide consistent results for their entire bioprocess.

However, the Good Food Institute has teamed up with Kerafast, a leading reagent manufacturer, to create a centralised biorepository for the industry, containing well-characterised, stable cell lines from a huge array of terrestrial and aquatic species readily available worldwide.

The cultivated meat industry uses cell lines that are appropriate to the particular meats they are seeking to replicate, e.g. bovine cells for beef, porcine cells for pork, and so forth. These cell lines are cultivated through a series of progressively larger bioreactors called a seed train, and ultimately introduced into an industrial-scale bioreactor to proliferate and differentiate into the desired final cell types (muscle, fat, etc.). Once mature, these cells are harvested from the bioreactor. Any additional downstream processing that is required will look similar to processing used for conventional meat products.

The most studied cell lines in the world are human and, of course, mouse cell lines; the stalwarts of pharmaceutical and biomedical research. By comparison, studies into avian, ovine, porcine, bovine, and piscine cells, while accelerating, are still relatively limited.

Furthermore, little work has been performed with cells from different breeds of agriculturally relevant species, though this is changing. For example, JUST is working with cells from Wagyu beef cattle through a partnership with a famous farm in Japan, the Toriyama. Leveraging a diversity of cell sources – including from breeds with distinct genetics and geographic origins – can improve both the quality and the resilience of the future cultivated meat supply chain.

Once stable cell lines are established and thoroughly characterised, they can be used for the two main stages to the cultivated meat production process: proliferation and differentiation

## PROLIFERATION

In order to produce large numbers of cells, selecting the most appropriate starting cell is particularly important. This is because the cells described above have different attributes. Some cells can continue doubling indefinitely (an immortal cell line) while others have limited replication potential. Cells that have limited potential are subject to the Hayflick Limit, which means they enter senescence when their telomeres (the caps at the end of chromosomes) wear away. A cell line is deemed to be immortalised when it has passed through 60 population doublings, capable of expanding from a single cell to $1.15 \times 10^{18}$ cells. To produce meat at scale, trillions of stem cells must be produced from a single cell line through the proliferation stages of the production process. Once sufficient cell numbers are achieved for a given batch, the cells will proceed into the differentiation phase of the production process.

## DIFFERENTIATION

After proliferation, which can occur within a conventional stirred tank bioreactor with the cells free-floating in suspension or attached to small beads called microcarriers, the stem cells are typically harvested and transferred to a new bioreactor for differentiation into the desired mature cells that compose meat. The bioreactor design for this stage of the process may be entirely different to the proliferation phase and will require a different media formulation, which we will get on to later.

This stage of the process typically involves the use of scaffolds, which are 3D structural supports that facilitate the cells' differentiation and arrangement into complex tissues. In order to produce dense pieces of tissue, such as a tasty steak, the cells need a material to adhere to. This material must be porous to facilitate the cells' access to oxygen and necessary nutrients and to prevent unwanted death (apoptosis or anoikis) of cells. Alternatively or in addition, nutrient access can be facilitated by introducing vaculature into the scaffold, thus mimicking the way in which cells are nourished within animal tissue.

As *in vivo*, i.e. in normal circumstances in the body, cells situate themselves in what is known as the extra cellular matrix (ECM). This consists of proteins and proteoglycans combining to create a 3D microenvironment that provides a number of biomechanical cues to the cell, defined by parameters like the architecture and stiffness of the ECM.

Cell adhesion and interactions within this matrix are modulated in part by integrins, which are a class of cell membrane proteins. These membrane proteins act as both adhesive and sensing agents and allow individual cells to respond to their external surroundings, such as guiding their differentiation based on the mechanical properties and chemical signals they perceive. Cultivated meat companies are exploring several avenues for mimicking these precise properties within their scaffolding materials, to improve the efficiency of differentiation and to enable exquisite spatial control of the arrangement of mature cells.

Companies looking to provide unstructured products, such as ground beef for burger patties or cultivated fat cells to be used as flavouring ingredients, need not worry about use of scaffolding. However, those that do have to think carefully about the scaffolding material; selecting and designing it to be safe and edible; and considering whether natural or synthetic materials are most appropriate.

Scaffolds can be made of natural substances such as fibrin, hyaluronic acid and gelatin, or prepared commercial mixes such as Matrigel. They can also be prepared from silk, chitosan (a sugar obtained from the exoskeletons of shellfish), alginate (a sugar from certain species of seaweed), yeast or other fungi, or plant-derived cellulose. In some cases, the scaffolds may be intended to remain integrated at some level in the final product, where they may contribute to the texture or perhaps even the flavour of the product. But other product developers may seek biodegradable materials that will not be detectable at the point of final harvest, as the cells will break down the scaffold and replace it with their own secreted ECM as they mature.

Decellularisation of plant tissues, including celery and green onion, has possible applications here, to mimic the native ECM of animal tissue. Plant tissues are favourable as scaffolds because they have a large surface area and existing vascular networks, as well as being edible and very cheap. In addition, hydrogels – water-dense (absorbing upwards of 1,000 times their weight), cross-linked polymeric networks, used extensively in tissue engineering to permeate oxygen and enable the flow of water-soluble nutrients – can also be employed here.

Computational modelling, in some cases employing machine learning techniques, is increasingly used to anticipate and predict the optimum conditions for cell cultivation, including the appropriate signaling influences to direct cellular behavior and metabolism. Throughout their growth and maturation, cells send chemical signals using factors that either encourage or inhibit growth in their neighbours or that otherwise influence behavior of cells near and far. These factors can be filtered out or supplemented to the medium to create the desired mixture of signals at each stage of the process. Exerting control over these signaling processes provides another point of potential IP protection for the cultivated meat industry.

# BIOPROCESS DESIGN

There is no specific timeline from start to finish – cell to product – for cultivated meat, as it comes in multiple forms and processes differ. However, it is generally a matter of a few weeks, with the cells going from smaller vessels *ab initio* into progressively larger ones as the biomass develops.

There is some debate in the industry as to whether large scale production (scaling up) is preferable to smaller scale, more localised projects (scaling out), and no doubt the answer is dependent on individual products and corporate strategies. So for instance, in scaling out, smaller bioreactors (100-1000 litres) might, in a decade or so, be placed in shops or restaurants, with the feedstock, technology, and equipment being provided by the company that invented the production method. By contrast, in scaling up, a single company would produce the food *en masse* with larger bioreactors (possibly up to 100,000 litres, though animal cell culture has not yet been demonstrated at scales larger than 20,000 litres), package it and distribute it to the retail, restaurant, or food service trade. This would be roughly equivalent to the difference between a microbrewery in a pub and a massive centralised brewing facility.

There are broadly three bioprocess strategies for large-scale production of cell-cultured foods: batch, batch-fed and continuous.

The batch method involves the transfer of densely-grown cell cultures into progressively larger vessels. With the batch-fed approach, a "feeder" vessel transfers carefully monitored amounts of appropriate nutrients into the mother vessel where the entirety of the process takes place. Continuous processes involve continuous monitoring and replacement of cells, nutrients, growth factors and buffers, and harvesting of biomass occurs in an ongoing fashion. In all three approaches, continuous mechanical mixing ensures that nutrients and dissolved gases are uniformly distributed within the cultivator.

No single method is dominant, and no-one has yet scaled up production to large quantities, although the technologies involved are well-established and scale-up should be a readily achievable ambition for most cellular agriculture companies, subject to addressing the issue of production cost.

Whatever the size of the bioreactor, a precise monitoring system through smart sensors is required to achieve optimum results. Regulation of the pH levels using unique buffering solutions, monitoring of temperatures in the reactors, cell proliferation and health measurements are all extremely important, and becoming increasingly sophisticated. Typically, fish cells are grown at much lower temperatures than those needed for land-based animals, whose optimal temperature tends to be around 37 degrees Celsius. Oxygen, which is normally transported by blood in living animals, must be introduced in significant and accurate quantities into the process; equally, carbon dioxide levels must be monitored and controlled as cells respire. The pH levels must be maintained, and excess production of ammonium and lactic acid must be avoided, as too much of either could cause apoptosis.

High standards of hygiene and contamination control are required in the process, as for any foodstuff, though it is noteworthy that these standards are likely to be much less stringent than those required for current industrial-scale animal cell culture processes to produce pharmaceuticals. To combat the threats of bacteria, viruses, and fungi, the cell-based meat industry will adhere to strict operational controls for maintaining closed containment. Between batches, cleaning-in-place protocols may entail steam cleaning or acidic/alkaline solutions, as are typical in many food-processing and fermentation cleaning practices. Typically, bioreactors are made of stainless steel, and these can either be used on repeat and thoroughly cleaned after each batch, or a disposable liner (preferably biodegradable) can be used each time. The former is likely preferable at large scale, as it avoids unnecessary waste from the process.

# THE MEDIA USED TO FEED CELLS IS OF INCREDIBLE IMPORTANCE TO THE PROCESS

In 1882-1883, Sydney Ringer, a British biologist, became the first recorded person to keep tissues alive *ex vivo*. Using a solution of saline, sodium bicarbonate, calcium chloride, and potassium chloride, he successfully recreated the chemical conditions of an animal's body, and by doing so was able to keep a frog's heart beating for several hours.

In later years, researchers worked out that keeping cells in blood plasma allowed the cells to persist and proliferate. The addition of glucose, insulin, vitamins, amino acids and glutathione were subsequently identified as being important to the cultivation of cells.

By the 1950s, Harry Eagle, an American physician, had developed a Minimum Essential Medium (MEM) formula, which identified the 13 amino acids required for cell survival and viability in a serum. In addition, he included glucose, inorganic salts and vitamins, and dialyzed serum. Over the years, Eagle's MEM has been refined and modified into multiple related formulations but remains in use today. Many of these formulation changes have aimed to replace the serum component with synthetic alternatives, since the serum is animal-derived.

The variations on Eagle's medium include Ham's F12, Leibovitz's L15, and Dulbecco's Modified Eagle Medium (DMEM). These are known as basal cell culture media, which provide the basic nutrients for growing animal cells.

The components of these basal media broadly include the same ones used in nature to produce meat – in other words, the same basic building blocks of life, which result from the digestion of food by animals. Among the primary energy sources are glucose or related sugar metabolites, such as pyruvate or galactose. These can be readily derived from starch-rich crops such as maize, potatoes and wheat. These sugars enter the cells and convert into ATP via glycolysis as the cells' principal source of energy, just like in humans.

The concentration of glucose is very important to the process of cell proliferation. Concentrations used for cultivated meat production will vary according to the type of cell that is being cultured and the stage of the process. It is extremely important to monitor glucose levels very carefully in order to avoid excess production of lactic acid in the cultured cells.

The second class of key components in basal cell culture media are the amino acids needed to produce proteins, nucleotides and other cellular machinery, whose vital importance was first identified by Dr. Eagle. Some of these are non-essential, which can be synthesised by animals (including by humans), while others are essential and thus must be introduced through diet.

Non-essential amino acid production applies across most mammalian species, meaning it has been preserved through evolution. The human essential amino acids (EEAs) consist of histidine, lysine, asparagine, phenylalanine, valine, threonine, tryptophan, leucine, and isoleucine, though different species of animal require different essential animal acids and in somewhat different ratios. Cats and chickens, for instance, need the same EEAs as humans, plus taurine and glycine; and dogs and pigs need the same ones as humans, plus arginine. And L-glutamine, while non-essential, is used ubiquitously in cell culture media across multiple mammalian and insect cell cultures because it also serves as a key energy source.

Not everything which is essential to a living organism is similarly essential in cell culture, and *vice versa*. For instance, arginine must often be added to *in vitro* cultivation of certain cells, whereas *in vivo* it is biosynthesised.

The basic point is that the key ingredients of glucose (or its equivalents) and of the correct

## ESSENTIAL AND NON-ESSENTIAL AMINO ACIDS

| ESSENTIAL | CONDITIONALLY NON-ESSENTIAL | NON-ESSENTIAL |
|---|---|---|
| HISTIDINE | ARGININE | ALANINE |
| ISOLEUCINE | CYSTEINE | ASPARAGINE |
| LEUCINE | GLUTAMINE | ASPARTATE |
| LYSINE | GLYCINE | GLUTAMATE |
| METHIONINE | PROLINE | SERINE |
| PHENYLALANINE | TYROSINE | |
| THREONINE | | |
| TRYPTOPHAN | | |
| VALINE | | |

amino acids must be present in the right quantities in the basal cell media to allow cell proliferation, just as occurs in nature. In addition, inorganic salts are important to the composition of the feedstock media, to maintain osmotic balance and to provide key micronutrients and trace minerals, such as iron, copper and zinc. Vitamins are also added, including riboflavin (B2), pantothenic acid (B5), folic acid (B9), and cyanocobalamin (B12).

Modelling of concentrations and metabolic rates for each of these media components is important for optimizing media formulations for cultivated meat production. The different combinations of ingredients is one of the distinguishing features of the various approaches, and will potentially lead to defensible IP applied to differing types of media for different species and cell types.

The media used currently in cultivated meat research is typically bought in fully-prepared form from specialist providers, including MilliporeSigma and Thermo Fisher Scientific, but companies are looking to find cheaper alternatives and make their own media in-house. The media can come in powdered form (which is cheaper) or in liquid form, and modern formulations typically have a long shelf life. Anticipated to account for between 55 and 90 per cent of the cost of the final product, media is often the most expensive component of the cell culture process, due largely to the expensive growth factors that most formulations contain. Media price is therefore a vital constituent of Moo's Law™.

# GROWTH FACTOR SERUMS USED IN CELL CULTURED FOOD PRODUCTION

Basal media is typically not sufficient on its own to make cells proliferate enough to grow meat. In the past, animal sera, mostly derived from cows, have been used. These sera normally come from cows during slaughter (about eight per cent of all cattle on their way to dispatch are pregnant) who are identified as carrying a foetus. Increasingly, this source of what is known as foetal bovine serum (FBS) is considered cruel, unethical and potentially dangerous because of pathogenic risk. Non-serum replacements have become more prevalent and are the focus of extensive research by the cultured meat industry.

FBS is often a good starting serum for companies, given that it is rich in growth factors as well as hormones, antioxidants, and lipids that replicate the foetal state of early animal development. Foetal bovine serum has been described as a "miracle juice" by Michael Selden, CEO of Finless Foods, a cultured fish startup, as it can be used in cultivating virtually any species. FBS is widely used in biomedical research as it supports and accelerates the growth of nearly any animal, fish or insect cell line. However, it is expensive (US $1000 per litre) and, despite multiple quality checks, it can be a source of viruses and other contaminants, including Bovine Spongiform Encephalopathy (BSE, or mad cow disease). In some geographies, up to 70 per cent of samples are contaminated. It is also variable in potency and effect.

For this reason, every single cultured meat company is either using recombinant versions of the key growth factors found in FBS; are seeking to produce their own growth factors; or finding novel equivalents to mimic the growth factor activity, all without using animal material. Most commonly-used growth factor ingredients are TGF-β, FGF-2, insulin, and the proteins albumin and transferrin. TGF-β and FGF-2 are the most expensive components, at US$ 80 million per gram and US$ 2 million per gram, respectively. While these two only comprise a small fraction of the total media volume, they currently account for 96 per cent of the total media cost, which is too high for use in the final production. For many companies, the cost of media and other components are the main bottlenecks to commercially viable production.

As we go through individual companies in the next chapter, I will examine the differing types of technology employed by our favourite companies.

# THE KEY
# PLAYERS IN THE
# NEW AGRARIAN
# REVOLUTION

—

**T**HIS BOOK WAS LARGELY WRITTEN DURING THE 2020 COVID-19 LOCKDOWN IN EUROPE. ONE OF THE FACTORS WHICH IMPELLED ME TO GET IT OUT QUICKLY IS THAT THE FOOD SUPPLY CHAIN THAT WE CURRENTLY RELY ON IS DEFECTIVE AND HAS TO BE CHANGED – AND FAST.

There are an increasing number of companies seeking to be a part of this change, be they plant-based food manufacturers, startups in the field of cellular agriculture, 'picks and shovels' manufacturers, or indeed, established large food companies looking to break into an expanding market.

There is also a coterie of experienced and well-heeled investors in the sector (the 'vegan mafia'), as well as thought-leaders involved in advocacy and planning. Many of these people have kindly given me their time – often on Zoom – to discuss what they do and how they do it. Very few face-to-face interviews have taken place, due to restrictions on travel, but there have been some; most, however, involve getting a feel for key industry players over the telephone.

What strikes me and my colleagues on the investment side of the industry is just how motivated most of the people involved in every aspect of new agriculture really are. There are, of course, a few charlatans, as there are in every nascent industry, but almost everyone I have spoken to and actually met shines with a passion, be it based on the potential abolition of animal cruelty (the most cited factor), a commitment to reducing environmental impact in farming (the second most listed factor), or a belief that human health can be improved by diet.

Profit and scale are, of course, important to the most impressive of these businesspeople and commentators, otherwise I would not be recommending their companies as potential investments. After all, this is a book primarily geared to investors; but it is good to know that the people behind these firms are almost vocational – and certainly devotional – to their cause.

In this chapter, I am going to describe and triage what I think are the best companies worthy of investors' consideration, and I will divide them into categories along the lines described in the preceding chapter.

First, there are the plant-based food companies, which are far more numerous than those in the other categories, numbering, at last count, about 430 worldwide.

Second, there are the companies providing tools to enhance the quality of plant-based products, either by using fermentation or cell culture techniques to add valuable ingredients.

Then there are the companies solely utilising cell culture, none of which yet have a widely-dispersed product, but some will in the next few years, and many already have prototype samples. The cell-based food companies, although small now, have the capacity to be very big indeed. This is because they are likely to benefit more from Moo's Law™ than plant-based or fermentation-based food companies.

The principal obstacles to their future success are technical barriers, which include replacing the animal-derived serums and expensive growth factors needed to proliferate cells and to grow tissues with cheaper and non-animal-related alternatives.

Also, the problems of scaling up to large bioreactors, getting consumers used to eating what have been called 'Frankenfoods' in the past, and getting regulators used to regulating them, are all being addressed. There are currently bioreactors available to produce cell-cultured food in very large quantities, but none have yet been used.

As a result, the larger, more established food companies are seeking to become a part of the revolution, some for reasons that are less noble than the upstarts. Here, it is a case of if you can't beat 'em, you might as well join 'em.

And lastly, there are companies involved in what I call the 'adventurous periphery' of the industry – companies involved in producing novel plant strains, for instance, or companies involved in vertical farming or new irrigation systems.

Overall, the food industry is going through a massive revolution. In this respect, as in so many others, Winston Churchill was prescient in his prediction in 1931 that in 'fifty years', 'we shall escape the absurdity of growing a whole chicken in order to eat the breast or the wing, by growing these parts separately'. A bit early in his forecast perhaps but, as in so much else, wise.

The industry likely to be most disrupted by this New Agrarian Revolution will be the global meat sector. In 2019, this industry was estimated to be worth US $1.4 trillion, which is about the size of the entire Spanish economy. By 2040, fuelled by demand from developing economies and rising populations, the market for all meats (including 'new' ones) is expected to be US $2.7 trillion, which is approximately the current size of the whole UK economy. Indeed, in the period 1990-2018, world meat consumption per capita grew by 93 per cent, with a commensurate increase in harm to the environment.

Jefferies, the US investment bank, estimates that alternative meats could be worth as much as US $490 billion in sales by 2040, and as 'little' as US $90 billion in a worst-case scenario, with the best guess at US $240 billion, or nine per cent of the market.

The two conventional meat categories growing fastest are pork and poultry, with beef and mutton lagging behind. The highest penetration of alternative meats so far is in the beef category, but that is about to change, with the ramping up of poultry and pork substitutes, both plant-based and cell-cultured.

The latter, produced by the cell-cultured companies, need to achieve dramatic – but attainable – cuts to their cost of production to become competitive. This is of course, *Moo's Law*™. Companies in the plant-based category are already familiar to consumers in many parts of the world – Impossible Foods, Beyond Meat, Good Catch Foods, Quorn Foods and Eat JUST are among the preeminent examples.

But others, employing cell-based technologies, will achieve prominence in due course. BlueNalu, Shiok Meats, Wildtype, Finless Foods and Avant Meats in seafood; Memphis Meats, Mosa Meat, SuperMeat, JUST and Aleph Farms in meats, and Mission Barns and Cubiq Foods in fats. In dairy, LegenDairy Foods, Perfect Day and TurtleTree Labs; in eggs, Clara Foods. In leather goods, VitroLabs; and in cotton, GALY. All of these are contenders, and in total, globally, there are about 70 of them, with multiple new corporate formations every year.

In due course, there will be plenty for us as investors to choose from, and I will regularly update the book's website to add any interesting new companies that come along – or indeed, to remove any that are acquired, are merged or, sadly, in the grand scheme of capitalism, fail.

I will also incorporate into this section information gleaned from interviews with key industry players, to give a better sense of the founders' backstories, current plans, distinguishing technologies, and aspirations.

It is worth explaining to the reader who is unfamiliar with early stage, venture capital investing, what is meant below when I refer to 'Seed' or 'Series X' funding. Seed funding is the early equity funding into a company which provides the initial capital to grow the business from a concept. Typically, in this sector, it provides funding for the company to hire its first employees, develop a lab space and create their first prototypes.

Series A funding comes later, once the business model has been more firmly established and investors can better see the commercial potential of the company and its product offerings. Typically, Series A funding rounds raise anywhere from US $2 million to US $15 million.

Series B, C, and beyond all follow, as the companies expand their teams, establish pilot facilities and seek large scale commercial production. Once substantial capital has been raised from the private markets, companies may look to IPO to attract public capital, or be acquired by big food players, which I will talk about later in this book.

# PLANT-BASED FOODS

There is a multiplicity of plant-based companies and – pardon the pun – they have sprouted everywhere in the past decade or so. There are now plant-formed imitator products of beef, pork, chicken, eggs, seafood, dairy, snack bars and much, much more for increasingly flexitarian consumers to choose from.

And consumers *are* so choosing, as confirmed by multiple metrics including sales, expressed preferences, and the switch by food producers to different and more appropriate plant crops.

For instance, the *de rigueur* protein source of choice now used in plant-based foods, the humble pea, has doubled in production from 2015 to 2019, with worldwide tonnage currently nearly 300,000 tonnes for the purposes of producing plant-based foods. Henk Hoogenkamp, a leading forecaster in the food sector, expects pea production for clean food to almost double to 580,000 tonnes by 2025.

Indeed, it is possible that within the next ten years the twin-pronged assault on conventional meat from plant-based and cell-cultured alternatives could have completely altered the food industry as it currently stands, and there are plenty of sober forecasters who make that prediction.

The recent pandemic will no doubt have proved an accelerant to this process, as, in the future, might a tax on meat, either imposed globally or by individual countries. Any meat taxes would be levied in order – rather like sugar or tobacco taxes – to discourage harms, be they direct ones to human health, or indirect ones to the environment.

Consumers are now much more engaged and attuned to the possibilities that animal-free proteins represent, with McKinsey & Company, the large management consulting firm, estimating that the compound annual growth rate (CAGR) in online searches for vegan products was 16 per cent between 2004 and 2019.

The Covid-19 crisis, as with so much else, has acted as a booster for the adoption of clean meats and alternative proteins. This is partly due to the outbreak of the disease in the slaughterhouses of the US and elsewhere, whose mass closures sharply curtailed conventional meat production during the period, and partly due to the fact that people were staying at home, and were prepared to try 'new' foods.

The first few months of the coronavirus pandemic were especially difficult for conventional meat producers in the US, Germany, the UK and parts of Asia. In the US alone, over 20,000 processing plant workers contracted the virus and over 200 died. Because of the closure of many plants, and the highly consolidated nature of the meat-packing industry, severe shortages of fresh meat occurred in many parts of the US. Analysts predicted, as of the time of writing, that losses for the US industry would be over US $20 billion.

Plant-based meats, by contrast, grew in sales by almost three times in the eight weeks up to April 2020, according to Nielsen. Beyond Meat sold US $97 million worth of its burgers, sausages and chicken plant-based foods, up 141 per cent year on year, and with a total of 25,000 grocery stores in the US stocking its products. Indeed, Beyond Meat's US grocery sales nearly doubled during the quarter ended June 27, 2020. But offsetting this, food service sales understandably slid, as restaurants, universities and office buildings temporarily closed. Across the Atlantic, a survey by Mintel found that nearly eight million people in the UK reported eating more vegan food since the start of the pandemic. This phenomenon of eating less meat per capita is spreading in most developed parts of the world, although meat consumption is growing in developing countries such as Brazil.

Furthermore, as Beyond Meat and others increase the scale of their production, they will become even more profitable relative to conventional meat producers than they already are (except in the peak pandemic period when restaurants and institutions were shuttered). In Q1 2020 Beyond Meat achieved a gross margin of almost 40 per cent, almost unheard-of in the food industry, and double the best margin Tyson, the world's second largest meat processor, has ever achieved in its history. Beyond Meat did lose money in the second quarter of 2020, entirely due to restaurant and food service sales collapsing in the face of the pandemic.

Beyond Meat, along with other plant-based food producers, is spreading its wings internationally. In June 2020 it opened its first European co-manufacturing plant in Holland, owned and operated by its European distribution partner, Zandbergen World's Finest Meat.

I spoke to Ethan Brown in California, where he was surrounded by a menagerie including his pig, Wilbur, and his bloodhound, Duke. Ethan, who is charming and articulate, has been eating a plant-based diet for a long time and he told me he was in the middle of writing to his best friend's daughter about his reasons for not eating animals. His family owned a farm in Maryland, although they mostly lived in Washington DC as he was growing up. He felt that his father, a philosopher, never really answered the question of why some animals lived in the house, and others were kept outside. He became vegan in his late 20s, eventually making the connection between climate change and animals, and changed his career from an involvement in hydrogen fuel cells, to what he does now. He is the founder and CEO of the most valuable plant-based food company on the planet.

Beyond Meat was founded in 2009 and started with a plant-based chicken strip product, which attempted to imitate the muscle of animal-based chickens, in 2012. He was inspired by the Buddhist tradition of prohibiting meat consumption and of trying to imitate it by using plants. He put together a programme at the University of Missouri with Harold Huff and Fu-Hung Hsieh of the university's department of agriculture. These two highly-ranked academics had been working on creating chicken strips from soy isolate for over 20 years.

He took a deep dive with them into the composition of plant material at a molecular -level understanding that we too are made of 99 per cent of the same elements as plants – oxygen, carbon, hydrogen, nitrogen, calcium and phosphorous – the primordial soup!

Humans are organised differently to plants, of course, but we can easily skip the process of using animals as processors of plants and producers of proteins. With his Missouri collaborators, Ethan organised experiments to break the molecular bonds of plants and to reset them, by using heating, cooling and pressure to create an approximation of animal muscle.

So, Beyond Meat started its chicken with a regional launch in the US grocery chain Whole Foods in 2012. It got a big break that very same year when Mark Bittman, the *New York Times*' food columnist, wrote that he could not tell the difference between the real thing and the Beyond Chicken Strip, when both were used in wraps.

Beyond Meat has always been against genetically modified products, not because they are evil but because the unintended consequences could be severe. Ethan used the example of GM soy – in itself fine – requiring Roundup, a controversial weed killer, to grow efficiently.

The company has since moved on to its famous burgers, which are sold just about everywhere now. Ethan says that iterations of these will get better and better, driving down sodium and saturated fat contents – making them healthier, and without the addition of any "gimmicks" (such as the haem in Impossible Burgers!).

Beyond Meat has two distinct types of consumer: the first category are the over-40s who are concerned about their health and the undoubted harm that excessive animal proteins, trans fats, and saturated animal fats can do. The second category is the younger generation, of school or college age, who understand the environmental damage of conventional meat production and are also motivated by animal cruelty.

The company now has a very good repeat purchase business - nearly 50 per cent in Q2 2020, which is very high in the food industry – and is looking at several line extensions. Ethan thinks that cultured meat will have an important place, but that it is some years away. He admires Uma Valeti (who he initially called Uma Thurman by mistake!) of Memphis. For sure, if Moo's Law™ begins to apply, Ethan will be looking for Beyond to get involved in the cell ag side of the industry.

He believes that Griddle Parity™ will be achievable for Beyond products in about three years' time, as the company's supply chains mature.

The Agro-Luddites, in his opinion, are misguided in not realising that plant-based foods can empower farmers and create wealth. This would stand in contrast to the dire economics of most cattle production – and the consequent addiction of many poverty-line farmers to OxyContin and other prescription opioids. Growing crops for human consumption is much more profitable than growing them for animals, as he points out.

Luckily, the evening I spoke to Ethan was our burger night, and I was able to show him the Beyond Burger packets we had lined up as well as, of course, our own hounds; Juno, Juniper and Twisis!

Even on the Isle of Man, small as it is, we enjoyed Beyond Burgers while in lockdown, and Beyond is trying to extend its reach even further through fast food outlets. Because Beyond products are non-GM, unlike the Impossible Burger, which uses a GM process in the production of its haem, Beyond Meat will be able to sell through European fast food outlets, and the company claims it is in discussions with a number of them already.

Beyond is already tied with Starbucks and Yum! Brands in China, which means that soon its products will soon be in KFC, Pizza Hut and Taco Bell in the world's second largest economy.

Impossible Foods, the second largest of the new US meat disruptors, has been making significant inroads with its plant-based burgers as well. As of the end of June 2020, they were on sale in more than 3,000 stores in the US, having been much stronger in the food service industry prior to the pandemic, including, as mentioned before, in Burger King. Impossible recently completed a Series G round of US $200 million, at an estimated valuation of US $4 billion, making it the second most valuable of the New Agrarian companies. Investors included Temasek Holdings, Mirae Financial Asset Group of Korea and Coatue, a large US investment fund.

*Meatless Farm advert in London. Reproduced courtesy of Meatless Farm.*

In the UK, the private company Meatless Farm offers plant-based meats, which it bills as cleaner and less calorific than those of Impossible and Beyond, using some pretty irreverent advertising. Meatless Farm has made inroads into the UK grocery market, including in supermarket giants Sainsbury's and Morrisons. Meatless Farm burgers contain about half the levels of saturated fat (a major cause of heart disease) found in Beyond and Impossible burgers, and currently the company is producing over 1,000 tonnes of minced plant meat a month for use in burgers, sold either in pubs or restaurants (with an obvious interruption for Covid-19) and on grocery shelves. Meatless Farm products are also now sold in Whole Foods in the US, joining Quorn at the forefront of a plant-based British expeditionary food force to America.

I spoke to Morten Toft Bech, the Danish-born but UK-based founder and CEO, and thought that he articulated the company's defining strategy of being "healthier" than other plant-based meat companies very well. Sales are currently running at a 300% growth rate, and while there are no current plans to raise further capital, this is a UK company with strong prospects, and I advise investors to closely look out for Meatless Farm. Meatless has just raised US $31 million in a Series B round, making total funding to date about US $50 million. In Q1 of 2021 it expects to do an even larger round, and so far, the key investors are Whole Foods (as a strategic partner) and Stray Dog Capital.

So, sales of alternative plant-based foods are booming, and alongside this is a rapidly increasing level of investment in the sector. Just under US $1 billion was invested worldwide in alternative protein companies in Q1 2020, according to the Good Food Institute (GFI), with Impossible Foods alone raising US $500 million and the brand holding company. The LIVEKINDLY Co., raised US $220 million. By June 2020, a total of US $1 billion had been invested in cell ag companies worldwide, marking a significant milestone for the nascent industry.

And the pace of sales and investment continues to astonish. Until recently, Bernstein, a leading US research house, believed that Beyond Meat and its ilk would have a much slower uptake of their products than is currently the case. For example, they thought that Beyond Meat's annual sales would be tracking at about US $1 billion by 2030 but have now revised that view so that it will be a decade earlier; i.e. by the end of 2020.

This is a phenomenal rate of growth, and as more and more distribution outlets stock the products of the plant-based food companies, both in the US and elsewhere, and as these companies begin to sell directly to consumers, sales growth will compound even higher.

Ethan, of Beyond Meat, expects his plant-based meats to soon be price-competitive with conventional meats, possibly as soon as the end of 2023. This is Griddle Parity™, and this parity is now well within sight for the plant-based meats industry. This is extremely important, as the key determinants for mass consumer take up of clean meat products will be taste and price. Only a minority of people, save for company founders, are primarily motivated by animal-related or environmental factors, and most of these people are already converted to the cause and, in any case, do not represent more than a fraction of the potential market.

This market potential is described by almost everybody I have interviewed as being primarily with consumers who are vaguely aware of the harms that conventional animal farming causes but are much more influenced by taste, mouthfeel, and price. They are prepared to move away from a largely carnivore diet to one that is more flexitarian if the products measure up.

Meantime, Ethan's fiercest rival, Pat (also Brown), of Impossible, is gearing up to take on the pork market, pork being the most consumed meat in the world, largely due to sales in China – in which, incredible though it may sound, half of all the animals in the world bred for food live. (Pat, incidentally, does not believe that cultured meat will ever take off, due to its expense. I beg to differ.)

Although Impossible, along with many others, has its eyes on the Chinese market and hopes to be in it by the end of 2020, it, along with all foreign interlopers, will face intense domestic competition.

Local Chinese companies are equally looking at pork-equivalent plant-based substitutes, particularly as more educated consumers become aware of the evident health dangers of intensive swine farming.

New Chinese plant-based companies are springing up, among them being Zhenmeat, a two-year-old startup making mooncakes with plant-based pork. Green Monday, which has raised a recent equity round of US $70 million and is based in Hong Kong, is another producer of plant-based pork, which it has dubbed OmniPork. Its product range is due to be introduced to vegan restaurants across China late in 2020.

The Chinese government appears to understand full well the need to improve the quality of food in the country, especially after recent pandemics, and is actively encouraging the development of a home-grown plant-based foods industry. Sun Junmao, the deputy director of Food and Nutrition at the Chinese Ministry of Agriculture, is on record as saying: 'The development of the plant-based food industry is a good way of nurturing our people's nutrition and health'.

There is typically not much IP in plant-based foods, and no reason to suppose that Chinese companies will not eventually be dominant in their own market, in combination with, or independent of, foreign companies. Green Monday is working on a plant-based fish and pork taco to be sold in China through Yum! Brands' Taco Bell subsidiary and is also partnered with White Castle of the US. Beyond Meat hopes to have two production facilities in China before the end of 2021, from which it can satisfy growing local demand for its products, including those sold through fast food outlets.

Dao Foods, part of a socially-aware fund, has teamed up with New Crop Capital, one of the most important – and philanthropic – investors in the clean meat space. Chris Kerr, the chief investment officer of New Crop, is possibly the most famous of the 'vegan mafia'.

He lives with his wife Kirsti in Woodstock, New York, and credits her with giving him an entirely new outlook on life. Growing up on a farm, where the slaughter of animals was part of the fabric of life, he did not become a vegan till much later in life – and after he met Kirsti.

His early work at the Humane Society of the United States (HSUS) proved too nebulous, so he started to help in raising capital for what are now leaders in the field – Beyond Meat, JUST, Daiya Foods and Miyoko's Creamery. He teamed up with Bruce Friedrich, head of the Good Food Institute, and formed New Crop Capital. Chris is a director of the LIVEKINDLY Collective and he also helped establish, and is a director of, cell-based seafood company BlueNalu (one of my featured and favourite companies), as well as a director of Good Catch Foods, a plant-based fish company.

He and Kirsti are motivated by changing the world and by reorienting attitudes to animals. They do not have children and are not money-oriented. His passion and devotion to the cause is evident in speaking to him and, clearly, he is also pretty good at spotting entrepreneurial brilliance.

Chris is mostly focussed on plant-based foods, believing that in 10 years' time, consumers will taste no difference between plant-based meats and conventional ones. He is somewhat sceptical of the ability of cell ag companies to scale, but sees huge opportunity in plant-based foods, which will enable novel extruded forms and tastes over time, as new forms of production are devised and optimised. This is interesting as New Crop was part of Memphis Meats' seed round, BlueNalu's seed round, and Aleph Farm's seed round...but I suppose this is called hedging your bets!

Chris is particularly enthusiastic about Good Catch, a plant-based fish company, and is keen that 'comfort foods' (e.g. tuna melts, which he loves) can be as convenient in plant form as those using wild-caught tuna.

His family – as mentioned, farm-country folk – is now reconciled to what he does and recognises that his mission to end the suffering of animals is a heartfelt and noble one. Kirsti is concerned about conventional meat production for the same reasons, but also expressed her concern for the welfare of abattoir workers who, working in close proximity in cold conditions (ideal for the spread of disease), are particularly susceptible to diseases such as Covid-19.

Chris points out that recent developments in dairy alternatives provide a clear pathway for other alternative foods. In just the past decade, alternative milks, such as almond, soy, oat, and rice, have captured almost a sixth of the US liquid milk market, up from a minuscule proportion in 2010.

He recognises that plant-based food products generally have less defensible IP than cultured food products but thinks that this might be less of a disadvantage than is commonly perceived, as the plant-based companies increasingly utilise new and patentable technologies, rather than off-the-shelf (OTS) machinery. He points to the first iteration of the Beyond Burger, dubbed the 'Beast', which he describes as having been awful, but now superseded by an infinitely better and more palatable burger. Chris is a big believer in the role of in-house chefs to tweak taste and texture to continuously upgrade products. Indeed, chefs prominently feature in the publicity of many of the companies I describe in this book.

As far as cultured meats are concerned, he thinks that BlueNalu could have a fish-based product, albeit relatively expensively priced, within two years; in land-based cell ag meat alternatives, he thinks that Memphis Meats could be at the same point in roughly the same timeframe.

In plant-based meats, he regards Impossible and Beyond as being light-years ahead of the others, and in fish, Good Catch as the clear leader in a less-packed field. He is also a fan of The Protein Brewery. This Dutch-based platform which is trying to make proteins using microorganisms to create a brewed fibrous protein, hopefully more affordable than soy, which, along with pea, is the stalwart plant of the clean meat revolution.

Chris recognises that certain markets are currently off limits to some plant-based products. For instance the EU's territory is verboten to GMO derivatives such as Impossible's haem, or the algae oil used in a few of Good Catch's products. But generally, the plant-based industry has a clearer path to regulatory approval around the world than the cultured meat industry. I explore the regulatory barriers to novel foods in the next chapter.

He understands that the clean foods industry may in some instances need to partner with the conventional players, who have been, in his eyes, the 'bad guys' in the past. These unholy partnerships are the result of a need for scale and reach which is why, for instance, Good Catch has signed a deal with Bumble Bee Foods, one of the world's largest seafood companies. Bumble Bee reaches 60 per cent of US households and thereby allows Good Catch to expand much faster rather than by building from scratch.

Chris and Kirsti have built an animal utopia and what sounds like an idyllic life for themselves, while all the time advancing what is an essential cause. Bears, squirrels, turkeys, deer, and chipmunks – not to mention six cats – are amongst the animals that come and visit their ranch regularly.

Bruce Friedrich is also highly prominent in the field, and is the co-founder and executive director of the Good Food Institute. GFI, which is fuelled entirely by philanthropy, has more than 100 full-time scientists, lobbyists and corporate engagement specialists all over the world, including India, Israel, Brazil, Europe, and Asia Pacific, and is central to the development of the industry.

The Good Food Institute's conferences, workshops, newsletters and publications are indispensable to anyone seriously interested in investing in, supporting, or otherwise observing this New Agrarian Revolution. As an aside, GFI's scientists reviewed the science in this book to ensure accuracy.

Bruce is an accomplished public speaker (he has a TED talk that has been viewed more than 2 million times and translated into 30 languages) and an acclaimed author. He lives with his wife and cats in Washington DC. In our discussions we have veered into feline territory, with me describing our neighbourhood cat visitor Marmaduke, who lives in the Isle of Man, where rare tail-less (Manx) cats are sometimes to be found, and of which Marmaduke is one. Bruce responds with photos and tales (tails?) of Rena, Tigger, and Angie, his three cats.

Bruce is central to the story of this industry, and on a connect-the-dots matrix he is the Kevin Bacon (possibly inappropriate word given the context!) of the clean foods world.

Another interviewee, Chuck Laue of Stray Dog Capital, high in the pantheon of the greats of this new industry, was quick to acknowledge the influence of both Chris Kerr and Bruce Friedrich in propelling the industry forward. Chuck made a fortune in the mobile phone insurance industry, and again was heavily influenced by his wife, Jennifer, to change his life for the better. He grew up in the US with no pets, as his mother was set against them, and it was not until he met his future wife's dogs that he was converted, and his heart melted. When he got his own dog, Quinn, a big white fluffy mix of Eskimo and Samoyed, his modern journey began.

His life with Jennifer in Kansas City revolved around her and Quinn (Quinn has sadly passed away), and gradually he ended up a vegan – as are most people in this industry.

On 10th February 2006, he ate his last meat meal. It is interesting that that date is seared in his memory, rather like the date of an alcoholic's last drink.

He and Jennifer instituted a mass spaying and neutering programme for local dogs and then merged their efforts with those of a large animal shelter, before Chuck joined the board of the Humane Society of the United States (HSUS) in 2013. It was around then that he was introduced to Chris Kerr, who happened to be working there.

Chris was at that time, *entrepreneur in residence* at HSUS, tasked with investing in startup companies that were trying to take animals out of the food supply chain. The HSUS eventually stopped making those investments, so Chuck and Jennifer, using their own investment vehicle Quinn Capital, named after their beloved dog, took over the funding of some of Chris's ideas. Quinn Capital was superseded by Stray Dog Capital, which is now one of the most important investors in the space. For the sake of balance, they also have an investment vehicle called Stray Cat Capital!

They now have about 30 investments in the clean foods space, and have also assembled a syndicate of about 140 individuals and institutions to invest alongside Stray Dog Capital. This syndicate is called 'Glass Wall', named after Paul McCartney's quote that 'if slaughterhouses had glass walls, everyone would be a vegetarian'. In 2008 the Humane Society of the United States conducted an underground investigation which exposed multiple atrocities in slaughterhouses including, heartbreakingly, the use of forklift trucks to take "downer cows" (cows unable to walk to their deaths due to sickness) to their place of destruction. Think about it.

Roger Lienhard, a prominent forward thinker in clean foods, is another important link in the chain of achievement in the clean food space. He acknowledges Chris Kerr with giving him inspiration to create his own portfolio, set up Blue Horizon Ventures and establish the LIVEKINDLY collective, which appears to be on track for a billion-dollar-plus IPO.

He is Swiss, and still speaks with a Germanic accent, though he lives quite a lot of the time in the US. He is a veteran entrepreneur, with all the scars that those of us with long careers in the hard-scrabble business world are familiar with – but he has deservedly picked up quite a few plaudits as well. He freely admits that not all his investments (mostly in IT) have worked, which is a humble admission I admire, but he clearly has made enough to fund a succession of clean meat forays.

He is 52, and his conversion to the righteous came from travels he undertook at the age of 45; travels he said were much needed, to refresh his spirit from an exhausting routine. He recognised that there was something to the food revolution early on and characterises it as like the internet 20 years ago. Funnily enough, this is exactly how I describe the longevity industry, and the analogies are well suited to both 'meta thematics', longevity and food.

Over a meandering career, Roger has eventually settled on developing novel companies in the clean foods business, and in this he has been remarkably successful. His vehicle, LIVEKINDLY, is one of the best-capitalised in the field, recently having raised US $200 million, the largest founders' round in food history, and the firm is headed up by a highly experienced management team. LIVEKINDLY is likely to be a big IPO in the US, and investors should avidly watch out for this.

Roger's Damascene moment was influenced by the ubiquitous Chris Kerr, and he was early enough on the scene that he now can go to lunch (vegan of course!) with any of the key people in the industry. He started by making about 40 (small) seed investments over five years, and the strain that this put on his finances was quickly alleviated when Beyond Meat, one of his early investments, went public. Apparently, his banker in Zurich was struck dumb by its success, and never questioned Roger's moves after that.

He then started Blue Horizon, a venture capital fund with about EUR 200 million, staffed by 10 people based in Zurich. It was this fund that was the anchor investor in LIVEKINDLY.

Roger firmly believes that, in 10 years' time, meat, as we know it, will be a niche product, and that animal farmers will be the equivalent of high-end hobbyists. He is focussed on plant-based products as he thinks cell-based products are possibly eight years away from commercialisation, which is more pessimistic than my view. He expects to be a big investor in cultured products in a couple of years' time, when he sees the path to scale and price more clearly, but for now LIVEKINDLY is focused on acquiring plant-based chicken brands.

He absolutely abhors the so-called 'blended' products – conventional meat and plants mixed up – as he sees them as a way for a uniquely cruel industry to survive longer than it should.

Roger admires the Beyond Meat model and is a big booster of Ethan Brown, its founder. He also likes Veestro, a plant-based meal delivery company in LA that is rapidly expanding. He is a fan of Alpha Foods, a company specialising in plant-based burritos and 'chicken' nuggets. This company sells its foods through retailers such as Costco in the US.

The business model of Roger's LIVEKINDLY is essentially to build a portfolio of geographically-dispersed brands focussed on plant-based foods. They have acquired several established vegan brands and they are actively engaged in buying more. One of these acquisitions is LikeMeat, a German plant-based foods company based in Dusseldorf, selling throughout Europe. LikeMeat complements the main focus of LIVEKINDLY, the replacement of chicken protein, partly by working with family-run farms producing chickens and pivoting them towards clean meat. At any time there are about 23 billion chickens on the planet, and imitation chicken meat made from plants requires fewer ingredients than imitation beef, because chicken meat doesn't need to 'bleed'. Chicken is a huge market and it is easier to replicate in a lab than beef.

# MOO'S LAW

LIVEKINDLY has an investment in PURIS, the largest pea protein producer in North America.

PURIS was founded by Jerry Lorenzen in 1985, and although it has received an investment of US $75 million from the huge food conglomerate Cargill, it remains essentially a family-owned company. PURIS uses non-GMO seeds, on which it holds multiple patents, to breed high-yield, disease-resistant crops that have the effect of leaving land in better shape than when the crops are sown. In 2020, PURIS expects to produce yellow field peas on 300,000 acres of land across 14 US states, as well as other pulses on other large tracts of land.

PURIS also owns a large soy protein isolate factory in Turtle Lake, Wisconsin, as part of what it calls its World Food System, which is an end-to-end food production system. The company also operates plants in Iowa and Minnesota.

Among many other customers, PURIS sells pea protein to Beyond Meat, and is actively encouraging farmers to move from soy monocultures to pea, which it regards as the future of plant-based foods, as does Roger.

Pea is better for the soil than comparable crops, including soy and sugarcane. Although soy is currently much cheaper (about one-third of the cost), this is largely because production of soy has huge economies of scale. As it will be with pea production, according to Roger, and in the relatively near future.

Roger believes that his chicken alternatives made with soy are already potentially cheaper than the cheapest chicken anywhere in the world (Brazilian) and that before too long they will be 20 to 30 per cent cheaper.

Currently, LIVEKINDLY has three plant-based chicken brands and is looking to expand its portfolio in South Africa. Price competition against Brazilian frozen chicken meat is the principal selling point – which Roger hopes will encourage South African farmers to sign up to the LIVEKINDLY ecosystem. In South Africa, LIVEKINDLY operates The Fry Family Food Company and in Germany, the aforementioned LikeMeat. Recently the company acquired five-year old Oumph! a Swedish maker of plant-based burgers, strips, fillets and pulled meat. Oumph! sells these products in the UK and the Nordics. This latest acquisition is part of LIVEKINDLY's strategy of assembling a collection of heritage and startup vegan brands to create a global yet local ecosystem of plant-based food companies.

Plant-based chicken is the main focus of LIVEKINDLY, at least *ab initio*, because chicken meat production will shortly overtake that of pork, as the world's most popular source of animal protein. Economists at the International Poultry Council support this view, stating that poultry production will overtake pork and beef production combined by 2050, and will remain the dominant individual meat category for the foreseeable future. Consumers have the highest acceptance for chicken and are very willing to switch from other animal proteins to chicken. Plant-based chicken is free of hormones and antibiotics, and there is no waste, unlike conventional chicken. Vitamins and other supplements can be added to make it even healthier, and standards of hygiene are deemed to be considerably better.

I do not know for sure, of course, but I imagine that LIVEKINDLY will join Beyond Meat as another plant-based food company to go public, and as a result this is absolutely a company to watch. They have adopted a clever policy of acquiring localised brands, adapting them to be price- and taste-competitive with localised requirements, but also garnering cost and branding synergies across the world. Their allying of this strategy to an ability to raise substantial funds from smart investors is, to my mind, their winning formula.

Another philanthropic key player in the clean food space is New Harvest, a non-profit driven entirely by donations. Originally founded in 2004 by Jason Matheny (who now runs an institute at Georgetown focused on existential risks to humanity), the first to donate was Mark Shuttleworth, a hugely-successful South African technology entrepreneur.

New Harvest is focussed on cellular agriculture and specifically on research, where it funds promising new ideas such as new culture media formulations, bioreactors, and methods of tissue assembly to produce cultured meat. It is also involved in community-building; bringing together scientists, academics, funders, policy makers and regulatory authorities with a view to fostering collaborative effort.

I spoke to Isha Datar, the impressive Executive Director of New Harvest, who has been in post since 2013. She is also the co-founder of Perfect Day, originally called Muufri, in April 2014, as well as Clara Foods in November of the same year (I discuss both companies in this chapter).

Isha was early to the field; having got her BSc in Cell and Molecular Biology from the University of Alberta in Canada, and subsequently a Master's in Biotechnology from the University of Toronto, she was among the first to recognise the potential of cell-cultured meat. Indeed, in 2010, which in the context of this industry was aeons ago, her paper 'Possibilities for an *in-vitro* meat production system' was published in the food science journal Innovative Food Science and Emerging Technologies.

Isha got into the space relatively early, firstly as author of the keystone publication mentioned above, and secondly as the full-time Executive Director of New Harvest, the first non-profit dedicated to producing foods from cells instead of animals. In her second year at New Harvest, eager to go beyond community building and instead see advancements in the lab, Isha connected the co-founders to establish Perfect Day, a company producing dairy proteins using precision fermentation. Committed to growing the cellular agriculture ecosystem at large, Isha gave her founding stake in Perfect Day to New Harvest so that the non-profit organisation had an endowment to fund future research. This model was followed with Clara Foods. Isha has been happy with the evolution of the cellular agriculture sector over the last decade, seeing that it has steadily been gaining momentum, with increasing differentiation. For example, Isha points to new trends in fish-based companies – Wildtype, Finless Foods, BlueNalu and Shiok Meats – as well as in enabling technologies; the 'picks and shovels' companies working on supply chains, serum-free media, and bioreactor designs.

On the question of defensibility of IP between plant-based and cell-based meat, Isha explains that, while biotechnology investment historically has relied on the robustness of patents to exclude competition, this sector will be different. Marketing is going to be such a big differentiator in this space, as companies build loyalty with future customers and tell the stories of their products. Another source of competitive advantage will simply be the artisanal handling of cell cultures – there is a know-how to cell culture which simply comes from experience, not from documentable intellectual property. Lastly, the food industry relies heavily on trade secrets as opposed to patents – as the innovations in cultured meats may not come from the growing of cells as much as the food science of turning those cells into marketable food products. Furthermore, in terms of getting these products to market, Isha sees a continuum between plant-based and cell-based meat, predicting that the transition will begin with something akin to a veggie burger sprinkled with cells (a hybrid product), followed through generations of product innovation by completely novel, structured foods consisting of 100 per cent cell culture, such as fillets of steak. Even beyond this could be products that break the mold of meat-as-we-know-it, towards new versions of meat with heightened nutritional compositions and improved textures and tastes. Roger Lienhard will be horrified with this line of thinking!

The leaders in the alternative protein space are similar in that they all have back stories that have led them to what was a form of conversion, almost always influenced by a desire to reduce the suffering of animals. In my interviews, I got the sense of a chain of happy coincidences as people met, compared notes on their passions, and joined forces to create what will become a huge industry.

Within the clean foods sector we have a number of players which stand out as significant.

I discuss them under their product subcategories below.

# PLANT-BASED CHICKEN SUBSTITUTES

Along with LIVEKINDLY, companies such as Rebellyous Foods and Beyond Meat are addressing the chicken market, which in terms of output volume has almost caught up with pork as the world's favourite source of animal protein.

## REBELLYOUS FOODS

Rebellyous Foods produces chicken nuggets initially for consumers and food-service distribution (restaurants, institutions, schools etc.). It is so far a relatively small, Seattle-based company, having raised about US $11 million in funding, including US $6 million in a Series A.

I spoke to Christie Lagally, the founder and CEO of Rebellyous. Christie has a background in mechanical and aerospace engineering and, early on in her adult life, recognised that the food system was intrinsically broken. I must say, I wish I had the same insights when I was young – better late than never though.

She was an early employee at GFI, working as a senior scientist focussing on modelling plant-based meat and, having caught the entrepreneurial urge, went off to start her own company, which is now Rebellyous.

Christie is a real advocate of what I have dubbed Moo's Law™ – my rule that the take-up of alternative foods will be driven by scale, which in turn will lead to lower prices. In the US, over 100 billion pounds of animal meat is produced annually, of which less than one per cent is plant-based, and so far none is produced by cultured methods. The market potential is therefore vast. Even in the UK, over one billion chickens are eaten every year.

She chose chicken as the company's initial product as the bird's meat represents nearly half of the US meat industry by volume, but is still under-represented by plant-based alternatives. In the US, chicken is generally prepared with batter or bread, fried, then served. This is the market that Rebellyous is seeking to serve with its chicken alternatives.

Rebellyous has been using teenagers (who better?) to test its products for key characteristics – juiciness, springiness, and dryness – to best replicate the taste of chicken. The company believes that the problem with plant-based foods and chicken analogues is an engineering one, and that previous purveyors of iterations of vegetarian 'meats' did not think through the unique problems of getting plant proteins to be as nearly indistinguishable as possible from the texture and taste of conventional meats.

Christie has therefore designed her own equipment and will, when scale and money permit, eschew the traditional OTS equipment used by most competitors. She is not a strong believer in the extrusion technology used by companies such as Impossible and Beyond, believing it to be inappropriate for chicken substitutes, mismatched for the types of products Rebellyous produces, as well as too slow and expensive.

She believes that the OTS equipment used by most plant-based products is basically a rerun of techniques used in conventional meat processing – e.g. bowl choppers, tumblers and frying systems – with the manufacturers of plant-based foods making these bits of equipment conform to the production of plant-based foods – and not very effectively.

A bowl chopper is designed to chop normal meat into tiny pieces but is reconfigured in plant-based meat production to add methylcellulose to the mix, as well as to emulsify the protein with oil and water.

Tumblers are fundamentally designed for incorporating seasoning and flavour into cuts of meat – but problems arise when used for plant-based protein, because of the different material properties, protein cell structure, and surface area of plant fibres compared to meat protein.

Similarly, frying equipment is not exactly fit for purpose, despite being widely used. This is because the characteristics of plant-based protein versus meat protein mean that thermal properties differ.

So, Christie has designed an entirely different system, based on a desire to get the cost of plant-based chicken below that of the cheapest 'real' stuff.

Rebellyous' equipment, she claims, will improve the efficiency, energy usage, wastage, production time and safety of the chicken-substitute production process. Given that the company is competing with highly automated chicken slaughterhouses, Christie believes that the company needs to produce its own equipment to dramatically drive down the cost of production. It is in their business model to eventually out-licence this equipment to converted slaughterhouses or, indeed, to other plant-based companies. Rebellyous is also already producing its own chicken products, which it now sells in retail, having made a swift pivot from food service in light of Covid-19.

However, the company is primarily a re-inventor of the manufacturing process, and it is in this area that it will stand or fall. Rebellyous currently uses a version of the 'mix and form' method of producing plant-based meat, where plants are mixed with other ingredients then 'formed' into shapes. This is different to the high moisture extrusion methods used by companies like Beyond and Impossible, and the Rebellyous method is faster, more energy-efficient and the meat loses less moisture.

At the moment, because of limited scale, Rebellyous chicken is still about twice as expensive per kilo as conventional chicken meat, but Christie expects that the two prices will converge in a matter of two or three years.

This will happen with a ramped-up production scale and the removal of some of the meat processing equipment currently used, including the bowl chopper, the kneading equipment and the hydration process. Apparently, this will significantly reduce the cost of goods sold (COGS), and Rebellyous thereby takes another step towards the holy grail of getting the price of their plant-based chicken to parity with the cheapest version of the real thing.

The prospect of incorporating healthy ingredients into the meat as a point of differentiation for Rebellyous – for instance by using canola oil and by reducing sodium content – is not lost on Christie. This will eventually be a major unique selling point for plant- and cell-based companies in presenting their products to consumers. Included in this proposition, of course, is the fact that all these products from the new wave of companies are hormone- and antibiotic-free and, unless we want the world to be at serious risk of a microbial pandemic, this is certainly very important.

Rebellyous intends to do a Series B round in mid-2021, and I like this company, so investors should watch out for that and contact the company directly if they want to be alerted to any investment opportunity. As with all the companies in this book, a website link is provided in Chapter 5.

## SIMULATE

Another American plant-based chicken substitute maker, SIMULATE, which owns the brand NUGGS, claims to be on the path to reducing the price of its plant-based chicken breast product, which is made of pea protein, to that of conventional chicken on a kilo-for-kilo basis by the end of 2021, which is roughly the same objective of LIVEKINDLY.

One striking thing about NUGGS is the youth of its founder: Ben Pasternak is only 21, and appears to be something of a polymath. In the case of NUGGS, he raised US $7 million in early stage funding, including from McCain Foods, the huge Canadian potato company, and more recently another US $4.1 million in a round led by Lerer Hippeau in July 2020. They intend to launch a DOGGs line of hot dog replacements and chicken patties before the end of the year.

NUGGS' marketing keys off the health benefits of its product, which it claims to contain twice as much protein as conventional chicken meat, with 20% fewer calories and zero cholesterol. 'Kills you slower' is the advertising tagline, as the company positions itself against the conventional chicken behemoths – and, as yet, on an exclusively direct-to-consumer basis.

# PLANT-BASED BEEF

So far, this is the biggest category in the clean meat space, reflecting the size of the minced beef market in the US, still the largest market for conventional meats. In the US, the two largest and most famous companies in plant-based meats are Beyond Meat and Impossible, but almost everyone else in the food industry is getting in on the act, alongside the many new entrants.

New production techniques, greater consumer acceptance, first-rate marketing, and a conjunction of positive events, are pushing people to become flexitarian and to 'try' plant-based beef products. Even though penetration is only about one per cent, it is growing rapidly.

But the fiercest competition to plant-based beef will soon come from cell-cultured beef, and the juicy margins enjoyed by companies like Beyond Meat will surely be eroded as competition from multiple entrants into the clean meat arena explodes. As I will seek to explain later, meat produced directly from cells (without whole animals) will perfectly replicate what we know as meat and will have the capability, in due course to be priced significantly lower than conventional meat, whilst tasting the same.

There is, of course, the additional issue with the healthiness (or otherwise!) of these plant-based meats; it is not the case that eating Impossible's or Beyond Meat's beef patties is necessarily better for you. They are, according to Lightlife Foods President Dan Curtin, 'hyper processed', and it is true that they contain a fair bit of sodium and fats. Lightlife, a Massachusetts, US, company that is part of Maple Leaf Foods of Canada, says: 'We've gone Beyond and it's not Impossible'. Its 'Clean Break' campaign against the two market leaders is clever. Lightlife products are made with tempeh (cooked soybeans) and contain simpler ingredients. Lightlife is competing against relative giants, as its estimated sales are only about US $40 million per annum.

But, more significantly, the plant-based food companies are beginning to face serious competition from the behemoths, such as Nestlé, Unilever, JBS, Tyson, Conagra,

Kellogg's, Perdue and Smithfield, as well as from smaller but established players such as Quorn and The Meatless Farm - and this competition will be brutal.

Regulatory and marketing hurdles are faced by everyone in the field, whether they be involved in plant-based or, especially, cultivated meat. They are not trivial, and I will discuss them in the next chapter.

Notwithstanding this, plant-based meats are accelerating in popularity, partly based on improvements in taste and reductions in relative pricing, but also on health factors. There is no doubt that plant-based meats *can be* (but are not always) better for human health than conventional meats, particularly red meat.

Plant-based meat typically has much more fibre and roughly equivalent levels of nutrients, excluding the full range of amino acids, than animal meats. Conventional meat of all types contains a wide range of amino acids, as well as key vitamins, including B12, niacin, thiamine, B5, B6 and B7, and vitamins A and K. Plants provide all of those except vitamin B12, which most plants cannot produce. Seaweed and some fortified cereals can, as can supplements.

Fibre helps digestion, reduces cardiovascular risk, and is vital to a healthy gut microbiome.

This is one of the reasons why studies suggest that vegetarians and vegans live longer and healthier, with reduced cardiac disease and cancer risk, than regular meat eaters.

So, reducing or eliminating meat intake (unless it is cultured and 'clean', in which case healthy fats can be incorporated and cholesterol can remain absent) is important for human health. But people tend to love the taste of meat, so replicating those characteristics that give meat its taste and mouthfeel is a key goal of the plant-based meat industry. That is why fat and sodium content can be on the high side in some of the plant-based foods, partially mitigating the health benefits.

The technologies employed by Impossible (haem for enhancing its meaty characteristics) and Beyond (coconut oil and cocoa butter fat globules that give its burger the marbled look of the real thing) are innovative and in the case of haem, revolutionary. Other companies, of course, mix in different plants and ingredients to improve taste. This includes the use of barley malt and yeast extract for a browning effect when burgers are grilled, as well as for a crunchier mouthfeel. In addition, consumers are increasingly looking for health benefits (e.g. less sodium and less cholesterol) in the plant-based burgers, and plenty of companies are making such claims.

As the vegetarian meat and seafood markets expand, I think there is a danger that it might become commoditised; where products lose their differentiation as a result of cut-throat price competition, mass production, and consolidation. The food service industry, both restaurants and institutions, is particularly susceptible to this pressure, due to their tight profit margins. In general, I do not believe the industry is anyway near this point yet, but we must anticipate casualties. Most recently, Ocean Hugger Foods, a plant-based seafood company, was sent to Davy Jones' Locker by the pandemic, and as I write there are rumours of another company sailing towards the rocks in the cell ag fish sector.

In plant-based beef (particularly minced beef) and seafood, distribution, consumer awareness, and engineered health benefits will be of paramount importance in gaining market share and in maintaining currently healthy margins.

Recently the *New York Times* did a helpful taste test of six major US brands of vegan burgers. While not scientific, it provided a useful guide to which ones were good and which were clunkers harking back to the days of insipid imitations of real meat.

The burgers were tasted as plain patties, and then as fully loaded hamburgers with cheese and condiments such as ketchup and pickles, and the results were conclusive. The Impossible Burger, which contains haem, scored best, and was described as a food with a 'brawny flavour' by the NYT restaurant critic Pete Wells. The problem, of course, is that we cannot get it in Europe, as its haem content is produced from GMO, though Impossible has recently applied to sell in Europe. It scored 4.5 points out of 5, losing half a point from perfection because, like all vegan burgers, it became a bit dry as the meal progressed.

The Impossible Burger is made primarily with soy protein, a bunch of added vitamins, coconut and other oils, methylcellulose, and of course soy leghaemoglobin (haem), among other ingredients.

Number two in the rankings was the Beyond Burger, scoring 4 out of 5 points, and about the same price by weight as the Impossible Burger (both in turn about twice the price of a conventional burger).

The Beyond Burger is soy-free, relying on pea protein for its bulk. It was described by the tasting panel as 'juicy with a convincing texture', with red juice provided by beets giving it an 'oozing look', as well as its added fat producing a 'marbled' appearance. This, again, has plenty of all-natural ingredients, including lemon juice, mung beans, sunflower, vinegar, and salt.

From the two market leaders downwards, the score card was none too impressive. Canadian company Maple Leaf Foods' 'Lightlife Burger' (see above for its CEO's catty comments) raked in 3 out of 5 points, despite being similarly-priced to the two leaders, with soy/tempeh as its key ingredient. The Uncut Burger, also soy-based, from Before the Butcher, a San Diego-based company, scored 3 out of 5 as well.

So, based on this test, it does appear that Beyond and Impossible deserve their lead in the US market, but some food giants, with their far-reaching distribution and financial muscle, are for sure going to encroach on this early success.

Recently, Kellogg's became another of the behemoths to launch its own line, in this case named Incogmeato (fire the branding manager!). It is supposed to 'bleed' like the Impossible Burger, but without the haem that Impossible uses to achieve the bleeding effect. This burger will be part of Kellogg's high-selling Morningstar Farms range of vegetarian products. This includes a line of chicken alternatives called Chick'n, made in the form of nuggets and tenders.

Meantime, British company Meatless Farm has products in Whole Foods outlets in the US and Hormel, another food giant, has recently launched its Happy Little Plants range. To add to the bustling line up, the US' largest supermarket company, Kroger, has launched an own-label vegan burger under its Simple Truth Brand, and is about to launch a wide range of vegan products under the same brand.

Meatless Farm is rumoured to be valued, in its recent Series C funding, at between US $200 and US $250 million pre-money, and to have raised US $31 million. This is a possible candidate for an IPO, so one to watch out for, and it could be that its differentiation as a 'healthier' provider of plant-based meats could make it successful.

As mentioned, Meatless is in the US (via Whole Foods), but also in Australia, and in the UK (Sainsbury's, Morrisons, Planet Organic and Ocado). Investors in the company include Channel 4, a UK TV company, Stray Dog Capital, Beyond Investing, and family office Elkstone Partners. Total funding is about US $55 million, including the recent Series C.

Tesco, the UK's largest supermarket, is targeting a four times increase in vegan product sales by 2025, and Mintel, the market research firm, expects UK sales of meat alternatives could reach US $1.5 billion by 2024.

With these plant-based meat companies, and a plethora of others, this is becoming a highly competitive and fast-growing space. From an investor's viewpoint, with Beyond, a public company, and Impossible, which is still private, both valued in the multi-billions, it is hard to see how they completely justify their current valuations, unless you have a very far-reaching investment horizon. Both are 'thematic' plays on a worldwide revolution in agriculture and are probably partly valued on this basis – a bit like Tesla, which seems to be crazily valued on fairly distant and highly optimistic future prospects.

But to be sure, current trends with food constitute a *real* revolution. Big international markets await the two leaders of plant-based beef, should they choose to expand their product range beyond minced beef – as Beyond in fact has done.

But these two will increasingly come up against the food giants, who, while not necessarily nimble, will be able to scale production aggressively and achieve further reach than either of these new(ish) companies. Therefore, margins will undoubtedly fall, and competition will intensify.

Of course, it is possible that one or both market leaders in this nascent category could themselves become behemoths, justifying current investor valuations, but the odds are, in my opinion, long.

The more likely outcome, to my mind, is that a giant such as Unilever or Nestlé just buys them, and at a decent premium. It seems unlikely (but not impossible) that either of the Messrs Brown would 'sell out' to a conventional meat producer, even assuming that one of those had sufficient financial firepower to buy Impossible or Beyond.

Both Impossible and Beyond are scrappy fighters though, and are prepared – at least for now – to take on the big boys; numbering among them their possible ultimate buyers. For instance, Nestlé has been forced to change the name of its 'Incredible Burger' to 'Sensational Burger' in Europe after it lost a court case against Impossible Foods, even though Impossible does not yet actually sell its products in Europe. Nestlé has bypassed this challenge in the US by calling its veggie burger 'Awesome' – presumably the consumer is to be the judge of that!

This 'Awesomeness' is up against a mighty front row of competition: Unilever's The Vegetarian Butcher collaboration is one example and, of course, Gardein and Quorn are impressive competitors also. Tyson Foods, one of the conventional meat giants, is launching its Raised & Rooted (where do these people get these truly awful names from?) range. This initially consists of chicken nuggets made of pea protein and, much more controversially, a 'blended' burger made of conventional beef and pea protein. Neither in nor out; a most unwholesome combination for my palate.

So, plant-based minced meat substitutes abound, but making a plant-based 'cut' of beef, rather than just a mince-like ingredient, is much, much harder. As I shall describe later, cultured meat companies also have this opportunity firmly in their sights, and are, frankly, more likely to succeed in this tricky endeavour.

There are plant-based meat companies out there that have gone beyond the minced meat replicas and are utilising 3D printing technology to recreate steaks.

Spanish company NovaMeat is developing a 3D printed beefsteak, pork, and chicken skewer product. It appears to be in an early stage of development, and its objective is to licence out its technology to other plant-based meat producers. NovaMeat believes that in a few years their steak will be cheaper than the real thing, since their input costs and plants are cheaper than raising cattle. At the moment, printing a seven-ounce steak prototype costs about US $4, but NovaMeat expects that cost to fall to US $2 by the end of 2021.

Redefine Meat of Israel is doing much the same thing as NovaMeat; using a 3D printing method to create a plant-based facsimile of the real thing. The general idea is to create a model of a steak with proprietary software, then 'print' the meat using a variety of plant-based 'inks'. In September 2019, Redefine received US $6 million in venture funding from big German chicken producer PHW Group, as well as from Jeremy Coller's CPT Capital. A limiting factor to scaled-up production currently is the speed of the extruder/printer, which is dictated by the size of the nozzles. At the moment these can produce five seven-ounce steaks in an hour, which will shortly be upgraded to about 50 an hour at the end of 2020. That is not enough to create a viable business.

Another area in which replicates are being developed is fats, which are vital to the taste and texture of conventional meats, particularly beef and pork. The idea is to produce cell-cultured fats for use in plant-based meat substitutes, creating a more authentic experience.

Future Meat Technologies of Israel is an example of a company working to produce cell-cultured fats that can be added to plant-based proteins to create hybrid meat products, including chicken, beef, pork, and lamb.

I spoke to Future Meat's CEO, Rom Kshuk, in June 2020, and was mightily impressed by his business plan and vision. The company was founded in 2018, based on technology from the lab of Professor Yaakov Nahmias at the Hebrew University of Jerusalem. Professor Nahmias is a tissue engineer, and Rom is a food entrepreneur with a background in chemistry and biology.

This company's product, although entirely cell-cultured, forms a bridge between the plant-based and cell-cultured categories, as several of the investment opportunities in the clean food space do. Its cell-derived fat products will act as 'bolsters' to plant-based products.

Rom believes that the important thing for cell-based companies is to get the cost of cell culturing down as fast as possible (Moo's Law™). As I shall describe, that is the self-avowed goal of every single cell-based company I have looked at. Future Meat's way of doing this is divided into three: by developing more efficient biological processes;

by using novel engineering techniques; and by scaling up (the holy grail of all these companies, of course!).

Future Meat does not use stem cells in its production, unlike most other companies in cell ag. It uses fibroblasts – cells which produce the structural framework (stroma) for animal tissues, employing what are known as the extracellular matrices and collagen. Without fibroblasts, the connective tissue in animals would not exist. Fibroblasts are the most common cells of connective tissue in animals. According to Rom, fibroblasts have a low doubling (proliferation) time; they require less media (nutrients); and they can grow to a higher density than other cell types.

Future Meat is trying to get to the point of using food grade nutrients for its products, rather than the expensive biotech nutrients currently used by some other cell ag companies. Indeed, they are trying to develop a way of recycling the media for several uses, all of which would significantly reduce cost of goods sold. The way he describes this is as a form of dialysis, akin to what happens in the liver and kidneys of a cow.

The company is species-agnostic in terms of the fats they intend to produce – chicken, beef and lamb are their first targets. Their target customers are plant-based meat companies, using the cultivated fats to 'mix' with plants, and thereby to generate something more akin to the flavour and aroma of 'real' meat, through the recreation of the connective tissues and fats found in all types of meat.

Future Meat's first plant will open in late 2020 or early 2021 in Tel Aviv, funded by the company's recent US $14 million Series A, and will supposedly be the first full-scale cultivated meat production facility in the world. Future Meat's main goal, as with all plant-based and cell ag companies, is to get the cost of goods down. Currently cell ag companies claim the cost of producing cultivated chicken is around US $150 per pound and beef US $200 per pound, both of which are unaffordable except to highly-committed early adopters. Mosa Meat is claiming an even lower price than this, in fairness.

Rom rightly points out that cell cultivation processes are not new – they have been used in biotech for decades – but only now are scale and affordability becoming more than a possibility in the production of food.

Future Meat has its own proprietary bioreactor technology (a claim made by several other companies), allowing it to scale well beyond the 5,000-litre level that is the 'standard' future aspiration in the industry thus far. Large-scale bioreactors needed for mass industrial production of foods don't currently exist, so this is a big deal.

Future Meat expects to do a Series B round in 2021, and investors should contact the company directly if they want to know more. I am intrigued by this company, as its business model lends itself to wide dispersal of its product. Industry giant Tyson was a seed investor through its venture arm in 2018 and is apparently being very helpful to what the company is seeking to do. Other investors, through the Series A round, include Henry Soesanto, an Asian tycoon, as well as Emerald Technology Ventures and Manta Ray Ventures from the UK and Neto, the largest importer of meat into Israel.

The company's IP appears to be strong, and patents cover growing fibroblasts in suspension, the recycling system for nutrients, and protocols for differentiating fibroblasts into fat and muscle. By using fibroblasts, there is no need for at least one of the ultra-expensive growth factors used by most other companies. These growth factors would normally include TGF-$\beta$, which Future Meat does not use, although it does use FGF-2, which it is seeking to replace with small molecules and/or plant- or cell-based solutions – few details exist as yet, however.

Future Meat's new pilot production plant will be able to produce one tonne of fats per month at first, which may not sound a lot, but is considerably ahead of most competitors who still struggle with scale.

# SOYLENT

Soylent makes more or less what it says on the tin. A mixture of soy and lentils with other stuff added; designed to be a meal replacement for people on the go who do not have time to cook, shop or spend time eating. The name was first coined in a 1966 science fiction novel called 'Make Room' by Harry Harrison.

Initially, the powder was sold as a time-saver to the bros of Silicon Valley, too busy changing the world with their app developments, but it has since become mainstream, and is sold in Walmart, Kroger, 7-Eleven and Safeway. All you do is add water.

The company behind this goop is Soylent Nutrition Inc., founded by a software engineer called Rob Rhinehart in 2013, which was *ab initio* crowdfunded, before getting more substantial funding. Rob worked out what proteins, carbohydrates, fats, minerals and vitamins were necessary for human survival and went ahead and produced the original concoction and has since refined it quite a bit.

He tried it out on himself first and drank only Soylent for 30 days, adjusting the formula in response to his body's reaction.

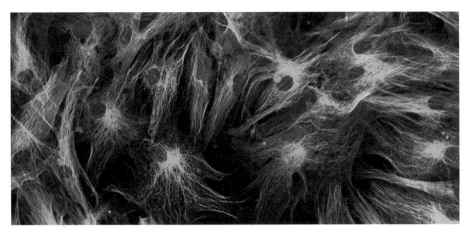

*Fibroblast cells.*

The company got a US $20 million injection in 2015, led by VC firm Andreessen Horowitz.

It appears that the funding has dried up as the company has shuttered some operations and withdrawn from the UK market.

This might be partly due to complaints about gastrointestinal issues in some people, or that it is fundamentally very boring to drink a powder three times a day, even if it saves you time. Farhad Manjoo of the *New York Times* once wrote that he 'found Soylent to be a punishingly boring, joyless product'. Chris Ziegler of The Verge, who experimented with substituting all conventional food for Soylent for almost a month, reported that, though he found it to be fairly palatable, said that 'Soylent isn't living, it's merely surviving'.

Soylent comes in a variety of flavours, one of which, Nectar, has been described as 'lemon flavoured aspartame'. Other flavours include Café Chai, Coffiest, and Cacao. The company has raised a total of US $72 million since inception, but seems to be running out of road.

It has competitors in the form of Huel from the UK. Huel is well-funded, with a £20 million injection in 2019, and has now sold well over 40 million meals in 85 countries. Indeed, they sold me a couple of packets, which I have recently thrown away, unopened. They do seem to be in better shape than Soylent, as they have done a deal with Chinese internet giant JD.com to partner in the Chinese market.

I honestly would not bother to invest in any of these companies. They are the Army K-ration equivalents of foods for people so busy making money or 'changing the world' that they can never enjoy themselves, even by eating.

# DAIRY

In some ways, the last decade's advance of plant-based milk substitutes relative to conventional milk and cheeses provides a template of how things might work out in other parts of the food industry, with the lightning speed disruption that is happening.

Research and Markets recently released a comprehensive report on this. Their forecast is that, the global market for the categories of soy, almond, oat, coconut and rice-based milks (excluding others, which are much smaller) for the period 2020-2024, will grow at a compound annual rate of over 10 per cent to a worldwide total of nearly US $22 billion. This is on top of dramatic growth over the previous decade, when milk alternatives' market share in the US rose from about 0.5 per cent to over 14 per cent.

In the UK market, the share is currently just over four per cent, but the key 16-24 year old demographic is increasingly turning to alternatives, with about a third of that group saying that they use milk substitutes.

Other milk substitutes not included in this forecast include cashew, macadamia, quinoa and hemp, all of which are fast-growing, but from small bases.

It is rare to go to a coffee shop, almost anywhere in the world, and not be offered at least one alternative to regular milk. Increasingly consumers, particularly in developed countries, are aware of potential health benefits of reducing regular dairy consumption. These benefits include higher protein content and added vitamins, for instance. In addition, those with lactose intolerance are clearly attracted to milk alternatives, and particularly to the two category leaders, soy and almond milk.

Corporate leaders in the alternative milks field include Coca-Cola, Danone, PepsiCo, Keurig, Hain Celestial, SunOpta and Blue Diamond. In fact, French giant Danone paid US $12 billion in 2016 to buy US WhiteWave Foods and get its hands on Alpro, a Belgian maker of plant-based milk alternatives.

Other leaders in the alternative plant-based milks business are Califia Farms, the third-largest in the US after Danone, as well as second-ranked and privately owned Blue Diamond. Califia is an example of how funding has grown in the area, and real disruption has followed. Founded in 2012, Califia sells its beverages in distinctive curved bottles, and has raised a good deal of money. In 2018, it raised

US $225 million in a round led by Ambrosia Investments, along Temasek Holdings, the Singaporean sovereign wealth fund which appears in the rosters of many food startups, Sun Pacific, and the Qatar Investment Authority as shareholders. The founder Greg Steltenpohl is well known as an innovator in product designs and packaging.

Likewise, Ripple Foods, a California-based maker of yogurt and milk alternatives, has been successful in raising large amounts of money, including US $65 million in 2018 in a Series C round led by Euclidean Capital, Goldman Sachs, and Fall Line Capital.

REBBL, a California-based maker of coconut milk-based drinks with added 'super herbs' and 'adaptogens', has raised substantial institutional funding as well, totalling at least US $34 million, from such investors as Stripes Group and Sun Pacific.

There are plenty of others who are in the startup alternative milks category, offering milk-type products or protein milkshakes based on plants. Rebel Kitchen in the UK is prominent, as is CytoSport's Evolve line of protein shakes in the US.

Other startups, all reasonably funded, in this field include Mooala from Texas, a maker of Organic Banana Milk, as well as almond milk producer New Barn Organics, from Modesto in California – which just happens to be where the almonds are! New Barn's operations probably don't help California's water shortages, of course, as almonds are not particularly environmentally-friendly, to say the least.

## THE NOT COMPANY

I spoke to the CEO and co-founder of The Not Company, also known more simply as NotCo, a Santiago, Chile, based maker of plant-based milk. This company is about to launch its products in the US, and has done very well in raising funds and in gaining market share in Latin American markets. Matias Muchnick is an engaging entrepreneur, moving from finance to food in the past decade or so. He is committed to changing people's lives for the better and has used AI to work out how to replicate dairy products entirely from plant-based ingredients. Early efforts to make vegan products proved difficult, and he quickly realised that up-to-date R&D methods were required to make a product that consumers liked, road-tested by chefs and constantly improved by machine learning and AI techniques. This realisation came after he sold his first company, Eggless, and he moved to the US for his postgraduate studies at UC Berkeley and Harvard. It was at Harvard that he joined up with NotCo's other co-founder, Karim Pichara and, together with plant bioscientist Pablo Zamora, they set out to use data science to better understand plants. The three men, all Chilean, returned to their homeland and started the company, founded on an AI platform they named Giuseppe.

Their first product was a plant-based mayonnaise, formulated by using Giuseppe to work out which plants created which flavour molecules right for mayo, which happened to be chickpeas and lupin. These form a combined structure which is like egg whites. This is different to the formula used by JUST, which uses pea protein and, according to tasters, is not comparable. Matias pointed out that in a mass spectrometry analysis of cheese and chocolate, the two foods share 73 molecules of flavour but do not taste anything alike; so to recreate familiar flavours accurately, physiochemical data and molecular composition are especially important. This data is also used to work out reactions to cooking for their various products.

NotCo's initial product focus on mayo was made because Chileans consume large amounts of the stuff (the world's third highest volume, apparently). Sales have been very good, and particularly encouraging Is the fact that the vast majority of consumers are not vegan, and that there is an excellent repurchase rate.

Initially, the company was funded by a well-known Latin American venture capital fund, Kaszek Ventures, which led the seed through Series B rounds. This funding enabled the young company to add milk to its product line at the beginning of 2020. NotCo already has a two per cent share of the dairy category in Chile and one per cent in Argentina. Brazil has imposed a punitively high import tax on plant-based foods to protect domestic farmers, making it a tough cookie at first. However, after putting the right team in place, Brazil has become one of their biggest businesses. Additionally, a US launch, involving a major retailer and a coffee chain, which we surmised was Starbucks, is imminent.

Currently, the company is producing 200,000 litres of milk a month at its plant, a figure that is about to be scaled even further, although specific details were not forthcoming. They have also launched a chocolate milk.

Apparently, their partners in the US have described them as the Beyond Meat of milk as the taste – evolved by Giuseppe and in part generated by cabbage and pineapple – is identical to the real thing, because the combination creates lactones. Furthermore, some of the problems encountered in foaming and heating alternative milks, such as almond or soy, do not happen with NotCo milk.

NotCo recently closed an US $85 million round, and while not at the same level as Perfect Day (total funding now of US $380 million), this is an impressive haul, especially for a non-US based company. NotCo has assembled a credible team from companies such as Nestlé, Danone and Chobani and is preparing vegan cheese products for the next phase of its rollout.

# MOO'S LAW

## OATLY

Then there is the Swedish company Oatly. This outfit has garnered huge attention in Europe and recently closed a funding round of US $200 million, on a rumoured valuation of US $2 billion. This round was fronted by Jay-Z, Oprah Winfrey, Natalie Portman and, presumably on a larger scale, Blackstone, the US investment powerhouse. This was not well-received by Oatly's target consumers, as Blackstone's founder was a major donor to President Trump and the firm is linked to two Brazilian companies supposedly involved in deforestation of the Amazon.

Oatly, obviously, uses oats for its milks (oat milk now being the second most popular alternative milk worldwide) and has a quirky marketing strategy. Comments about the products are printed on the cartons (including one that 'it tastes like shit') and it uses founder and CEO Toni Petersson in ads which are offbeat or downright weird. Sales have been soaring, with US $200 million in 2019 and double that forecast for 2020, despite coronavirus. The latest cash raised will be used to build more factories in the US and UK, where sales growth has been particularly strong. In the UK, consumers tried plant-based milks in droves during lockdown, and Oatly's sales rose by over 120 per cent in the period, easily outpacing the growth of current market leader, Alpro. In fact, Oatly products have recently appeared in my own household, to considerable acclaim.

It will not be long, in my view, before Oatly hits the market as an IPO. Warning to investors, however; this is a very crowded field and will be much harder to make money in than in cellular agriculture companies, which as yet don't sport very high valuations, and who don't seek, nor get, celebrity endorsements.

## PERFECT DAY

Perfect Day is based in Berkeley, California, and has raised over a whopping US $360 million of total funding to further their goal of producing non-animal whey and casein, vital ingredients in cow's milk. Casein is addictive – it is the protein in milk that gives it its white colour, and when digested it turns into casomorphins. The 'morphins' part gives the clue – they attach to the same brain receptors that heroin does!

Casomorphins occur in human and cow milk and encourage infants and calves to suckle, and they are amplified in potency when milk is fermented to create cheese. This is why some people are 'addicted' to cheese.

Temasek, the giant investing arm of the Singapore government, has invested in every round including the most recent Series C, which gathered US $300 million, with the Canada Pension Plan Investment Board (CPP Investments) also participating. Perfect

Day makes its proteins by using an engineered 'flora' to sell to food service companies as well as to food producers.

The process is akin to brewing beer or making insulin, using an engineered strain of fungus, namely *Trichoderma reesei* (which they call 'flora', presumably to dampen the 'yuck' factor associated with fungi), which is fermented to produce the key whey proteins found in cow's milk. *T. reesei* is modified to contain the DNA sequence from a cow that causes the production of the whey proteins – specifically β-lactoglobulin. During the process, the microbes are 'fed' on nutrients, including sugars, in large-scale fermentation tanks. It is this process that forms the basis of the Perfect Day's patent estate, and presumably proved to be a key factor in their raising so much money.

Perfect Day was founded by Ryan Pandya, Perumal Gandhi and Isha Datar, who is New Harvest's executive director. The three co-founders emerged from a clean food biotech accelerator called RebelBio (the pre-seed accelerator of SOSV that is now merged with SOSV's larger food tech accelerator, IndieBio). It was announced that former Disney CEO Bob Iger will be joining the board in an executive role in 2020: a huge deal. Perfect Day produced a limited release, animal-free ice cream in 2019 in order to showcase their technology. From now on they will partner with The Urgent Company, a spin off from Perfect Day, to sell to consumers, while they themselves sell ingredients directly to other food producers.

Perfect Day's founders started The Urgent Company, to launch their ice cream through the brand Brave Robot, using Perfect Day proteins, initially in California. I am not quite sure how this is not a conflict, but the explanation appears to be that The Urgent Company is a vehicle to popularise the Perfect Day product in an initial ice cream range, and to encourage other food producers to use the proteins as well.

The range of substitute dairy foods that Perfect Day expects their ingredients to be part of includes cheese (mozzarella, feta, cream cheese etc.) as well as milk. Archer-Daniel-Midland (ADM), a huge conglomerate in the agricultural space, was an early (2018) partner of the company and will be involved in scaling up production of the proteins, to tens of thousands of tonnes by 2022.

Perumal Gandhi spoke to me in lockdown, describing his own journey. This is the typical pattern of a clean foods founder, which is to move gradually from eating everything to becoming either vegetarian or vegan. Perumal, along with his co-founder, Ryan, who is also the CEO, has a scientific background. Perumal is a biomedical engineer and Ryan is a chemical engineer. Introduced by Isha, together they examined the difficulties of making alternative milks taste more like the real thing and settled on the idea that whey and casein were the missing ingredients in ersatz products. They opted to use a

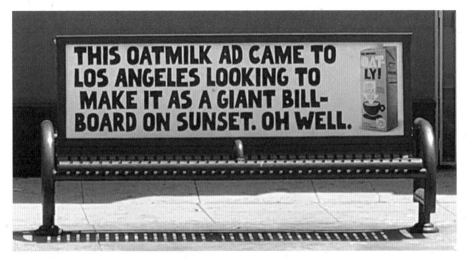

*Oatly advert in Los Angeles. Reproduced courtesy of Joe Stamey via Reddit (u/itsplanty).*

There are six proteins found in milk, of which the two most important are whey and casein. They have cracked whey, and are indeed already commercialising their version, and they say that they will have a casein product – the 'addictive' component – on the market in two years or so.

Perumal says that, although most plant-based milks are not yet perfect replicas, they are generally fine from the point of view of taste. However, they leave a lot to be desired when used in things like cheese, yoghurt, and ice cream.

Their ingredients business, selling fermentation-produced whey, is already at commercial scale, and while the price point is still too high for dramatic scale-up, the cost is falling fast (Moo's Law™). One avenue for the company to grow faster, at least as an aspiration, is to partner with dairy farmers, substituting cows with bioreactors, where the technology is licensed by the farmer from Perfect Day. I am guessing it is because Perfect Day wants dairy farmers to embrace and benefit from the food revolution.

Their whey protein, β-lactoglobulin, has received Generally Recognised As Safe (GRAS) designation from the US Food and Drug Administration (FDA) and will not require further regulation. For the moment, the company is focussed on the North American market, but in due course they will work with international partners. Perumal thinks the RethinkX report that suggests that 90 per cent of US dairy proteins will come from fermentation or plants by 2030 is optimistic and would cost vast amounts of money to achieve. But he does agree with the general direction of travel, and believes that if farmers join the story the process will be accelerated, so that by the end of this decade half of all dairy in the US could be fermented, presumably putting the conventional dairy business into a death spiral, unless they do indeed collaborate.

Indeed, Borden Dairy Co., the second largest dairy company in the US, recently filed for bankruptcy, within months of the largest US milk producer, Dean Foods, doing the same. High debts, declining interest in drinking conventional cow's milk and the rise of alternative milks did it for both of them. Their assets will no doubt be restructured, but the days of milk's ascendancy as a key food in the US diet are well and truly over. The average American has reduced consumption of fluid milk by more than 40 per cent since 1975.

In the past year, as of publication, about US $1.5 billion has been invested worldwide in alternative proteins, of which almost a third has gone into companies using fermentation, according to the Good Food Institute. 44 fermentation companies exist globally, of which the grandaddy is Quorn.

## LEGENDAIRY FOODS

LegenDairy Foods is one of the cell ag companies I like very much. It is focussed on producing cheese by cellular means. It has several key competitors: Remilk, Better Dairy, New Culture, Motif Foodworks and Perfect Day, the last of which is featured above. Noquo, based in Sweden, is seed funded by Northzone and Inventure to the tune of US $3.6 million, and roughly speaking has the same objective as LegenDairy, which is based in Berlin, Germany, but uses plant-based proteins to make its products. All three of them are culturing cheeses using fermentation techniques, though Perfect Day has a broader range of products.

Anja Leissner, the co-founder and head of R&D at Noquo, has said that 'we are starting with cheese, because there is so much culture and craftsmanship behind it. Casein has a very complex structure; we know how it behaves and we are learning how to mimic it. Melted cheese is the Holy Grail we are aiming for'.

LegenDairy, New Culture and Perfect Day have similar objectives; vegan cheese has been notoriously bad up till now. It does not melt well or stretch properly or even really look like real cheese. This is because cheese production is dependent on the coagulation of the proteins in milk into a gel matrix after the addition of rennet, which is found in the stomachs of ruminant animals. Rennet is composed of a very complex set of enzymes that is hard to mimic, and this is the challenge for all three companies. Rennet, known chemically as the chymosin enzyme, is key to all professionally made cheeses, and produced by fermentation.

Noquo, whose other founder is entrepreneur Sorosh Tavakoli, is based in Sweden and is using a 'protein study' approach to combining pulses and other legumes to create a realistic version of cheese. LegenDairy and Perfect Day are using a cellular fermentation technique to achieve the same objective – animal-free cheese.

Noquo has identified casein as the key nut to crack, as it is found in concentrations seven times higher in cheese than in human breast milk, where it is the key factor in getting infants to suckle. This requirement – to mimic casein by using plant-based combinations – is the Noquo path.

LegenDairy, fronted and founded by Raffael Wohlgensinger, whom I have met on a number of occasions, is pursuing a molecular path, as are New Culture and Perfect Day. LegenDairy's process uses 'microbial fermentation'; growing dairy proteins by using yeast, with beer brewing being a sort of template. LegenDairy has raised EUR 4 million so far and will no doubt be raising further funding; again, if investors are interested, they should contact the company directly.

New Culture, founded by Matt Gibson and Inja Radman, is San Francisco-based and is seeking, like LegenDairy, to make a cultivated mozzarella. The conventional version of which is apparently the world's best-selling cheese, with worldwide sales of US $10 billion in 2019, and a compound annual growth rate of about five per cent. This is largely down to the popularity of pizza, and to the manufacture of mozzarella using cow's milk rather than the traditional, but more expensive, buffalo milk. New Culture raised US $3.5 million from, amongst others, the investing arm of Kraft Heinz, the food behemoth.

Interestingly, though Perfect Day has raised US $380 million, the other three have raised roughly identical, but much smaller, amounts (US $3-4 million), but LegenDairy appears further ahead than the other two minnows, and is likely to be raising more money relatively soon. LegenDairy's seed round was co-led by Agronomics and M Ventures (the venture capital arm of Merck KGaA), with CPT Capital participating.

Bel Group, one of the biggest cheese groups in the world, is about to launch a range of cheeses based on plants and suitable for vegans, so even the established order is sitting up and taking notice!

# TURTLETREE LABS AND BIOMILQ

TurtleTree Labs is based in Singapore, which is emerging as a hub for new food technologies. This company is not going after the dairy market *per se*, but the large and growing infant formula business. About 10 per cent of the world's conventional milk production ends up as infant formula, so this is big business, especially in Asia.

Many women are unable or unwilling to breastfeed their babies – about 80 per cent have to stop breastfeeding before the generally recommended period of six months. TurtleTree, along with competitor BIOMILQ of Durham, North Carolina, are developing alternatives to infant formula.

Infant formula as currently sold is an imperfect solution, as it does not contain all of the key ingredients in human milk. Both TurtleTree and BIOMILQ are working on using cell culture techniques to grow human mammary cells *in vitro*; cells which will be able to produce all the components of breast milk, which number over 2,500. BIOMILQ recently announced that they have managed to make human casein and lactose using human mammary epithelial cells, and are well on the way to producing breast milk.

Founded by Michelle Egger and Leila Strickland, the company has raised US $3.5 million in a seed round led by Breakthrough Energy Ventures, a large impact fund co-founded by Bill Gates. Leila is a cell biologist by background and Michelle a food scientist.

TurtleTree Labs was founded by Fengru Lin, Max Rye, Mkulima Britt and Rabail Toor, and is currently led by Fengru and Max, whom we spoke to. Both of them have backgrounds in the tech industry and have evolved to be proponents of lab-developed breast milk, with similar aspirations to BIOMILQ. They use proprietary and patented stem cell lines, and force their differentiation into mammary cells which make milk. These cells are 'fed' on nutrients and insulin, suspended in a water-based media which they say is recyclable.

They settled on human breast milk as a scientific and business opportunity because of discussions they had with Ryan Bethencourt, founder of Wild Earth and also of IndieBio. He guided them to the 'white space' (as yet unexploited markets) available in infant formula. Raw milk is difficult to produce in many parts of Asia, and in Singapore they found the perfect location to establish their business. Milk, like all other food, is mostly imported, due to space limitations and the absence of any farms, and the government is keen to encourage greater food security. In fact, the Singapore government has an ambitious plan to produce 30 per cent of all food consumed there by 2030.

TurtleTree's product will be free of pathogens and contaminants and, if necessary, the lactose can be removed, to be used for infants who are intolerant. Vitamins and minerals will be added, and cholesterol will be reduced, and there will be no hormones, although insulin is used in the feed media.

The key to both TurtleTree and BIOMILQ's ambitions is to closely replicate the human milk oligosaccharides (HMOs, also known as human milk glycans) that form the third largest component (after lactose and fats) of human milk. There are about 200 of these oligosaccharides in human milk; they are indigestible by infants, but they cause a prebiotic reaction and are the food source for 'good' bacteria. This allows for a healthy intestinal microbiome, which reduces the incidence of diarrhoea, as well as viral and bacterial infections.

The BIOMILQ sales model is as yet apparently undeveloped. TurtleTree expects to have a demo plant in Singapore by the end of 2020 and they want to partner with established formula companies such as Nestlé, Danone, and Unilever. They see China and India as huge markets but in particular they will focus on China, which currently imports 89 per cent of its milk from New Zealand.

This raises an interesting concept: selling short the New Zealand milk producers, such as Fonterra, Open Country Dairy and The Tatua Co-operative Dairy Company, and buying into the upstarts, with a particular liking for NotCo, Perfect Day, LegenDairy, and either of TurtleTree or BIOMILQ.

# NOVEL PROTEINS

Camille Delbecque, an IndieBio alumnus, founded Afineur in New York in 2014 with Sophie Deterre. Camille is an agronomic engineer by background, trained at both Harvard and Paris Descartes Universities, and has been a serial entrepreneur prior to Afineur. Sophie, also a PhD from France, is a food and flavour expert, having previously worked on developing a new distillery for Grand Marnier, the French liqueur brand.

Afineur is using fermentation to improve the protein profile of various foods, and works with by-products from the food industry to create new proteins. It piloted its first project with a company producing stevia, utilising the left-over plant biomass to make a new cultured protein with better functionality than conventional protein. This project was acquired by Ingredion.

They leverage fermentation to upcycle existing biological waste; helping farmers and brewers get rid of unwanted by-products by turning them into valuable protein products. Recently they have been working to produce a bitterless coffee and a protein called Afineur Cultured Protein. They aim to improve the taste of plant-based foods by engineering their synthetic microbes to feed on the foods in a fermentation process, thus enhancing nutrition and flavour. They have recently signed a partnership with Lavazza to supply their gourmet bitterless Arabica coffee.

IndieBio offered the seed funding in 2014, and they reached their Kickstarter funding target within six hours in 2015. In 2016 TechStars invested an undisclosed amount in Afineur and will be looking to raise a Series A round of US $2.5-3 million next year. Commercial success in their past projects means they have been generating revenues.

I mention this company, not because it is one that I have invested in or will invest in just yet, but because it is a further example of a 'white space' opportunity in the clean ag sector, with a differentiated proposition of using existing biomass to create exciting products.

# FOOD FROM THIN AIR

There are two companies I have spoken to who are working on ways of turning air into proteins, using electricity. If this sounds too good to be true, I have to tell you that it is happening, and it might well revolutionise a lot of stuff in the food industry.

It is absolutely a fact that electricity and carbon dioxide and hydrogen can be used to produce edible calories. These calories take the form of a mush that can go into fake meats or be used to 'feed' the bioreactors that make real meats from cell ag processes.

The basic process for both these two companies is similar. Carbon dioxide, oxygen, hydrogen and nitrogen are combined with water and minerals, put into fermenters alongside microorganisms and then fermented, using high energy inputs in the form of low-cost renewable electricity.

## AIR PROTEIN

The first of these companies, is a spin off out of a Bay Area company called Kiverdi, although the two companies share the same management and founders. Air Protein is trying to produce air-based 'meat' and, just as with its Finnish rival, Solar Foods, it is using a technology first developed by NASA in the 1960s.

Back then, the basic concept was that astronauts would breathe out carbon dioxide which would be converted into food by using hydrogenotrophs, which are a type of microorganism.

Air Protein, as does Solar, has refined this original concept. Fermentation tanks are employed by both companies, and hydrogenotrophs are 'fed' on carbon dioxide, hydrogen, and nitrogen as well as vitamins and minerals.

Dr Lisa Dyson, to whom I have spoken, is an impressive evangelist for her industry. Her CV reads like a tour through the world's top institutions, including Stanford, MIT and UCL amongst others. Her co-founder, Dr John Reed, was the inventor of Air Protein's core technology. John is an expert on the chemical and biological energy storage as well as in conversion technologies, which are the core competence of Kiverdi, Air Protein's parent company. John has developed a way of mitigating carbon emissions that is a hybrid of chemical and microbial processes, which can capture and recycle inorganic carbon into high energy biofuels using conventional bioreactors. This technique is now being applied to the production of proteins, in a similar fashion to yogurt or beer production. The key advantages of this process are obvious – less land and production is much quicker than growing conventional crops without any consideration of weather and water conditions.

Air Protein's business model is to sell a chicken-like protein product (which they emphasise is a meat-like product not an ingredient) directly to the food service industry. The company believes that its proteins will be cheaper at scale than soy or pea protein, and it holds patents under exclusive licence from Kiverdi on the use of hydrogenotrophs to excrete protein via electrolysis. It does this by splitting water into carbon dioxide and hydrogen, using renewable electricity to produce a protein isolate.

As of our latest contact with the company, it was in the early stages of raising funds, and I would say its round is definitely worth looking at. The key variable costs for both Air Protein and Solar Foods are the electricity (to split water and get hydrogen), and the fermentation tanks, added vitamins, minerals, and nitrogen, as well as the hydrogenotrophs, which are readily found in nature but cost money to harvest.

Air Protein also has patents pending on its bioreactor technology and expects to be producing about 2,000 tonnes a year from its first plant. This is forecast to cost US $10 million to build and which it anticipates being highly profitable.

## SOLAR FOODS

Solar Foods and Air Protein are direct competitors using variants of the same technology. They both use microorganisms to metabolise hydrogen and carbon dioxide to produce their protein: 'Solein'. The differences in their methods and IP lie in the specific species of microorganism they employ, and in their gas processing and equipment designs.

I spoke to Dr Pasi Vainikka, the CEO of Solar Foods, a couple of times during the writing of this book, and as soon as it becomes possible, I will be off to Finland with my colleagues to visit this extremely exciting company.

Pasi speaks with typical Scandinavian deliberation, but his passion for the company's mission shines through every sentence. He used to work in developing renewable energy systems and, since energy costs are a critical component of the economics of Solar Foods' proposition, this has come in handy as he and his team develop the company. It was founded in March 2018 by a team of scientists who worked at VTT (the Finnish technical and research institute) and LUT University, including Pasi himself, Dr Juha-Pekka Pitkanen, CTO, and Sami Holmstrom, the Production Manager.

The basic premise of Solar Foods and Air Protein is to turn electricity and carbon dioxide into edible calories. This is necessary, Pasi points out, because about a quarter of all emissions-related environmental damage is caused by our current eating habits – especially the farming of animals.

Pasi's early motivation to change the food supply was as a result of environmental impact, but he has now added a concern for animals and their welfare to this list as well.

He says that although Finland has a green image, the eutrophication, or algal growth as a result of saturation with nutrients in the Baltic Sea, is terrible, and a large part of this is due to animal farming and pesticides.

Solar Foods have therefore come up with Solein, their protein product. This is a single cell protein (SCP), as well as being microbial protein (MP).

So, by definition, Solein is actually a microbial cell, containing a variety of different proteins within it that are not secreted and remain intracellular. This is important, as it means Solein is not a GMO, therefore if approved by the EU Novel Food Regulation, it will be able to be sold in Europe.

Solar Foods uses a process of gas fermentation to produce its proteins, as does Air Protein. Bacterial microorganisms are introduced into a fermenter vessel, along with a small amount of minerals, and the principal growth media is provided by hydrogen and by carbon dioxide, which are created by electrolysis, and by carbon dioxide. About 90 per cent of the growth media is provided by these two gases, which interact with the added ammonia, minerals and microorganisms to form a basic protein, which consists of fats, carbohydrates, and vitamins.

Once the organisms, which are known as hydrogenotrophs (of which there are different types), in the fermenter have grown, the product liquid is extracted, centrifuged, and eventually forms a dry, nutritious powder. This is roughly the same path that Air Protein has taken, and is based on the aforementioned research done by NASA in the 1960s, to feed astronauts while in space.

These hydrogenotrophs are found naturally in Finland, and Pasi believes that wind power in the country can produce cheap electricity to enable the liberation of hydrogen. Carbon dioxide is likely to come from carbon capture from the air outside the facility. Indeed, as the price of wind power has come down, it no longer requires subsidy in Finland.

The idea is to replicate the Solar Foods process – producing a protein called Solein – around the world, particularly in places such as the Middle East where energy is cheap and food sources are lacking. The company has researched where the ideal production locations might be, explaining that cheaper electricity is a key factor.

Pasi believes that in ideal production scenarios, Solein could sell for EUR 2.20/kg, which is comparable to the lowest-cost chicken. Solein will be used as an alternative to soy or pea in plant-based meats and dairy, and will supposedly be healthier and more sustainable than either of them.

Ultimately, when the company has secured further funding, the protein could be used to 'feed' cultivated meat, if processed further to isolate the amino acids from the current powder formulation.

Solein is about 65 per cent protein and also boasts high levels of Vitamin B, a low sugar content and no saturated fats. It is also likely that it will contain rather high levels of beneficial omega-6 fatty polyunsaturated acids.

Solar Foods recently closed a EUR 15 million Series A round led by Fazer Group, a Finnish confectionary and food company, with participation from Agronomics, CPT Capital and Lifeline Ventures. This takes its total funds raised to just over EUR20 million.

The company is about to submit a dossier to enter the European Food Safety Agency novel foods pathway (see Chapter Four on regulation) by the end of 2020, and anticipates that its proteins will be approved for sale in the latter part of 2022.

Solar Foods anticipate in their pilot facility they will be able to produce 300kg of Solein a day, at approximately EUR 20-25/kg. They have conducted cost estimate models to show how the cost of production will decrease with economies of scale. When at a full-scale industrial process with 10 fermenters, the cost of production will be down to EUR 5/kg on a 100 percent protein basis, including post-processing steps. Conventional soy costs around EUR 3/kg to produce. Series A funding will be used to run the pilot demonstrator for at least 12 months.

# EGGS

Eggs are another food category ripe for disruption. Most people are aware of the cruel and intensive techniques used in producing the bulk of the world's eggs, and that 'free range' is not as benign a label as it sounds. China is by far the world's biggest egg producer, accounting for 42 per cent of global production, with the US at seven per cent and India at six per cent. Most eggs worldwide are still produced from caged hens, where the birds live in cramped and filthy conditions. In the US, 97 per cent of laying hens are kept in such cages. The EU is more enlightened, in that barren (empty and uncomfortable) cages are now banned, and labelling has to specify exactly the conditions in which the birds producing eggs live. However, all over the world, the words "fresh" or "natural" are highly misleading when it comes to eggs. Eggs are of course also used in almost all baked goods, mayonnaise and pasta, and they are more than likely to come from caged birds.

Two French entrepreneurs, Philippine Souleres and Sheryline Thavisouk, have apparently come up with vegan eggs, with a shell-like covering and a realistic-looking plant-based yolk, which they have called Les Merveilloeufs (marvellous eggs). That would be marvellous indeed if it came to fruition, as the egg business, as with so much in agriculture, needs to change. Now.

## CLARA FOODS

There are several players in this field, both plant-based and cell ag companies. One of them, Clara Foods, a startup based in San Francisco, is using fermentation to produce animal-free egg white proteins. This is done by using yeast to grow proteins that are identical to some of those found in eggs.

Clara, founded by Arturo Elizondo and David Anchel, was recently funded for a second round in a rumoured US $50 million Series B, led by Ingredion, a global ingredients distributor with operations in 120 countries, which is partnering with Clara to distribute its range. Not surprisingly, Clara's products will be, at least in part, sold to food producers as components of products, ranging from baked goods to prepared meals, where conventional eggs would normally serve. To emphasise the point, another investor in the Clara Series B round was B37, an arm of Grupo Bimbo, the world's largest baking company. Clara's Series A was completed in 2016 and amounted to US $15 million, led by holding company The Production Board.

This is close to the largest amount of money raised in the cell ag space, behind only a few companies such as Mosa Meat, Memphis Meats, Geltor, Perfect Day and ingredient producer Motif FoodWorks. Interestingly, Clara was started at the accelerator IndieBio, which is the progenitor of a number of notable cell ag startups such as Memphis Meats, Geltor and the less notable Finless Foods.

The first products from Clara are likely to be a baking-friendly egg white foam and an egg white product as a substitute for whey in sports nutrition drinks and powders.

I spoke to Arturo in lockdown. Texas-born, he was raised eating two eggs every day and, with a Mexican heritage, his diet was heavy in animal protein. Prior to going to Harvard, he spent a summer working at the United States Department for Agriculture (USDA). Astonished and disturbed by the fact that a million animals are slaughtered every hour in the US, he elected to study food security and ways of disrupting the food supply chain.

He was interested in both plant-based and cell ag forms of food production as far back as 2012, when remarkably, the only companies of note in the US were Hampton Creek (now JUST) and Beyond Meat. A chance meeting with Isha of New Harvest and Dave at a conference in 2014 led to the foundation of Clara.

The ubiquity of eggs in the food supply chain and the lack of competition both conspired to draw Arturo into the market. Over one trillion eggs are consumed worldwide every year – at least 125 for every person on the planet – and alternatives to conventional eggs account for only 0.1 per cent of the global market.

There are about 100 proteins in egg white, which is the key binding agent in baked goods, and each of those proteins has a specific function. Clara is focussed on producing the most important of those proteins; the ones that provide the nutritional content designed to feed a baby chick.

Clara is already in production at quite a high scale – Arturo told me tens of thousands of litres – but even at that level, cost remains an issue. These are falling rapidly, however, and today, on an egg-for-egg basis, Clara's end price is only a few cents more than the conventional product. Happily, egg whites are 90 per cent water, so once the key proteins are isolated and produced at scale, the price should actually begin to undercut that of conventional eggs.

Interaction with the FDA in the US has been smooth, so far as they work to achieve

GRAS designation for their products. Clara Foods is optimistic it will have ingredients on the US market very soon, with Asia the second area that they are looking at closely.

Arturo expects that 70 per cent of the US 'egg' market will be cage-free by 2025, only five years away, and that the Clara egg price equivalent will be similar to the farmed egg by then. This is a company to follow – it is well-capitalised, well-partnered and, in an area where the competition is not yet too fierce, has a significant head start.

## JUST

Then there is JUST, which is controversial to say the least, but it is also the first of the cell ag companies to reach a valuation over US $1 billion. A public offering in the near future is very likely. It is definitely worth going to the JUST (*né* Hampton Creek, full name Eat JUST) website, as it is slick and informative, though a bit long on as yet mostly unfulfilled promises. JUST started as a purveyor of plant-based vegan condiments and of egg substitutes made with mung beans, but has latterly been promoting its potential role in cultivated meats.

The company (as Hampton Creek) was started by close friends Josh Tetrick and Josh Balk in 2011 – aeons ago in cell ag terms. Tetrick is now the front man, and has attracted considerable coverage, some of it outlined in a 2020 book called *Billion Dollar Burger* by journalist Chase Purdy. Balk ended his involvement with the company shortly after its establishment and now runs Farm Animal Protection at HSUS.

Purdy clearly admires Tetrick but pulls no punches in reporting on the unorthodox culture of JUST, where there seems to be a fair bit of hectoring, cursing, and pushiness. A few years ago, there was some negative publicity about JUST, involving an alleged scheme to buy its own products to bolster its sales at the time of a funding round. An investigation by the SEC and the Department of Justice was closed, and no wrongdoing was found.

This more or less coincided with an attempted coup by three high-level employees as well as a director of the company. Khosla Ventures, a very prominent Silicon Valley funding group, and the early backer of Tetrick, was not involved in this failed coup, which ended up with Tetrick firmly in control of the company. The combination of these events has always left a bit of a cloud over JUST, which may partly be down to competitors' jealousy, or the reported abrasiveness and intense earnestness of Tetrick, or the fact that he has no scientific background. Or, perhaps, it is down to the fact that as far as cultivated meat is concerned, the company has been way behind on fulfilling its promises.

But the fact of the matter is that JUST is a true disruptor, has raised substantial funds,

*Scrambled eggs with JUST. Image reproduced courtesy of JUST.*

has substantial sales of its vegan plant-based products and huge ambition. Based on my review of the company, it could well be one of the big winners, and my conversation with Josh Tetrick was nothing other than cordial, informative and inspiring.

Tetrick, a dog-loving 39-year-old Alabamian, is of the opinion that the main obstacle to the widespread introduction of cultivated meat is and will continue to be, regulatory. JUST is San Francisco-based, as are so many of the New Agrarian startups, and is scaled for success. Apparently its office is 90,000 square feet, reflecting its ambitions to add meat lines, including cultivated Wagyu beef and chicken, to its impressive line-up of plant-based vegan products.

JUST originally planned to have a cultivated chicken line by 2018, but at the time of writing (2020), the company has no cultivated products on the market. In 2019, JUST demonstrated its avian alternative on a small scale, producing 40 pounds of cultivated chicken nuggets. Josh told me that the price has subsequently fallen from thousands of dollars per nugget to about US $50. Josh thinks cultured meats will be widely and globally available in about 15 years' time. He is now saying that the JUST chicken will be available in a limited way in 2022-2023.

Production is now being scaled in a 1,000-litre bioreactor, using primarily non-GMO techniques. This will be important for market acceptance, particularly in Europe, where GMO is banned.

Tetrick thinks that Asia will be the first major market for cell-cultivated meats, as the path to regulatory approval will be faster (see the next chapter), and he cites Singapore as the most advanced in terms of its industrial policy in this respect.

He says that if a clear regulatory path existed JUST meats would already be on the market, with either its Wagyu beef line (derived from cell lines from Toriyama, the famous Japanese farm) or with chicken, supposedly derived from the feather of a single chicken, Eric.

JUST's business model for cultivated meats is one of upstream production; partnering with food companies and distributors to take care of the downstream, or consumer-facing, end. This means that the JUST's plan is to sell technology, from media to bioreactors, to partners around the world. This is in contrast to its model for selling vegan plant-based foods where it directly produces and sells its products.

Josh is another successful food entrepreneur whose motivation is to avoid animal suffering and slaughter. He had been an athlete (and remains super-fit) but was not good enough, by his own admission, to be a professional athlete, so he stumbled on the food revolution to make his career.

JUST's egg substitute product is a major success and is based on mung bean protein. The company uses this plant because it allows the end product to gel at the same temperature and time as a regular egg. JUST settled on mung bean after screening a host of plants, and found a way of milling the mung beans into flour, using centrifugation.

JUST egg liquids are now sold by most of the major US food retailers, such as Kroger, Walmart and Safeway, and are also used by many restaurant chains. Apparently, the JUST product is in the top 20 per cent of all egg brands sold in the US, and sells alongside conventional eggs, rather than in the vegan section of stores.

The company is enjoying considerable self-proclaimed success, despite the fact that on an egg-for-egg basis its product is about twice the price of conventional eggs, which typically sell for US \$0.08 apiece. The company wants to get the price of its egg equivalents down to about US \$0.05 each, which would be cheaper than the cheapest conventional eggs found anywhere (currently in India at US \$0.068 per egg). Apparently about half the cost of regular eggs is represented by soy and corn, which is what the bulk of chickens feed on. JUST's facility for making its egg liquid is in Western Minnesota, and the company has partnered with Michael Foods, a division of Post Holdings and the largest supplier of eggs to the foodservice industry in the US. A similar relationship has been established with Eurovo and PHW (partner of LIVEKINDLY and Beyond Meat) in Europe as well, and in Korea with SPC, and in Thailand with Betagro Group.

The supply chain of mung beans has been expanded in recent years, and JUST is developing relationships in Africa, Thailand, and China to ensure an adequate supply of these beans, which are traditionally used to make dhal. Apparently, there is no problem in finding sufficient mung beans for its production of liquid eggs.

The inflection point for JUST will come when its cultivated meat products begin to be commercialised, and that will take a few years. Through adroit marketing and a good backstory, the company has raised about US $300 million in its history, and the most recent valuation is rumoured to be about US $1.2 billion, far outstripping any of the other cell ag companies. The company has established a European headquarters in London and is working through regulatory issues, which will likely not be onerous for its mung bean egg products but will inevitably be difficult for its clean meat lines, once those emerge.

The company was producing about 50 million eggs equivalent a month as of June 2020 according to Tetrick, which, in a very rough calculation with vegan condiments added on top, implies a sales run rate of about US $100 million per annum. This is not enough to justify the substantial valuation, so everything depends on cultured meat.

And there is some formidable competition coming up on the rails.

Nonetheless, Tetrick told Reuters in August 2020 that the company was heading to profitability in the near future and that an IPO was on the cards. Tetrick also says that the company owns 99 per cent of the plant-based egg category in the US and that the egg liquids are in about 12,000 stores in the US. Let's see how this plays out.

# CELL-BASED MEAT AND FATS

## FOIE GRAS

Foie gras is one of the most disgusting foods on the planet. The method by which 'real' foie gras is made is demonstrated in a link at the back of this book and is illustrated by a single photo here. Suffice it to say, in my younger days, I used to visit a friend in France who relished the stuff and, ignorant as I was, I joined in as he stuffed the goose or duck

*Force-feeding during foie gras production. Reproduced courtesy of Animal Equality.*

liver down his throat. The goose's throat had no such choice.

The foie gras, from what I can remember, was delicious, and plenty of others still find it so. It has worldwide sales of over US $2 billion a year, with most of it coming from France – not a country known for its animal welfare concerns. Some is also made in the US, using duck liver, and New York City is proposing a ban on its sale by the year 2022. Good for them.

If a way of producing this food without cruelty can be found, then I applaud it. Scientists at a French company called GOURMEY, presumably in atonement for the sins of its compatriots, are developing what they call 'ethical' foie gras, using cells derived from duck eggs as its foundation. GOURMEY is hoping to grow several types of meat in its labs, which look impressive in their promotional video.

I think it is clever to go for a niche and 'French' market to begin with.

Another company, Peace of Meat, in Belgium, is working on a duck liver pâté – apparently easier to make as well as being cheaper than duck or goose foie gras. They, rather like Future Meat, are a hybrid company, in that their principal products will be fats sold to plant-based meat companies. Their fats will be produced from cell cultures, but the principal ingredients in the end products will be plants.

# MOO'S LAW

Peace of Meat have developed a GMO-free stem cell line for their fat and liver products, and have already produced a 20g proof of concept that will supposedly be enough to produce ten times the amount of final product, which will be plant-based plus cell-cultured fat meat alternatives.

On the issue of scale, the company thinks they could be producing up to 100,000 tonnes of fat within ten years. Their technique also involves bulking up the individual fat cells, rather in the same way a bodybuilder does with his or her muscle cells.

This is interesting because, as with all cell ag companies, the scale up from tiny quantities will surely be the hard part. The scaling up from 100,000 tonnes to, say, a million tonnes will be considerably easier, and that is why, although the market currently looks tiny, I can confidently predict it will be huge – and within about a decade.

## MOSA MEAT

Mosa Meat is the company founded by Mark Post, one of the leviathans of the clean meat space, and a gentleman whom I interviewed for the purposes of this book. Peter Verstrate, a veteran food scientist, is the other co-founder, and the 35 full-time employees at Mosa are led by CEO Maarten Bosch, whom I have also met. Mark is Chief Scientist of the Netherlands-based company, and was heavily influenced by Willem van Eelen, who died in 2015 having worked for much of his life in trying to promote and develop cell-based meat production. Willem had seen and experienced starvation first-hand as a prisoner of the Japanese in Indonesia during the Second World War, and from that point had fantasised about growing meat from stem cells.

Willem, who only retired at the age of 86, did not manage to do it by himself, so in 2004 he convened a group of Dutch scientists, including Mark Post. Backed by government funding, they began to address the problem of using labs to grow meat.

Mark immediately became enthusiastic about the prospects and, based at the Eindhoven University of Technology, eventually attracted the attention of Sergey Brin, the co-founder of Google, whom I have also met through my work on longevity.

Sergey asked Mark to develop what became the world-famous first cellular hamburger, which was unveiled in London with considerable press coverage in 2013. The purported price of this single patty was US $330,000, although in reality it was probably much higher. By the time Sergey approached Mark the Dutch government's funding had come to an end, and so Sergey's money was probably one of the key ingredients in facilitating what in the coming decades will undoubtedly be one of the world's most important industries.

This first burger was made of lean muscle alone, without fat and connective tissue. It was cooked at the London presentation without these now-critical ingredients, because adding all the key elements of minced beef would have extended the project by another one or two years.

As it was, not much happened news-wise after the London launch of the incomplete demonstrator hamburger, and it is only now that what is a complex and previously hard-to-scale technology is coming to the fore.

Mark and team have since been busy working out ways of eliminating foetal bovine serum (the earlier way of catalysing growth in bioreactor-grown meat; now replaced in the case of almost all cell ag companies by alternative, and currently very expensive, growth factors) and of scaling stem cell production. He has also been working on ways of adding fat tissue, and this is all now incorporated into what Mosa is working on.

Mosa uses biopsy-derived cells from anaesthetised cows (equivalent to 0.5g of tissue only)

*Professor Mark Post, Chief Scientific Officer, with a newer iteration of Mosa's cultured beef. Reproduced courtesy of Mosa Meat.*

to produce their beef meat, with one sample currently able to produce 20,000 burger equivalents. Mark believes that using cows to produce cell lines would reduce the global cow population – initially from about one billion to 125 million, with those 125 million living full lives – and make slaughterhouses things of the past. Theoretically we would only need 150 cows to satisfy the world's demand for meat. By contrast, the worldwide herd is currently 1.5 billion cows. Improvement in the cell doubling technology would eventually lead, he believes, to only *two* cows being required to produce *all* of the world's beef.

The Mosa technology is similar to the techniques employed by most of the other companies, except those using immortalised cell lines, so it is worth reviewing.

Mosa's technique uses cell biopsies from living cows, which they identify as the best pathway to avoid the use of genetic modification and therefore maximise the possibility of their entering the more or less GM-forbidden European market.

First of all, stem cells are harvested from a sedated cow by a veterinarian. This biopsy sample is placed in ice and moved to Mosa's lab. It is then processed using fluorescence activated cell sorting (FACS) based on cell-specific markers to separate the muscle stem cells from the adipose fat stem cells. Both are the key to the eventual product. This sorting is now optimised at Mosa for muscle stem cells, and they expect it to be so optimised for fat cells in the near future. Having taken the initial cultures, the cells are cryogenically stored. Upon retrieval, the stem cells are checked for contaminants and/or disease.

These muscle (myosatellite) and fat (preadipocyte) stem cells are then expanded – i.e. allowed to divide and replicate – for a short period, before starting their journey to making meat.

This journey is initiated in a series of 'seeding trains' to increase the cell numbers. To do this, they are moved between a series of ever-larger vessels, each of which can accommodate between four and six population doublings. By the time this process is finished, the number of population doublings is between 30 and 35.

In the final step, the cells are transferred to a vessel (bioreactor) of 100 litres or more, where the cells are suspended in a culture medium. The cells are placed in microcarriers within the bioreactor to allow them a surface on which to grow, fed by nutrients and growth factors. The bioreactors are optimised to provide the ideal temperature, pH and oxygen levels.

The fat and muscle precursor cells are grown in separate tanks, with somewhat different nutrient mixtures for each category. Once the cells have been sufficiently expanded, they are removed from their microcarriers using a process of filtration and possibly, in the future, a centrifuge.

The respective cell lines, divided into muscle and fat, are then induced to go into the 'formation' stage, where they begin to produce tissue. All these steps of cell separation, cell amplification, and tissue formation are performed in a semi-automated and aseptic process.

In the formation phase, the fat and muscle precursor cells remain separated in different vessels, with biochemical triggers used to induce muscle stem cells into primitive muscle fibres. The fibres are merged with a gel that forces them to attach to one another to form a tissue, this process being known as 'self-organisation'. These aligned muscle fibres are generally about 2.5cm long and 1mm in diameter, and start to contract spontaneously and become tense. At the same time muscle protein synthesis begins.

Muscle tissue formation takes two to three weeks, during which the tissue is fed by an optimised nutrient mix.

Meanwhile, in separate tanks, the fat stem cells are induced by biochemical means to mature into adipose cells. These are also encased in a gel, and over a two to three-week period – happily coinciding with the time it takes to grow muscle tissue – the fat is grown.

This fat is then harvested and mixed with the muscle tissue, in a conventional food industry process, to produce the hamburger patty mix.

As with all other cell ag companies, including fish ones, the medium that the cells feed on is key to the end product. In Mosa's case, it is a solution of amino acids, vitamins, and minerals. The medium is currently pharmaceutical-grade and too expensive, and it is on reducing this cost, as well as that of the growth factors, which Mosa, along with all the other producers, are focussed on reducing (Moo's Law™).

The replacement of foetal bovine serum (FBS) – the original way in which cells in cell ag were induced to amplify – is fundamentally necessary. This is because of the way in which the serum is derived (from slaughterhouses), as well as the possibility of contamination, and the generally high cost. The use of FBS would go against everything cell ag companies represent: the attempt to remove animals entirely from supply chains and improve the overall sustainability of meat production.

Alternative growth factors remain very expensive, but huge progress is being made, including by Mosa. Currently, sets of these growth factors, which are naturally-occurring proteins, are needed to trigger cells to expand and then to produce tissue. Typically, five or six such factors are required, depending on the cells being expanded and the phases of the production process. Scientists are working on making recombinantly-produced growth factors, and indeed Mosa is developing these factors in-house as a back-up to externally-sourced ones. Companies, including Mosa, are also looking at optimising ways of recycling media and microcarriers. The latter are made of non-degradable and non-edible synthetic material, so it is important to reuse them once they have been separated from their harvested cells.

The stainless-steel bioreactors are sterilised between cycles and are reusable for many years of service.

Mosa was founded in 2016 and is based in Maastricht in the Netherlands. It recently closed the second Series B in the cultivated meat sector, raising a first close of EUR 55 million led by Blue Horizon Ventures, with support from Bell Food Group, M Ventures and Agronomics.

Mosa's first scaled production of about 10,000 tonnes of meat a year is expected in 2025, and the company will also outlicense its technology to third-party production. Forecasted revenues of EUR 350 million a year are expected by 2030, with about ten production facilities around the world.

In the case of nutrients, development also proceeds at an exciting pace. For instance, the protein made by companies such as Solar Foods (see earlier) is a likely source of cheap nutrients for cellular meat and fish production, and the recycling of nutrients, along with growth factors, will be another key factor in reducing costs (see Future Fields later).

As with all of these companies, reaching Griddle Parity™ will require much cheaper growth factors and feed media than is currently the case. Some pharma-grade growth factors can cost as much as US $80 million per gram (TGF-$\beta$) at the moment, but Mark Post is optimistic (in part based on discussions with biotech giant Genentech) that the cost can come down precipitously in the near future. These much cheaper growth factors would come from recombinant processes used in the biotech industry, and Mark estimates that Mosa would need only about two kilos of these much cheaper proteins to satisfy the company's production needs for centuries.

At the moment, Mosa is focussed on minced beef, but ultimately will try to produce more complex products such as steak. This it will do by using 3D techniques, possible use of sacrificial moulding, and using scaffolds in the production process.

The company is also looking at ways of co-culturing the fat and muscle cells, which will be another development important in reducing cost throughout the cell ag space. Mosa, along with other companies, notably Aleph Farms, is also trying to create a channel and perfusion system for more complex meat production. This is necessary because whenever tissue becomes thicker than 1mm, it needs a blood vessel analogue to deliver oxygen and nutrients to all parts of the tissue. This is also important to remove metabolic waste.

Mosa is going to address the European market first, and will soon file their initial application to the regulators. They expect to be able to commercialise on a small scale in about 18 months after that submission. If the European process takes too long, then they are likely to go to Singapore to obtain regulatory approval faster, but their expectation is that the European market will welcome their products in a limited quantity in about late 2022.

This is an ambitious target as the company is still at lab scale in terms of production, producing only about 0.5 kg of 'meat' (divided into fat and muscle) a month at the moment.

Mosa is certainly ambitious and has set out plans to produce two million tonnes of beef per annum by 2030, which will save 10 million cows from the slaughterhouse. Importantly, it will stop the production of 70 million tonnes of carbon dioxide, free up 19 million hectares of arable land, reduce water use by 25 gigalitres and, in the company's opinion, represent about 22 per cent of the worldwide cultured meat market at that point.

Worldwide sales of meat substitutes, all plant-based, were EUR 3.1 billion in 2017 and are expected to grow to an astonishing EUR 24.6 billion by 2025. Surprisingly, despite the success of Beyond and Impossible, Europe remains the largest market for meat substitutes, accounting for nearly 40 per cent of worldwide sales in 2017.

Mosa will launch first in European markets, selling minced beef, which will be its sole launch product. Of course, other companies, including Memphis and JUST (both interviewed) are working on multiple meat lines including beef, but Mosa and Aleph Farms of Israel are the only ones of substance purely focussed on beef. Meatable is currently focussed on pork, and several companies are interested in beef but focus primarily on poultry.

Some of these companies are producing undifferentiated products composed of loose cells, but Mosa has developed mature tissues, organised into structured muscle fibres. This is more complex than might be expected for minced meat, but it is apparently the way that the company's product achieves the real texture of meat.

# RETAIL SALES VALUE OF MEAT SUBSTITUTES IN WESTERN EUROPE

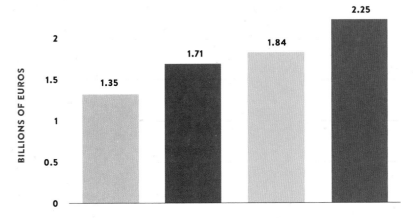

*Data reproduced courtesy of Nils-Gerrit Wunsch, 'Retail Sales Value of Meat Substitutes in Western Europe 2015-2022' (6 December 2019) statista.com.*

## MEMPHIS MEATS

Memphis Meats was founded in late 2015 and secured over US $20 million in initial seed and in a subsequent Series A funding in 2017. Early investors included Cargill and Bill Gates.

Fast forward to today, and Memphis has now raised over US $200 million in various funding rounds; with the bulk in a recent Series B of US $161 million that included investment from heavyweights such as Temasek, SoftBank, Bill Gates, Kimbal Musk and Richard Branson. It also has Cargill and Tyson as shareholders, both established 'old style' food companies.

Memphis, which is confusingly based in Berkeley, was very quick out of the gate after its foundation, and had produced a cell-cultured meatball by February 2016. Memphis is developing what it calls a 'species-agnostic' platform with the remarkable amount of money it has recently raised. The company expects to sell (presumably expensive) prototypes of its products within the coming years.

I spoke to Uma Valeti, the super nice founder and CEO of Memphis. Uma is of Indian origin, and while growing up in India he started to develop an aversion to animal slaughter at the age of 12, when he attended a birthday party where animals (unspecified) were killed. Later, while in the US, he had a shocking visit to a slaughterhouse, which surely is enough to put anyone, bar committed carnivores, off meat for life.

By then Uma had moved to the US to train as a cardiologist at the Mayo Clinic, and by working with cardiomyocyte stem cells to aid recovery in people who were recovering from heart attacks in his cardiology practice after his time at Mayo, he made the eureka connection that such cells could be used in food. It is a bit of a leap, but he had developed an interest in food, which grew into a full-time obsession – and into the company.

Having met Jason Matheney, the founder of New Harvest, he started the process by which Memphis was born. In 2015, he moved to San Francisco at the behest of a venture capital firm, and the company was started.

Uma and his team at Memphis identify cells that are akin to the best characteristics of the animal breeds they seek to replicate. They are looking principally for genomes that provide the best taste, texture, and what Uma calls 'organoleptic' experience, which elicits an individual's positive response to different foods.

Memphis Meats looks for cells that spontaneously grow into meat and have the ability to self-renew efficiently. Although they have made products without genetic engineering, they are open to it in future iterations, of their product, but using GM in a regulator-friendly way.

Publicly they have spoken about making chicken, beef and duck, and they are also looking at other species. Because chicken is the hardest meat to produce – basically because the cost of goods has to be very low to compete with conventionally-produced chicken – it would serve Memphis well if they crack this species. In that case, their platform could handle any other species very efficiently, including seafood.

Memphis is developing all three of the key components of cultured meat – connective tissue, fat, and muscle – so they are, on paper, ahead of most of the other companies in the space.

The company was one of the founders of the AMPS Innovation coalition, which was announced in August 2019. AMPS Innovation is short for the Alliance of Meat, Poultry and Seafood Innovation, and is an industry coalition for US-based companies involved in the field. Apart from Memphis Meats, members include JUST, Finless Food, New Age Meats, Artemys Foods, Fork & Goode, and BlueNalu. It is a complementary advocacy organisation to the Good Food Institute and New Harvest amongst others, and now consists of seven companies.

*Skewers of cultivated duck. Reproduced courtesy of Memphis Meats.*

Memphis works closely with regulators, of which it is very respectful (more on this in the next chapter), to prepare the way for the launch of a cultured meat product in the next couple of years. Uma would not commit to a date, sensibly, but it is clear that Memphis is one of the real contenders in this space.

It is well-financed, well led, has great science and is absolutely a company which investors should be keeping an eye out for. Despite there being no intention or mention of an IPO, and while Bruce Friedrich thinks they are likely to be acquired by investors Tyson or Cargill, I don't see why Memphis could not look to list in the next couple of years, most likely on a US exchange.

## MEATABLE

Meatable is a smaller company, at an earlier stage of development. I have spoken to Krijn de Nood, the founder and CEO, and actually met him, despite lockdown. It is an impressive outfit and is developing a unique cell ag technology based on induced pluripotent stem cells (iPSCs) derived from discarded animal umbilical cords. No samples are taken from live animals and umbilical cords present no ethical issues.

The proprietary technology that Meatable uses has been developed with Roger Pedersen, a Cambridge University-based stem cell biologist, as well as with Mark Kotter, a neurosurgical clinician also based in Cambridge.

Meatable raised an initial round of US $3.5 million in 2018 from venture capital firms Blue Yard Capital, Atlantic Food Labs and Backed. Krijn himself is an impressive leader. In December 2019 they raised a further US $10 million. More recently, in June 2020, Agronomics co-led a EUR 6 million funding round alongside Humboldt Fund, a venture capital firm based in Chile.

The technology developed along with Roger and Mark is named OPTi-OX cell reprogramming. According to Meatable, will offer a 25-fold improvement on the standard economics of cellular agriculture, due to improved efficiency of cell growth and differentiation. iPSCs are notoriously hard to direct in the right direction, in this case into fat and muscle cells, but the OPTi-OX technology can apparently accomplish this redirection within five days. The other great feature of iPSCs is that they are closer to an embryonic stem cell state and can infinitely proliferate without the addition of microcarriers.

## ALEPH FARMS

Aleph Farms, headquartered in Israel, works on cultured beef, and presented a whole cut of beef in 2018 that consisted of various types of cells which were co-cultured on a plant-based scaffold, a replacement to the extra cellular matrix found in animals. As such, it could be seen as a hybrid product, but the exact details of the product(s) are still under development, and so are not fully known to us. I spoke to Didier Toubia, the co-founder and CEO.

Didier, who has dual Israeli and French nationality, studied for a Master's degree in food engineering and biology, with a focus on malnutrition, and ended up working in agriculture for the International Finance Corporation (IFC) in Africa. He approaches the cultivated meats sector from the perspective of food security, explaining that the reason why 850 million people suffer from food scarcity today is not because of a lack of resources, but because of misallocation of those resources.

He is excited to be focussing on whole muscle meat (steaks), which he thinks will generate a real shift in consumer behaviour, due to the visual relationship that people have with the whole experience of eating meat on a plate, rather than just viewing it as mere protein. He sees Aleph's careful approach to design, along with reaching carbon neutrality by 2025, as emulating the way in which Apple, Google and Toyota (in hybrid cars) have managed to dominate the industry – not by being the first to market, but by being first to market with the right product positioned for the consumer.

Didier believes that Aleph will be able to achieve price parity with animal-based beef within three years of a large-scale production launch focussing first on steak, which typically is a premium product. He sees the future of the meat industry as being two-tiered, with cultivated meat taking the place of current intensive farming practices; leaving livestock farming the freedom to revert back to its more traditional, organic, grass-fed roots, without decreasing the overall meat supply. There will be separate categories for different consumer preferences – like red wine and white wine – and good quality conventional meat will not have to become a scarce luxury good.

Didier has led Aleph since 2016, after being involved with a couple of tech startups which led to an M&A and a successful IPO. Aleph was founded in association with the Kitchen Hub, an incubator owned by the Strauss Group, an Israel-based food group active in the US, Brazil, Europe, and China. Aleph acquired a licence from the Technion-Israel Institute of Technology, based in Israel, developed by Professor Shulamit Levenberg, who is an acclaimed tissue engineer.

He believes that Aleph will raise production to a very large scale in the next seven to ten years, and the company has committed to having zero carbon emissions in its operations by 2025. It is definitely a 'woke' organisation! In fact, they have been working with the International Space Station (ISS) to produce meat in space, to demonstrate that cultivated meat can be a solution to food security in the most remote places on Earth – and beyond. This strikes me as a bit of a PR stunt, but my overwhelming impression of Didier was that he was an entrepreneur firmly committed to doing good.

The technology that Aleph uses is cloaked behind a veil, which is fair enough, but I do know that they have been working with Russian company 3D Bioprinting Solutions to produce the 3D printed steak on the ISS. Last year, the Russian company announced that it would be working with KFC in Russia to 3D print chicken nuggets, nuggets that are supposedly a hybrid of cell-based meat and plant proteins. Incidentally, 3D Bioprinting Solutions has also been working with Finless Foods, a cell ag fish company (discussed later) in respect of producing fish on the ISS.

## MISSION BARNS

Mission Barns is focussed on creating animal fats (primarily duck, chicken, and pig) by cell ag techniques. The company is based in Berkeley, California, and has raised a total of US $7 million thus far, with a further round of US $20 million likely before year end 2020.

In May 2020, I talked with Eitan Fischer, the CEO and founder, who gave an overview of this impressive company.

In the small Israeli kibbutz where Eitan grew up, animal farming was emphasised, which he did not see as ethically problematic at the time. He moved to the US to study at Yale, where his views began to change.

He started to look at the environmental impact of intensive farming, as well as issues of animal welfare. He co-founded a non-profit called Animal Charity Evaluators, which he describes as a judge of charities involved in animal welfare, so that donors could better assess where to put their money.

Eitan continued his studies at Stanford in California, and from there joined JUST, when it was called Hampton Creek. In 2018, he left and started Mission Barns.

His team decided to start by focusing on fats, partly because it was a less complex technical challenge, and partly because the substitutes used by food companies for animal fats – for instance coconut and palm oils – are just not very good replicates of the real thing; they lack the juicy, meaty flavour that fatty tissues provide.

So far, the company has demonstrated two products – duck fat and pork fat – and has produced a hybrid bacon containing a mix of plant with 20 per cent pork fat grown in the lab.

The company has developed its own in-house production process, including customised bioreactors, and is building a species-agnostic process to grow all sorts of fats at scale.

Bacon, a US $65 billion market, is the first target of the company and once the company is at scale, Eitan thinks it will be much easier to produce fat cells than, for instance, muscle or connective tissue.

This creation of fat cells is known as adipogenesis and apparently uses much less media and batches are produced in much shorter time frames, compared to muscle tissue production.

Eitan expects that his cultivated fats will not just be used in foods, but also in personal care products such as soaps, makeup and cosmetics, and here he will go up against US-based Geltor, which makes collagen substitutes for use in personal care products and foods.

Mission Barns is looking to partner with other food producers and cosmetic producers rather than selling its own branded products. Eitan sees massive opportunity for the company in Asia and particularly in China, where pork dumplings, for instance, could be made using the company's fats.

Rather than relying entirely on an IP estate, the company has kept its cell line and seed train process as trade secrets, but what Eitan did tell me is that Mission Barns uses their proprietary bioreactors to grow very dense cells, and that this part of the process is patent-protected.

In academia, it has been established that soy protein scaffolds, which are nutritious and edible, can be used to generate three-dimensional bovine skeletal multiple tissue for cultivated meat.

Mission Barns harvests stem cells from cryogenically-frozen biopsies (from non-slaughtered pigs and ducks) and induces these stem cells to differentiate into fats by adding low-cost, food-safe molecules to the growth media.

Eitan imagines that the company will partner with multiple food producers, and has already scoped out a pilot plant in the Bay Area.

This company is absolutely worth watching. It appears to be eschewing the expensive and uncertain process of building a consumer brand in order to focus instead on making the vital ingredient required in both hybrid and fully-cultivated meats: fats.

## GELTOR

Geltor is another cell ag company out of San Francisco-based accelerator IndieBio. It was founded by Nick Ouzounov and Alex Lorestani and the company is focussed on producing animal-free collagen proteins for the food and personal care industries.

Geltor is well-funded and a recent Series B round brought in over US $91 million from such industry-leading investors as CPT Capital (Jeremy Coller's company), and RIT Capital Partners, Cultivian Sandbox, WTT Investment of Taiwan and collagen producer GELITA, as well as global food giant Archer-Daniel-Midlands (ADM).

This Series B, completed in mid-2020, was the largest funding round yet for any cell ag company, and took total funding for the sector to date to over US $1 billion.

Geltor is absolutely a company to watch. Its cell ag-derived collagen proteins have a huge potential market, evidenced by its partnership with GELITA, a German giant in collagen and other food products, which will produce dietary supplements made with animal-free collagens, with sales starting in 2021.

The worldwide collagen market is growing rapidly, and will reach US $7.5 billion by 2027, according to Grand View Research. Collagen is used in a wide variety of applications, including cosmetic surgery, wound healing and personal care products. In food, collagen is used as a stabiliser, in the form of gelatin. Most collagen comes from bovine sources, although porcine and marine sources are also used.

Geltor is already making waves, and has established partnerships with companies such as Kolmar Korea, a leading beauty products company for which it has already produced an Ageless Real Eye Cream for Face. I want some of that! It has many other products in development with partners around the globe as it designs proteins in a B2B model.

This is a really interesting company for an investor, and further details are available at the back of the book.

# CELL-BASED SEAFOOD

The imperative to do something about the state of the world's fisheries is, if anything, even more urgent than the case for transforming meat. The global seafood market is estimated at US $175 billion annually and is growing at a nine per cent compound annual rate.

An amazing fact, which I did not appreciate before starting this book, is that more fish are now farmed worldwide than are caught in the wild. About 53% of all fish harvested for human consumption in 2019 came from farms.

Most readers will already know about the overfishing of many fish species, the prevalence of contaminants in the water, including mercury and microplastics (mostly from tyre fragments), ocean acidification, viral and bacterial infection and the industrialisation of fisheries; all to the detriment of long-term supplies of this vital source of protein.

What many people do not realise is that many farmed fish eat wild-caught fish. About 12 per cent of the world's caught fish goes to feed fish and shrimps grown in farms (according to the IFFO, The Marine Ingredients Organisation). Basically, smaller fish such as anchovies and sardines are ground up into fishmeal and fed to larger fish such as salmon, as well as shrimp. This is because some fish, such as salmon, are carnivorous and plant-based foods hinder their growth. Also, farmed salmon require fishmeal to absorb Omega-3, which is not produced naturally in farmed fish.

Bluefin tuna, one of the most prized species on the planet, is imperilled by overfishing. Astronomical prices for the fish are often achieved in Japan's legendary fish markets, where a single fish has been known to sell for US $1 million. Global tuna sales total about US $40 billion per year, and its lucrative prices have attracted fraudsters and organised crime. Oceana, the American ocean conservation charity, estimates that about 20 per cent of all fish worldwide are mislabelled.

The trade in wild-caught fish is not alone in causing environmental and financial damage. Farmed fish are often raised in gruesome conditions and fed their wild-caught relatives in order to grow efficiently. Fish farms use all sorts of nasties to produce their output. Antibiotics, dyes (without which farmed salmon would be grey), hormones to promote growth and anti-parasitic drugs are just some of them. And the output of these farms is typically not as healthy as wild-caught fish; farmed fish are fattier and provide less protein than their wild cousins. Plus, if these farmed salmon escape they can wreak havoc with the wild salmon population, as they introduce "deformed" genes. This has recently happened in Scotland, where 50,000 salmon escaped captivity.

Alternative foods for farmed fish are being developed, using insects, algae, and canola, and a Californian company called Calysta, whose production facility is in Britain, is refining a protein designed to feed fish by converting natural gas using bacteria. Calysta has attracted investment from Temasek as well as BP.

This is welcome but will do little to improve the dire state of the world's fisheries. Species after species is being overfished, and there has never been a better case for cultivated fish. It is just as well that remarkable progress is being made by the relatively few companies involved in the field. Bluefin tuna stocks are down by over 90 per cent since the pre-industrial age, as just one example of the extraordinary destruction wreaked on the world's fish stocks. Most of the world's bluefin supplies are now farmed, and that is not a good thing.

There are, of course, plant-based fish companies, for instance Good Catch, which already has a range of fish cakes, but for my money the future of fish lies in labs.

Enter the cell ag fish companies, led by BlueNalu, but also Finless Foods and Wildtype, all based in California, and Shiok Meats of Singapore.

## BLUENALU

In my opinion, the standout company in fish meat cultivation is BlueNalu. The word "nalu" is the Hawaiian word for a 'wave' of the ocean, and the term "nalu it" is also local Hawaiian slang that means 'roll with it' or 'go with the flow' but be mindful and considerate at the same time. The leadership team, composed of food industry veterans as well as experts in tissue engineering, cell biology, regulatory strategy, and bioprocessing is impressive; the company is well-funded and the path to commercialisation is clear.

BlueNalu raised US $20 million in its Series A in late 2019 from investors such as Stray Dog Capital, Agronomics, New Crop Capital and CPT Capital – in other words, the who's who of the clean meat space. Previously, in early 2018, they had raised a seed round of US $4.5 million. BlueNalu currently has investors from 11 nations, demonstrating the global reach of the company, including strategic investments from five multinational organisations thus far (Sumitomo, based in Japan; Pulmuone, based in Korea; Nutreco, based in the Netherlands; and US-based Griffith Foods and Rich Products) with expertise in areas that include supply chain, operations, sales, marketing and distribution.

Through its 'cellular aquaculture' processes, BlueNalu has already made prototypes of its first seafood products, made from yellowtail amberjack. These whole muscle pieces were prepared using various techniques, resulting in fish tacos heated in frying oil, a poke, a kimchee product prepared in a typical acidified marinade, seafood soups, and more.

I have visited BlueNalu at its San Diego, California, facility and have met its CEO and co-founder, Lou Cooperhouse, on several occasions. Along with Chris Dammann, the

*BlueNalu's whole-muscle, cell-based yellowtail, prepared in four different recipes at a demonstration in December 2019. Clockwise from top left: roasted butternut squash and yellowtail bisque, poke bowl, fish taco, and kimchi. Image reproduced courtesy of BlueNalu.*

other co-founder and CTO, Lou is working on a platform that will eventually produce a diverse range of seafood. This will include Bluefin tuna, but also mahi-mahi, yellowtail amberjack, Chilean sea bass, red snapper and other finfish, and eventually crustaceans as well. Salmon is extensively farmed and wild-caught in US waters, so BlueNalu has strategically chosen not to pursue this species for American markets.

BlueNalu's species strategy is to go after fish that are overfished, imported (into the US), or difficult to farm.

Cultivating fish is waste-free, with no scales, tails, heads, entrails and, of course, no bones or shells. This results in a yield of nearly 100%, compared to an estimated 60% that may normally occur with conventional fish, resulting in considerable labour savings, convenience, and consistency. Furthermore, conventional fish is typically shipped very long distances and associated with very high amounts of bycatch and damage to our ocean floors, so the environmental and sustainability advantages of cell-based seafood are extraordinary. Because cultivated fish is largely free of bacteria, shelf life will be considerably longer than for regular seafood as well.

BlueNalu expects to have scaled up production to 2,000-litre batches by 2021, and 200,000-litre batches by 2024. They have successfully isolated and proliferated multiple species of fish muscle cells in stable cell lines. They do not use foetal bovine serum, nor any genetic modification in the process. They cryogenically preserve cell lines to be ready for scaling up. In the bioreactors, they do not use scaffolds, but rather an extrusion method to produce high-density fish and seafood tissues.

Each type of fish needs a tailored media formulation to support proliferation and growth. The company has chosen cell lines that go beyond the Hayflick Limit of about 50-60 divisions, and selects the lines to avoid mutations developing in proliferation. Their scientists isolate satellite cells, fibroblasts and preadipocytes, which will then go on to develop mature muscle fibres and fat components to make up fish tissue.

BlueNalu's technology allows for a rapid doubling rate which, for example, can be done in less than 48 hours in the case of yellowtail amberjack and its other finfish species.

At the same time as cells are busy proliferating, BlueNalu expects to ensure that the sensory attributes of its fish products are the same as conventional fish products – including taste, texture, smell, etc. The company has a partnership with Nutreco, a leading Dutch animal and aquatic feed company for media, as well as Griffith Foods, a leading culinary-based food ingredient company. Along with everyone else, BlueNalu is looking at ways of lowering media costs and avoiding pharmaceutical-grade media.

BlueNalu engaged with regulators from the outset, and has in fact hired a team of former senior FDA officials to guide it through the process of approval.

The company believes, and I agree with them, that they have great potential to be in the top 10 seafood producers worldwide in the next decade or two. The current top 10 producers each have revenues in the billions of dollars, so the prize is high. The leadership team wants to disrupt industrialised fishing, in which the top 13 companies are responsible for 10 million tonnes of wild catch annually. BlueNalu believes it can help small, artisanal fishing businesses to thrive, by facilitating a recovery in depleted fish stocks in many parts of the world.

BlueNalu has the strongest management and scientific bench in the cell ag fish business, led by Lou, a genial but laser-focussed food industry leader. Prior to BlueNalu, Lou was CEO of Food Spectrum, a well-recognised food industry consultancy, and before that he was the founder and executive director of Rutgers University's Food Innovation Center for 15 years.

Also on the team is Lauran Madden, who leads the company's R&D efforts and is key to their significant success in technology development, and Rami Nasrallah, known as the 'cell whisperer', which is either great branding or he is somebody every other company will want!

In an advisory capacity, the company also boasts Pierre-Yves Cousteau, son of the legendary Jacques.

BlueNalu is species-agnostic, in contrast to other companies in the field. Wild Type is working on Coho salmon; Finless on bluefin tuna (but has only demonstrated a carp croquette so far); but BlueNalu wants to cover everything in the edible marine world.

Lou has told his shareholders that BlueNalu will be profitable when its first large-scale factory is in full production during 2025, and that the company will initiate a string of production facilities worldwide shortly after this first commercial success.

BlueNalu is looking to produce whole muscle fish fillets, not blended hybrid versions, and nor is it looking to produce a fried or battered version of fish which is what most plant-based products currently are.

The global fishing industry is estimated to be worth about US $225 billion dollars a year by 2026, so it is a big prize. The President of People for the Ethical Treatment of Animals (PETA), Ingrid Newkirk, believes that a no-kill fish will be readily accepted by a large percentage of consumers, because of the ethical, environmental, and health boxes that cellular aquaculture ticks are of huge import.

Fish stocks and fish quality are under grave threat across the planet. Modern fishing techniques such as vast trawlers and nets have resulted in overfishing to the point where some species are close to collapse.

The harvest of wild fish caught in the seas is somewhere between 80 and 90 million metric tonnes a year, which some cell ag advocates have said is equivalent to the weight of all the humans in China.

The depletion of fish stocks has made for striking changes in our food supply. McDonald's Filet-O-Fish has been made from a variety of species over its history since 1963, when it was first launched. What started off as a halibut product is now made with Alaskan pollock, having run through the depleted stocks of cod, haddock, and hoki.

Of course, BlueNalu, as the leader in cellular aquaculture, would love to partner with McDonald's in its next iteration of fish, should the Alaskan pollock go the same way.

Humans are literally at war with fish – using quasi-military techniques to scoop up as many as possible of the creatures, depleting supplies and in many cases destroying them. Of the large predatory fish that roamed the oceans about a century ago – fish such as tuna and shark – 9 out of 10 of their population have gone due to factory fishing.

## WILDTYPE

Wildtype is well-funded, has a clear vision and is backed by capable investors including, notably, Spark Capital, which has backed numerous successful tech ventures. The company is focussed on a specific type of salmon, the Coho salmon, and is working on ways not to just grow the salmon cell lines into fish meat, but also to improve the health benefits of eating it, by introducing extra iron, omegas, and vitamins and minerals. The Coho salmon is very popular for sashimi and tuna rolls, and therefore has a very large potential market.

The company was founded in 2016 by Justin Kolbeck and Aryé Elfenbein, who met at Yale University in 2011. Justin spoke with me, and while he was realistic about the complexities and challenges of getting their Coho salmon to market, he was also enthusiastic about the company's prospects in the medium term. Aryé, the scientist in the team, has a background in molecular biology and cardiology. Justin was formerly a US diplomat for six years, including a tour in Afghanistan, and it was there that he realised how fragile the world's food system is.

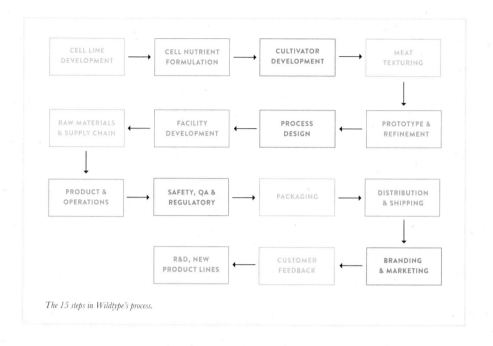

*The 15 steps in Wildtype's process.*

On the Wildtype website there is a 15-step chart encompassing the complexities of the process of producing foods such as fish filet, which highlights all the familiar steps in cell ag food production. These include nutrient composition, cell line identification and development, as well as meat texturing.

Originally, Wildtype looked at producing foie gras, but quickly pivoted to the much bigger fish market, which is the number one source of protein in the world. They settled on salmon, the most consumed finfish in the US and the second most consumed seafood after shrimp. Seafood is typically healthier than meat, and even the Beyond and Impossible burgers are high in sodium and saturated fats, which according to Justin do not help people seeking a healthier lifestyle.

Wildtype is going to produce salmon with no microplastics, no antibiotics, no parasites, and no mercury, and with as much Omega-3 as regular fish because of a proprietary process of introducing it via algae into the cell feed.

Justin thinks that consumers will be open to cell-cultivated salmon because of its purity, and that some consumers who cannot eat raw seafood (e.g. pregnant women) will be the early adopters, leading to wider public acceptance.

Since most farmed salmon in the US comes from Chile, Scotland or Norway, there is a domestic angle for Wildtype to exploit, especially as most salmon is frozen for a long time before landing on the consumer's plate. Wildtype is going to partner with existing salmon producers rather than fight them, according to Justin.

Cells are sourced from Pacific salmon and do not undergo any form of genetic modification. The company has regular conversations with the FDA, and the decision for a non-GM route should enable Wildtype to have a smoother time seeking regulatory approval in the US. That said, the FDA approved AquAdvantage, a genetically-engineered Atlantic salmon from AquaBounty Technologies in 2015. That process of overcoming political opposition and obtaining approval took around 30 years, however, exemplifying why it is not worth even attempting to use genetic modification for cell-based fish. AquAdvantage salmon is also not yet on the market in the US, although AquaBounty Technologies said they had sold 4.5 tonnes in Canada in 2017.

Wildtype has built a pilot plant in San Francisco, where it is based, and expects to have reasonable production capacity by the year end 2020. The salmon consists of both muscle and fat, with the latter consisting of between five and 20 per cent of the finished fish, roughly equivalent to regular salmon. No FBS is used. A specialised media has been developed using specific amino acids, along with salts and sugars. The company will integrate the vitamin astaxanthin to produce the colour of many variants of salmon, but the exact colour of its product is yet to be determined.

Its team currently consists of 20 full-time employees, of whom 18 are scientists. Justin is therefore one of only two non-scientists in the company!

Wildtype has raised a total of US $16 million between its seed funding round and its Series A. It has also got a venture debt line of US $4 million, so has snagged a total of US $20 million since foundation. Spark Capital led the seed round and Charles River Ventures, a VC firm based in Boston, led the Series A.

My own view on this company is positive; I would place it at number two in the cellular aquaculture space after BlueNalu. If investors are interested in taking things further with Wildtype, details are at the back of this book.

## SHIOK MEATS

Shiok Meats is a Singapore-based cellular aquaculture company focussed on making shrimp meat. It was founded and is headed up by Dr Sandhya Sriram (CEO), whom I have met, and Dr Ka Yi Ling (CTO).

Shiok produces muscle cells to create a shrimp meat mass, to be used mostly in Asian foods including shrimp pastes, which are used abundantly in Asia. Shiok is a fairly small organisation, with big plans. Its website is littered with exclamation marks and the company has the mark of hyperbole about it.

But there is some good sense in what they are doing. At present, shrimp caught in the oceans are caught alongside a lot of what is known as by-catch. In fact, for every kilo of shrimp caught, about 20 kilos of innocent bystanders are discarded. About 45 per cent of world shrimp production is caught, and 55 per cent is farmed in pretty awful conditions. Farmed shrimp are vulnerable to infectious diseases, due to the filthy and dense conditions, and are often heavily dosed with antibiotics.

Parasitic worms in raw seafood have increased in prevalence nearly three hundredfold in the past two decades, and farmed fish emit even more noxious emissions than the cultivation of farmed pork or poultry.

Because so much shrimp production has been moved to farms, mangrove swamps, which are often used for the farms, have decreased in size by 1.5 million hectares since 1980. Mangroves are excellent carbon sinks, so farmed shrimp production is even worse for the environment.

There are particular challenges of mass producing shrimp meat, including immunogenicity and the look and feel of the finished product. Shellfish in particular are known to be highly immunogenic, which means that an adverse reaction can be elicited by some people consuming shrimp. Supposedly, Shiok is working on ways of reducing the immunogenicity of its shrimp product. It is only producing muscle tissue at this point, and is buying in the fats, which are a key component of shrimp's taste. The flavour of shrimp meat is produced by the haemolymph (a kind of blood found in invertebrates), as well as by the high percentage of fat. (In mammalian meat, taste is also produced by these fat and blood components.) Shiok is working with Tyson Foods, which produces a form of plant-based shrimp meat, to perfect its cell-derived product.

Shiok's first product is shrimp dumplings, a very popular Asian dish, and has been working with a leading media specialist to drive down the costs of media as well as with the Japanese cell ag company IntegriCulture.

The company is interesting, and has raised venture funding from investors including Henry Soesanto, the CEO of Monde Nissin (the Filipino company which purchased Quorn Foods in 2015), along with Aqua Spark, who led their US $12.6 million Series A financing in 2020. However, in our dealings, we have found them to be somewhat opaque and prickly, so this may not be a company in which I would necessarily invest in future. Shiok may well be able to sell early products in Singapore in 2022, and they are also working on crab and lobster, so they are worth watching – with caveats.

## FINLESS FOODS

Finless Foods is a hard-charging cell ag fish-based company, but in my conversations relating to this book, it is generally seen as an also-ran behind BlueNalu and Wildtype. The perception of the company was not improved by an apparently botched initial tasting of its croquette product, which consisted of 75 per cent potato and 25 per cent carp (at least, carp cells).

The CEO and co-founder of the company is Mike Selden, who is under 30, and is a biologist and molecular scientist by training. It was he apparently who rushed the move to a poorly-received croquette tasting. He has admitted that a reporter from the Guardian who attended the tasting was 'fair in her negative opinion of the product'. Finless now claims to have a dozen cell lines of different species of fish, including what Mike claims is the only bluefin tuna line. This is the key to up-market sashimi and to the huge Japanese cuisine market.

He claims also that the cost per pound of their tuna line has fallen from US $19,000 to US $4,000 and will fall to US $20 per pound by 2025. Finless's initial funding was US $3.5 million in a seed round, from an impressive list of investors, including Draper Associates and Babel Ventures, but I cannot find evidence of any subsequent funding.

In 2019, Finless partnered with Russian 3D Bioprinting Solutions to print a small fish-like mass in space in the International Space Station, a gimmick it shares with Aleph Farms, which did the same thing for meat.

Finless is rumoured to be short of cash, and it is not on our preferred list.

## AVANT MEATS

I caught up with Carrie Chan and Mario Chin, co-founders of Avant Meats, a Hong Kong-based company, during lockdown. They came across as really nice people with a fascinating proposition. Carrie is an entrepreneur who 'found' Mario, formerly Professor at the School of Medicine at Pennsylvania's Temple University, and a specialist in molecular genetics.

This is a small company, but worth a look. They have been largely funded by angel investors thus far, but were recently seeking to raise about US $2 million of fresh capital.

They founded the company in Hong Kong because their product – fish maw, which is dried swim bladder – lends itself to local markets, and it is also where their employees are based - which I think, so far, is principally themselves!

Fish maw lends itself to both early scale up and commercialisation because it only uses one cell type. The early fish prototype they are working on is a fish maw derived from croaker cells, and they expect to have a pilot plant early next year and their first commercial product by the end of 2021 or the start of 2022. The fish maws can be grown at scale in approximately one and a half months per batch.

Maw is traditionally derived from two fish species, Bahaba and Totoaba, both of which are under threat from overfishing. The product is supposed to have health benefits according to Chinese tradition and the texture is loved by consumers. As a long-standing resident of Hong Kong, I must say truthfully that I have never knowingly tried it! Cultivated maw would also be traceable, as as from time to time traditional maw is mislabelled and mis-sold.

Apart from maw, they are also working on a fish fillet scaffold, and are looking at a variety of plant-based materials from which to make these structures.

Their business model is B2B, selling their maw to food producers and to the food service industry. Asia is likely to be the earliest adopter of technologies such as Avant's. Though this company is at a very early stage, it had raised US $1 million in seed funding as of mid-2020.

Still, it is innovative and worth keeping an eye out for any further fundraising.

# MATERIALS

The world of cellular agriculture goes beyond just food. Its application for materials is an area of considerable interest to me, as the path to market is clearer than with food. This is because materials don't require regulatory approvals in most cases, and yet the environmental case for these products is as strong, if not stronger, than that for cell ag made foods.

Several companies are employing cell ag techniques to 'grow' materials in labs. These include leather, silk, fur, and entirely novel materials that attempt to mimic the properties of leather.

## MODERN MEADOW

Modern Meadow, a company based in New Jersey, has already produced a material they call 'inspired by leather', using engineered proteins. Modern Meadow uses microbial fermentation to produce a collagen-like material in yeast; collagen is then separated from the yeast and aligned to form performance bio-alloys. This company has raised a total of US $53 million from a wide variety of investors, including Li Ka-shing's Horizons Ventures, Temasek, and Iconiq Capital.

Modern Meadow is trying to be a provider of alternative materials, that are superior to traditional leather in sustainability and performance, for fashion goods, sporting equipment, luggage, and furniture. Founder and CEO Andras Forgacs, formerly of Organovo, a company involved in printing human tissues, is trying – and I am not certain that he has been entirely successful in this – to use this 'biofabrication' by assembling collagen and other proteins to yield leather that is 'biologically identical' to the conventional material. This material has no fat or hairs on it, so is easier to put through a tanning process without liming, and as a result has considerably less environmental impact.

Modern Meadow is using synthetic biology to grow leather in labs, not from livestock.

## VITROLABS

VitroLabs is in the business of producing real leather by tissue engineering, forming the complete cellular composition of leather, unlike Modern Meadow, which is solely focused on the collagen component. VitroLabs already has prototypes, including leather watch straps and wallets, orders in hand, and a clear business strategy. This is a company that makes a whole load of sense to me as an investor, and I urge readers to follow its progress. It has made substantial progress in R&D since its inception, arguably at a much swifter pace than Modern Meadow.

They are raising Series A funding at the time of writing and as always, the details for investors to contact the company directly are in Chapter Five. The company has raised US $9 million in seed funding to date, including support from Agronomics, Firstminute Capital, Fifty Years and Khosla Ventures.

I have met the CEO of VitroLabs, Ingvar Helgason, who heads up a team of about 15 full-time employees and he has a clear plan towards making substantial volumes of the company's cell-derived leather - and substantial volumes of money.

It is clear that this is a no-brainer white space: cow hides limit the size of pieces of

*Leather watch straps made from VitroLabs' cultivated leather. Photo reproduced courtesy of VitroLabs.*

leather, whereas cell-derived leather can conceivably be grown to any size. Cow hides are difficult to get in a perfect condition for luxury goods (Vitro's initial market) as they are often scarred by barbed wire or have other imperfections. Cows or calves need to be slaughtered to produce leather, and of course VitroLabs's process involves no killing. Cowhides need extensive removal of hair and a great deal of liming and tanning. Vitro's leather has no hair (as with Modern Meadow), and their tanning process uses much less water, and creates much less pollution, than the conventional method.

VitroLabs uses a fairly conventional cell ag process to grow its leather. First, stem cells are proliferated into a sufficiently large biomass. The cells are then seeded onto a scaffold in their proprietary scalable bioreactor platform, which enables them to grow sheets of leather on vertically-stacked palettes.

Collagen, the most prevalent protein in skin, comes in a variety of forms, and VitroLabs is most likely to focus on Type I and Type III, along with other essential extracellular matrix proteins. These are among the five most common types of collagen. Type I is related to skin, tendons, vasculature, organs, and bone. Type III is the reticulate, which is the main component of reticular fibres which form networks in tissues, and is commonly found alongside Type I. The skin cells play a vital role in binding the matrix proteins into the specific structure found in bovine hides.

VitroLabs currently uses polyester scaffolding, although it is looking to ditch the polyester in the near future, probably using cellulose as a sustainable replacement. The company is also looking to optimise the cell seeding strategy, because not every cell sticks to the scaffold at present, and this represents unnecessary waste.

The proprietary platform is an automated, modular design, and can allow VitroLabs to scale up through the addition of multiple platform units. The company is working with Eppendorf and PBS Biotech (both of which are discussed later) and so far has been producing leather in its initial bioreactor platform, the three-litre "Nandini", which clearly has to grow dramatically for full commercialisation.

At the moment, 12 litres of media are needed to produce one square foot of leather, so another objective is to reduce the volume, and cost, of media. The company is also modelling ways to recycle media and extend its life, by adding glucose and glutamine and by removing waste products such as ammonia and lactic acid.

Once the tissue (which will be 0.8-1.3 mm thick) is harvested and separated from the scaffold, it is washed with water, packed in salt, and stored at 3 degrees Celsius before being sent to the tannery.

VitroLabs's process is partly automated and has already produced skin pieces equivalent to bovine tissue, with little manual intervention. VitroLabs expect their bioreactors to eventually be fully automated, with machines replacing all current human inputs, which include removing waste bags and adding media.

This luxury-standard leather has already attracted the attention of major fashion brands. As luxury brands are the biggest consumers of high-end leather, this is a big bonus for the upstart company. Already, one test product, a leather cardholder, has been made. A top-three global luxury brand is planning a 'capsule' range, and no doubt this will be highly sought-after and publicised.

One has to imagine that as scale goes up and prices go down, VitroLabs' products could rapidly gain share in the luxury goods market, where the producers are not as sensitive to cost of goods sold as, say, shoe manufacturers, but rather can revel in the virtue-signalling accompanying the use of cultivated leather.

VitroLabs is establishing barriers to entry partly through a patent-driven approach. In May 2016 they filed their first patent for 'Engineered Skin Equivalent, Method of Manufacture and Products Derived therefrom', which has been granted. They also have multiple provisional patents filed in the bioreactor and cell-line space.

They are developing a cell bank to minimise the need for animal biopsies, and are improving cell yields by reducing the number of cells in the seed train. They are trying ways of getting rid of microcarriers (purchased from Solaris) in the bioreactors by using alternative non-plastic methods, including hydrogels. Once the cells are seeded onto a scaffold, it is a combination of the 3D microenvironment and the addition of ascorbic acid (Vitamin C) and TGF-β to the culture media that triggers collagen production.

Over the next three years, VitroLabs expects to get its costs of goods sold down to a highly competitive US $10 per square foot, which is comparable to finished luxury hides. Producing the leather in their San Jose, California, production facility and the material shipped to tanneries in Normandy, France. VitroLabs's leather platform produces less than one per cent of the greenhouse gas emissions of conventional leather production, and the product can be used not only in luxury goods, but also in anything from aviation to saddles, sports equipment to high-end Tesla car seats. It could be adapted to produce furs and exotic materials such as crocodile, snake, or alligator skin.

Furthermore, Vitro's leather uses less than five per cent of the land needed to produce the same amount of conventional leather, and emerges from the factory in whatever size is needed, in perfect condition, and without discarded offcuts. And it is REAL leather.

Ultimately, VitroLabs envisages commercialising a Platform as a Service model (PaaS), where their technology is licensed out to, say, luxury goods manufacturers. Leather goods in the luxury market are big business, accounting for sales of US $52 billion globally. Hermès alone bought an estimated US $300 million of leather in 2018, so there is considerable potential.

Ingvar, from Iceland, spent 20 years in the high-end fashion industry before founding VitroLabs. He has been joined by Dr Craig Halberstadt, who is Chief Scientific Officer and has extensive experience in tissue engineering. Craig has been granted 10 patents over his 25 years in the field. The team is further augmented by Dr Dusco Ilic, who is a leader in stem cell technology and skin models, and also has over 25 years of experience.

This is a tightly-focussed, class act of a company. I highly recommend investors take a good look at VitroLabs.

## BOLT THREADS

Bolt Threads is a well-capitalised later stage company that currently makes spider silk from bugs but wants to use its platform technology to produce many different types of materials. Bolt Threads has raised significant funds, most recently a Series D round of US $123 million in 2020, which means that since its foundation it has raised US $213 million. The Series D was led by leading Scottish investment firm Baillie Gifford (the second largest investor in Tesla) as well as Fidelity Investments, and the ubiquitous Temasek.

Bolt Threads has operated since 2009 and currently makes synthetic spider silk, which is stronger than Teflon, durable, elastic, and soft at the same time. It has produced samples, and in 2017 unveiled a US $300 necktie as an example of what was possible.

Today, the company has partnerships with the likes of ethical clothing brands Patagonia and Stella McCartney. Bolt Thread's Microsilk is produced with far less environmental damage than conventional textile manufacturing, and it biodegrades at the end of its life. This Microsilk replicates something very hard to produce in nature – because the spiders end up eating each other before much can be produced. In fact, the longest ever production run of this silk using spiders was in Madagascar in 2009 – and that was only 80 feet.

Bolt Threads uses a fermentation process to produce its materials, which is not unlike brewing beer. Engineered yeast containing spider DNA (the IP) is fermented with sugars and water, and then expels a protein that is chemically identical to spider silk, which is spun into fibres.

Bolt Threads has a competitor in the form of Spiber, a company based in Yamagata, Japan, which makes a 'brewed protein' from plant-derived biomass using a fermentation process. Spiber makes silk fibres rather like Bolt and spun yarns similar to cashmere, as well as animal-free fur and leather alternatives.

Spiber, founded in 2007, has a rich history of research, and produced a 'Moon Parka' in 2015 as a demo of its skills with new materials. The company has about 250 employees and has raised around US $250 million since inception, so it is worth keeping an eye out for capital raises and IPOs for both Bolt Threads and Spiber, although, it has to be said, neither appears to be at the point of mass-scale production.

## GALY

GALY is working to produce high quality cotton through cellular means, at competitive prices compared to conventional cotton and with a much lighter environmental impact. The company is relatively new, having only been founded in 2019, and has so far raised US $4.8 million.

Cotton is highly water-intensive – 10,000 litres are required to make a single pair of jeans – so the crop is highly sensitive to droughts and other factors. It requires large quantities of pesticide to grow successfully, with over six per cent of the world's pesticides devoted to cotton. The monocultural nature of cotton farming also lends itself to the loss of biodiversity. For these reasons, it would be a significant achievement to grow it successfully in a lab.

GALY holds a couple of patents for the general technique of growing cotton in a lab, and has done a great job in a short space of time on the way to successfully producing cotton. The company has already conducted 1,000+ tests to develop different protocols, including the use of appropriate media.

Cotton is a disaster from the perspective of climate change and health. GALY estimates that, with the use of its technology, lab-grown cotton would eliminate US $12 billion of unnecessary costs worldwide, including nearly US $6 billion of logistical costs and US $4 billion of chemical costs.

Currently, cotton production uses up to 2,000 chemicals, including glyphosates, ethephon, trifluralin, sodium chlorate, paraquat, and diuron. The water requirements, as noted before, are astonishing. GALY claims it will be able to make Egyptian cotton-quality material at a much lower cost than conventional cotton, with 80 per cent less water and carbon dioxide, and at sites closer to the garment factories.

To grow 1,000 tonnes of cotton requires about 200 acres of farmland, but the same quantity produced in a factory will only require about 0.25 acres.

If ALL cotton were grown in factories, a dream admittedly a long way off, about 300 million acres of farmland would be freed up, or the equivalent of 154 million soccer fields.

At the moment, GALY uses lab-grade media, but when the company starts producing at scale, they expect to use sugar cane for the primary feedstock.

At this point, they expect the media to cost about US $0.50 to produce a kilo of cotton. The good news on cotton is that the cell which kicks off their production process is a meristem – in other words it is totipotent. This means that cells in the meristem can develop into all the tissues and organs that make up plants, including cotton.

The production process is similar to cell ag produced food. Cells are multiplied in a bioreactor and elongated into fibres, which are then matured, harvested and spun into the final product.

The full cycle of production at scale will last 40 days, including cell multiplication and cell elongation into fibres, versus the 180 day cycle for farm-produced cotton.

Cotton is a US $140 billion worldwide business, so the market has terrific potential. So much so that GALY is already in discussion with six 'ideal' partners.

I spoke to the CEO and co-founder Luciano Bueno, a Brazilian national, and although the company is based in Boston, Massachusetts, he was in his home country for lockdown. Luciano is joined on the leadership team by Dr. Paula Elbl, who has a PhD in biotech and 15 years of experience in cell culture and micropropagation, as well as 14 other scientists, business development, marketing and operations people.

Luciano has spent about a decade working in the VC and consulting world, including a stint at Deloitte as well as a prior startup jaunt working on the application of nanotechnology for textiles.

GALY was founded in 2019, so is an early stage startup. So far, the company has produced enough cotton for proof of concept and is looking to scale up very soon. But Moo's Law™ applies here as well, and I think this could be a real winner.

The company has raised a significant amount of money from a Seed round and this includes a grant from the H&M Foundation, linked to the giant Swedish retailer Hennes and Mauritz AB.

In the following years, the company expects to raise further rounds of investment to build a pilot facility. This will only produce a couple of kgs of cotton per year but will act as a proof of concept for a small-scale production and then massive international expansion.

Beyond clothes, there is strong demand for cotton in applications ranging from buds to bandages.

Apart from cotton used in clothes, the market for cotton in buds (Q-tips, for instance) is large, as is the market for medical cotton (bandages for instance).

GALY's labs are in Amherst, Massachusetts, and in Sao Paulo, Brazil.

GALY will require a great deal more funding to reach its goals, and no doubt will face resistance from the established cotton producers, which are principally in China, India and the US. Nonetheless, I think this is a company worth backing, and would urge investors to contact the company directly if they are interested.

# PET FOODS

Global pet food sales are absolutely enormous; this is another market ripe for disruption, though there are not many participants as yet in the cell ag space for pets, which gives early investors a potential opportunity. According to Grand View Research, the global pet food market was estimated to be worth US $86.6 billion in 2019 and is forecast to be worth US $90.4 billion in 2020.

There is absolutely no reason why at least some of this market cannot be converted to plant-based or cell ag foods. Dogs are omnivorous – they don't need to eat meat and are able to digest proteins from multiple sources. I can attest to this as the owner of three dogs who will generally eat ANYTHING!

Cats are another matter, being carnivores, and it will be some time before the meat replacements they would need to survive and thrive are available through cell ag methods. Dog food greatly outsells cat food globally.

Treats are the fastest-growing segment in pet food, and the fastest-growing markets are in Asia Pacific.

The pet food market is dominated by two US companies, namely Mars Petcare, a division of Mars (of confectionery fame), which had global pet food sales of US $18 billion in 2019, and Purina, the US subsidiary of Nestlé, with sales of US $14 billion. All other companies are much smaller, including J.M. Smucker of the US, with sales of about US $2.8 billion and Hill's Pet Nutrition, with US $2.4 billion, as well as Diamond Pet Foods, General Mills and Spectrum Brands of the US, Unicharm of Japan and Deuerer and Heristo of Germany.

In the US alone, the scale of pet ownership is staggering, with households owning 184 million cats and dogs, and 68 per cent of Americans owning one or more of them. As a result, US consumers spend US $30 billion a year on pet care and nutrition.

Pets are voracious consumers of meat, with a quarter of all meat eaten in the US sold in the form of pet food. If American pets were a meat-eating nation, they would be the fifth largest in the world.

I have identified two cell ag startups involved in pet food production and have met the founders of both. These are Wild Earth and Bond Pet Foods, with Wild Earth looking to produce a cultured protein and Bond Pet Foods starting with pet snacks, or as we call them in our household, 'meaty treaties'!

Conventional pet food can sometimes be contaminated. J.M. Smucker, for instance, had to recall over a hundred million cans of dog food in 2018 because some of the ingredients – possibly from dogs and cats from animal shelters and as well as horses – contained drugs to euthanise animals. As a committed pet owner, this fills me both with rage and fear.

And it does suggest that there must be a better way to produce healthy pet food.

## WILD EARTH

Ryan Bethencourt, a well-known figure in the cell ag business, and his friend Ron Shigeta started Wild Earth to pursue precisely this mission. These were the guys behind the widely-admired IndieBio clean ag accelerator, which has spawned such companies as Finless Foods, Memphis Meats, Clara Foods and Geltor, so they have extensive experience of the cell ag scene.

They joined up with two other co-founders, Kristin Wuhrman and Abril Estrada, and formed Wild Earth in March 2018, raising US $4 million of seed funding promptly thereafter.

They were subsequently joined by Dr Ernie Ward, a noted vet who has helped to formulate the company's first products, which include complete nutrition for dogs, as well as treats. Cats are so-called obligate carnivores, so they will have to wait for the mass-scale production of cultivated meat.

Total funding for the company, which is based in Berkeley, California, has now risen to US $16 million and has come from such people as Mark Cuban and Peter Thiel, funds such as Stray Dog Capital, VegInvest and Felicis Ventures and, presumably keeping an eye on the future, Mars Petcare!

The main ingredient (about 31 per cent) in Wild Earth's food for dogs is a yeast protein. Ryan Bethencourt, the company's CEO, has said that this yeast protein has all the 'umami (savoury) taste that dogs love'. He also says that the yeast protein provides all the nutritional benefits of meat, including the key amino acids that dogs need, without the contamination issues and environmental damage.

Wild Earth is already selling directly to consumers on a subscription basis. The founders of the company have written a book on the subject, the 'Clean Pet Food Revolution', which is worth checking out on Amazon. Ryan makes the point that if pet ownership in China reaches the level of the US there would be 500 million more dogs and cats in the country – all needing food. Hence the urgent need for new protein sources for pets.

A private British company, HOWND, has started fundraising to do more or less what Wild Earth is doing, though its current sales consist mostly of ethical grooming products.

## BOND PET FOODS

Bond Pet Foods, founded by the genial and articulate Rich Kelleman and based in Boulder, Colorado, uses what is essentially a brewing process to produce dog and cat foods. Since dogs and cats have no interest in the aesthetics, texture, or mouthfeel of food, they don't really care about how the food looks. This makes a pet food free of conventional meats much easier to produce. As a result, the company uses yeast to produce animal proteins without the involvement of any animals. Bond has recently announced a cultivated chicken line for dogs, which is very exciting.

According to the Pet Food Institute, nearly 3.8 million tonnes of conventionally farmed meat were used in pet foods in the US in 2018, so the need for alternatives is pressing.

Rich was originally an advertising strategist working on Burger King's account, and as time went on; travelling around and looking at (but not eating) burgers and chicken sandwiches, he became a vegan. Later, the arrival of a dog in the household of Rich and his wife meant that he started thinking about new ways of feeding dogs. Hence, the germ of an idea for Bond.

The first product from Bond is based on a biopsy-derived chicken muscle protein which is then formulated into a snack. In a nutshell, animal protein genes are taken humanely from a farm animal, added to yeast microbes, put into bioreactors, and fed vitamins, minerals and sugars to produce pet foods that are nutritionally identical to meat counterparts. At the end of 2019, Bond announced completion of its seed funding, raising a fairly small US $1.2 million in a round led by Lever VC, a leader in investment in alternative proteins, and joined by Agronomics, KBW Ventures and Andante Asset Management. 'What makes us so excited about Bond Pet Foods is that it is the first clean-meat company producing meat protein in a way that doesn't require major technological breakthroughs to get to price parity with conventional meat,' said Nick Cooney, founder and Managing Partner at Lever VC. 'We don't think there's any other company out there with the potential to disrupt the US $100 billion pet food market as much as Bond Pet Foods.'

As a side note, Because Animals, a startup creating both plant-based and cultured protein-based pet food, has already created a cultured-mouse meat prototype for cats, and is working on cultured rabbit meat for dogs also. This is another company to watch in the pet food space.

# EXOTIC FOODS JOIN THE NEW AGRARIAN REVOLUTION

## INSECTS

Many people find the idea of eating insects disgusting, but it has been going on for millennia in large parts of the world. Eating insects is known as entomophagy, from the Greek words 'entomon' (insect) and 'phagein' (to eat). Some noted ancients were partial to eating creepy crawlies, including Aristotle, who apparently loved cicadas for a snack. Pliny the Elder on the other hand was partial to beetle larvae.

It is estimated that about a third of the world's population still eats insects, and that over 2,000 species of insects are consumed by humans.

The consumption of insects is now becoming more than just a local pastime for people in poorer parts of the world. Chapul (an Aztec name for cricket – the insect, not the game) is a manufacturer of cricket flour in Salt Lake City, Utah. Chapul claims that its cricket protein powder is a clean, minimally-processed protein that contains all the essential amino acids for healthy muscle growth and development. Unlike soy, crickets do not have harmful phytoestrogens, and cricket powder is apparently rich in Omega-3 fatty acids, Vitamin B12 and iron (more than spinach!), and is also highly digestible. It is twice as dense in protein as beef.

Insects consume little water compared to livestock and are easy to farm, provided that they have a moist environment in which to thrive, so hot climates are better. Therefore Chapul, which used to sell protein bars until its co-packer JV partner went bust, produces insects and powders in Indonesia for sale in the US. These are fine to be sold as long as they are 'free from filth, pathogens and toxins' according to the US Department of Agriculture (USDA). Chapul Cricket Protein has raised an undisclosed amount in a seed round from Equilibria Capital. My view is that this is a struggling enterprise and I will not be rushing to invest.

In the UK, Sainsbury's already sells Smoky BBQ Crunchy Roasted Crickets made by small British startup Eat Grub.

Barclays, the bank, thinks that the global market for edible insects will be worth US $8 billion by 2030, partly driven by environmental and health considerations. One other big advantage insects have is that they cannot act as carriers of disease to humans in their edible form, say, cows and pigs, which can cause zoonotic transmission. Grub's up!

# FUNGI

Fungi, which are not plants, are becoming increasingly popular as a source of alternative proteins. Quorn, a British company with revenues over £200 million, which is one of the largest and oldest alternative meat producers in the world, uses *Fusarium venenatum* fungus to produce the mycoprotein that is the key ingredient in all of its products. This fungus culture is dried and mixed with egg albumen, which acts as a binder, and is then pressed into various forms, such as mince and sausages.

New forms of 'meat' are being developed using fungi, including a steak replica, and Emergy Foods, a company based in Boulder, Colorado, raised nearly US $5 million in a seed round to produce just such a thing. It has developed a range of meat alternatives including whole cuts of meat, based on fungi, under the brand Meati Foods.

Emergy was founded in 2016 by Justin (seems to be a very popular name for founders in this space!) Whitely and Tyler Huggins, who both have engineering backgrounds, and the company looks pretty interesting. Worth keeping an eye on.

There is also MushLabs, which comes out of the same Berlin-based accelerator as LegenDairy. This company has just raised US $10 million to produce a meat replacement using mycelium, another type of fungus. This company, headed by co-founder and CEO Mazen Rizkin, uses side streams from the agricultural industry as 'free' growth media to produce their meat substitute, in a circular process that takes just four or five days. MushLabs use fermentation technology to grow the mycelium, which are the 'roots' of mushrooms, and these supposedly provide 'complete and balanced nutrition'. Singapore-based VisVires New Protein and Swiss fund Redalpine led this recent Series A round, at an unspecified valuation.

I personally am not bullish on meat replicas made from fungi, as they will never be able to truly mimic the sensory experience of real meat. They do, however, have considerably smaller carbon footprints and offer overall a new sustainable category of 'meat', and as with Quorn, may be useful as 'fillers' for items such as sausages or sausage rolls.

# POND SCUM

The algae from ponds and the sea could be an important source of protein in the future, according to several observers. Best-known of these are spirulina and chlorella, which are popular offerings in health shops around the world and are increasingly incorporated into drinks and foods. These small algae are typically rich in iron, B vitamins, and protein, and can be grown relatively easily in dense urban environments. Spirulina can be used in baking, and IKEA (of furniture and meatball fame) is experimenting with the protein as a meat substitute. Better than horses, I guess!

A Cambridge University professor, Alison Smith, is a staunch advocate of using these algae more widely in food production. Innocent Smoothies (incidentally founded by Richard Reed, the chairman of Agronomics, a big investor in the cell ag space) has produced a bright blue drink based on spirulina, which is now sold widely in Europe. Aldi, the large German supermarket chain, purveys a soup made of microalgae and sweet potato in its vegan range.

# THE MANIPULATION OF THE GENOME FOR BETTER FOOD

Tropic Biosciences, a British company based in Norwich, was established in 2016 and is developing enhanced-performance crops, mostly grown in the tropics – hence the name. In 2020, the company raised US $28.5 million in a Series B round led by Temasek, the Singapore-based giant sovereign wealth company, which took the company's total funding to US $40 million.

Other investors in the company include Agronomics, Skyviews Life Science, Sumitomo Corporation, and Five Seasons Ventures.

Tropic has developed a technology platform, GEiGS (Gene Editing induced Gene Silencing) which is used by agricultural businesses to promote animal welfare and to develop disease resistance in key crops. The platform, according to the company, is compatible with all existing gene editing tools and allows for non-transgenic, i.e. non-GMO, editing of RNAi genes to enable a far greater set of crop protection and crop enhancement applications than existing technologies.

GEiGS builds upon available gene editing tools (e.g. CRISPR, TALEN) to edit existing RNAi genes and direct their silencing functions towards new targets, including insects, viruses, fungi, or even a plant's own genes.

Among these plants are rice, which is the staple food for about half of the world's population, and bananas, the most commonly eaten fruit worldwide. The Cavendish, the main banana species comprising 99 per cent of bananas consumed, is under threat from a disease known as TR4, or Panama Disease. This disease is caused by a soil-based fungus, which is easily spread and threatens bananas across the planet. Cavendish bananas have no resistance to TR4, but Tropic is using CRISPR gene editing techniques to counter this, and, indeed, to work on new banana variants that could partially supplant the Cavendish's hegemony. Interestingly, all Cavendish bananas (and therefore every banana most of us have ever eaten) came from a greenhouse in the grounds of Chatsworth, the home of the Duke of Devonshire, in 1834. His name was William Cavendish. Domestic bananas have long since lost the seeds that allowed their wild ancestors to reproduce – if you eat a banana today, you are eating a clone. Each banana plant is a genetic clone of a previous generation.

50 million tonnes of Cavendish are consumed across the globe annually for an approximate revenue of US $36 billion, so Tropic's work in preventing disease in these bananas is vitally important to the communities that produce them.

Coffee is another key target for Tropic. Again it is working on ways to induce disease resistance into coffee plants, as well as to remove caffeine from coffee beans. This is because the process of decaffeination interferes with the taste of coffee. Worldwide, coffee is estimated to be an US $80 billion industry, with about 60 per cent of production under threat due to disease.

Tropic, which now has over 60 full-time employees, is led by CEO and founder Gilad Gershon, and the company is one of the world's leaders in agricultural gene editing for the benefit of growers, mostly in developing countries. In addition, GEiGS, the platform technology, is being used to develop disease resistance in pigs and cows.

Already, Tropic's technology is being used by multiple international clients including BASF, the giant German company, which is one of the world's leading seed producers. The relationship with BASF is similar to the other ones that Tropic has with its clients – it out-licenses its substantial IP to its collaborators, looking to create an attractive and valuable revenue stream.

In my opinion, this is an exciting company well worth following. About half of the world's population will live in the tropics in the near future, and the engineering of their staple crops to provide greater protection against disease as well as a better nutritional profile will be of incredible importance.

Separately to Tropic, British scientists based in Cambridge are developing super-strains of fava and broad beans which are both derived from Vicia Faba, an ancient form of nutrition. This strain will be resistant to pests, richer in protein and suitable for growing in the damp and often cold UK.

# VERTICAL FARMING

Vertical farming is the name for growing crops in vertical stacks, using soilless techniques such as hydroponics, aeroponics and aquaponics. This is typically done in repurposed urban buildings because the practice is environmentally friendlier than growing crops in the traditional way. This is partly because vertical farming lends itself to dense urban environments and it also plays into consumer concerns about the carbon footprint of importing fruit and vegetables from farfetched locations.

Vertical farming uses very few, if any, fertilisers. Fertilisers are extremely damaging for the planet, with about half of the world's food supply dependent on nitrogen-based fertilisers, contributing to 500 oceanic dead zones, and causing about five per cent of global warming.

Vertical farming is an attractive way, on paper, of reducing land use for crops and the length of food supply chains. Worldwide, 800 million hectares are committed to soil-based agriculture, which represents nearly 40 per cent of Earth's total landmass.

However, vertical farming has been generally unprofitable, with only a quarter of vertical farms being cash-flow profitable, according to IDTechEx.

New types of vertical farming, for instance from well-funded German company Infarm, which situates vertical farms directly in supermarkets, are giving a boost to the technology. IDTechEx suggests that over the next ten years, the industry will grow to US $1.5 billion in revenues, a compound growth rate of about seven per cent per year, which seems light to me in the context of the capital intensity of the business and the rather large amounts being invested into vertical farming companies.

Some big money is flowing in the direction of this fairly established form of farming, with Berlin-based Infarm recently raising US $140 million of a total round of US $200 million for its Series C round, which is designed to fund further modular units of its vertical farms in supermarkets and restaurants. The attraction lies in the 'freshness' of the herbs and salads that these units grow, literally picked in front of shoppers and diners. The company has secured deals with Marks & Spencer Group of the UK, Kroger in the US, and Aldi in Germany.

The company has secured backing from Liechtenstein's royal family as well as from Atomico and Balderton Capital. The founders are Erez and Guy Galonska, brothers, and their competitors include startups Plenty (from San Francisco), Bowery Farming (from New York) and AeroFarms (from New Jersey). Bowery Farms is backed by Google and raised US $90 million of funds in late 2018. Bowery operates a giant farm outside

New York and specialises in leafy greens. AeroFarms raised US $100 million in 2019 to expand its operations from New Jersey, where it too operates a giant vertical farm. Plenty has been funded by SoftBank and former Google CEO and chairman Eric Schmidt, as well as Jeff Bezos of Amazon. Valuation of Plenty is over US $500 million, according to Pitchbook.

Vertical farming has attracted a fair amount of money, with the global market expected to attract over US $12 billion of funding by 2026. However, it is mainly used for only a limited range of crops, such as soft fruits and lettuces. Unlike the Haber-Bosch process of artificially fixing nitrogen to allow all crops to grow bigger and faster, vertical farming at the moment only really makes sense for a small number of expensive crops (like basil and parsley) – and that's hardly going to feed the world

Unfortunately, due to the capital intensity of this type of business, I cannot recommend it to investors, nor does it grab my attention as a genuine 'technology' business. Vertical farming businesses often go bankrupt because of the high energy costs of lighting and ventilation. Recently FarmedHere in the US went under the soil, as did Swedish outfit Plantagon after absorbing quite a lot of nutrients in the form of investors' money.

# NUTRACEUTICALS

Nutraceuticals are a big market that is growing quickly. The word is a catch-all for any foodstuff that provides actual or claimed health benefits to humans. These might include vitamins, minerals and probiotics for the general population, designed to relieve hypertension, diabetes or allergies as well as nutrients designed for specific patient types.

Total nutraceutical sales are expected to be US $722 billion by 2027, which represents a compound growth rate of over eight per cent between now and then, according to Grand View Research.

Consumers are increasingly aware of the health benefits (or otherwise) of specific foods, and emerging markets such as China or India, where rising affluence heightens awareness of health, are particularly attractive to nutraceutical companies.

Specialised diets such as paleo or keto have enhanced the attractions of nutraceuticals to food producers. My own day job as Chairman of Juvenescence, a longevity-focussed company, brings me into contact with Juv Life, its nutraceutical subsidiary, headed up by the formidable Colin Watts, who I interviewed for the book.

Colin was the head of The Vitamin Shoppe in the US, having earlier been in senior positions in WW (Weight Watchers) and Walgreens. He has launched, with his impressive team's help, the first of several nutraceuticals which will come from Juv Life over the coming years. These products – the first of which is a ketone ester – contain bioactive molecules or supplements developed in a biotech setting. The ketone ester, known as *Metabolic Switch*, is cardioprotective as well as being cognition-enhancing, with the added benefit of inducing ketosis, which dieters everywhere will like.

Ketone esters allow us to exogenously consume ketones that normally would only be produced during ketone fasting, which is difficult to do to say the very least. Ketones are a mechanism for survival in famine, as the human liver converts energy sources from fats stored in the body rather than converting ingested foodstuffs.

Nutraceuticals are not strictly in the purview of this book, but startup companies can make an impact and, when they do, they sell to the majors at multiples – quite often over 4x – of sales, so it is an area worth looking at.

And the big boys are buying. Nestlé recently bought Aimmune Therapeutics, a US company which has a treatment for peanut allergies, for US $2.6 billion. As the Financial Times reported, '[s]ales of highly processed foods are on the wane. Food and pharmaceutical groups are converging around high-margin, non-prescription health products for both humans and animals. Nestlé, for example, makes dog food that claims to fight dementia'.

According to the WHO, up to 240 million people suffer from food allergies. Therein lies a further opportunity for cell ag companies – engineering the causes of allergies out of the food supply.

# MEDIA AND MACHINERY

There are two key areas in the picks and shovels part of the cell ag and plant-based food and materials industries. One is the machinery that makes it all happen – the extruders, processing machinery, bioreactors, sensors and so forth, which allow for plants and cells to become edible foodstuffs. The second is the 'media' which goes to feed the cell-based products.

Both of these areas are dominated by divisions of big companies, which have typically served the biotech industry. There are only a handful of dedicated companies and most of those are not investable.

The method of making food via cell ag draws largely on established biotech methods.

To scale up from relatively small biotech production runs to mass-scale food production will require much bigger bioreactors and a whole new thinking around the problem. Some solutions will come from the cell ag companies themselves and some will come from new specialist companies as well as from the old order of biotech-focussed systems companies.

Computer modelling of the way that cells react in bioreactors will speed up the development process. Indeed the Cultivated Meat Modeling Consortium (CMMC), which consists of such partners as Merck KGaA, the Good Food Institute, Mosa Meat, Meatable, Biocellion and TurtleTree Labs, is using powerful software to model how scaling up might look.

The CMMC uses the analogy of the automotive industry, which uses computers to work out scenarios for car safety without having to go through time-consuming and costly physical experiments; so will it be with the design of bioreactors and equipment. They examine problems ranging from how cells will grow in different conditions, stirrer speeds and the effect of turbulence on growing tissues.

Bioreactors, scaffolds, and media are really important to cell ag and perfecting their designs will be vital to cutting down costs in this fledgeling industry.

I will mention names of some businesses, big and small, involved in both branches of the picks and shovels trade, and I will go on to look for more, which I will mention on the website in due course. For the moment, though, the pickings are thin for investors in this particular area.

The key large companies in the area are Sartorius AG, a German company which owns Danaher of the US, Germany's Merck and its US subsidiary MilliporeSigma, General Electric of the US and its Cytiva subsidiary, as well as Thermo Fisher Scientific, another American giant. These companies are all public, but the percentage of sales represented by clean foods or materials remains small.

Smaller companies include Canadian startup Future Fields, Japanese company IntegriCulture, Solaris Biotech USA, and contract manufacturer JOINN Biologics of the California Bay Area.

Sartorius, the smallest of the giants, is probably the purest play, and I think this company will undoubtedly be a leader in the scaling up of bioreactors, both for single and multiple use. It is listed in Germany, with a slightly complex capital structure. Thermo Fisher is strong in food extrusion equipment for the plant-based industry.

Merck KGaA is the leader in media, is making a concerted push into the new industries, and is definitely worth following, though for all these companies the performance of their biotech-related businesses will be much more important than the food/material business for some time to come.

In the case of the private companies, I like IntegriCulture, which is refining a whole-system approach to the production of clean meat. It raised a US $7.4 million Series A in 2020, bringing total funds raised to US $10.4 million. More recently, in September it received a further US $2.2 million as a grant from the Japanese government.

Solaris, which was founded in 2002, produces fermenters, bioreactors, gas analysers and tangential flow filtration systems, which incorporate microfiltration and reverse osmosis – in short, everything needed for clean meat except the media. It appears to be happily private and not in need of funds, so unlikely to be investable.

Future Fields is focussed on media, and uniquely is using insect larvae as an expression system for growth factors rather than fermentation. Growth factors are vital to the amplification of cells, rather than the conventional yeast. Future Fields is working with VitroLabs, but the concept of insect larvae – which should end up producing growth factors very cheaply (possibly US $4 per gram compared to current prices of up to US $1 million per gram) is very appealing, but as yet unproven for food production. The lower cost series because the insect larvae do not require expensive media and can be grown on cheap conventional foods, including sugars and cornmeal. This is a small company, raising small amounts of money – and in my opinion it is worth a punt.

There is also Heuros, producing media in Australia. On its website this startup describes itself as follows: 'Heuros produces high quality, GM-free media for the manufacture of cultivated (clean) meat. Our media is made without using genetic engineering to synthesise recombinant proteins – so products made using this media will be GM-free. Heuros media does not use antibiotics, hormones, or animal blood products (such as FBS)'.

Heuros media stimulates the growth of bird and mammal muscle cells. They are also developing novel bioreactors for the large-scale production of cultivated meat and can supply this technology commercially. They are able to work together with other cultivated meat companies to optimise production technology for their specific cell lines.

Other companies of note producing media are Multus Media, a London-based company which is using machine learning to develop optimised media for the cultivation of animal cells. There are also Cultured Blood, Back of the Yard Algae Sciences, Scinora, and CellulaREvolution, all startups in the media space, with further information in chapter five.

In the scaffolding space, important to most of cell ag, there are Matrix Meats and Cass Materials, with Matrix Meats probably ahead. This is an Ohio-based company with a proprietary custom-engineered animal-free matrix for meat to be grown on, and the company claims it will produce a steak in partnership with a cell ag meat company by the end of 2020.

CellulaREvolution, a company from Newcastle in the UK, is engaged in developing continuous-cycle production processes for cell-based meat, and has developed a peptide coating that increases cell proliferation in serum-free conditions. Its bioreactor is also capable of continuous production of adherent cells.

## INTEGRICULTURE

IntegriCulture is a smallish Japanese company that will probably be very difficult to invest in, at least at this stage. It has developed what it calls the CulNet System which is a general-purpose, large-scale cell culture technology that can be applied to bio-reagents, cosmetics, supplements, and cell-based meat. This is done by mimicking *in vivo* conditions, avoiding tank stirring but rather allowing cells to communicate via endocrine factors to efficiently proliferate cells. The best growth conditions for cells are found *in vivo*, inside living bodies.

## ORF GENETICS

This Icelandic company, founded in 2001, has used barley to produce human growth factors for 10 years or so, and is now progressing the development of animal free growth factors for use in the cell ag business with a recently awarded EU grant of EUR 2.5 million. Growth factor costs are a key factor in advancing Moo's Law™, so getting these costs down is a mighty challenge and opportunity. ORF claims that its barley-produced growth factors are uniquely pure and are grown in inert volcanic pumice stone with a negative carbon impact. Merits watching.

# REGULATIONS
# AND
# LOBBYING

———

# IN ALMOST EVERY COUNTRY IN THE WORLD, FOOD PRODUCTION AND DISTRIBUTION ARE REGULATED, AND POWERFUL FARMING LOBBIES OFTEN OPPOSE NOVEL FOODS THAT COMPETE, OR WILL COMPETE WITH THEIR CONVENTIONAL OUTPUT.

These two facts – regulation and lobbying – are potential hindrances to some of the more optimistic forecasts, such as those in the RethinkX report, coming true at the speed supporters of the demise of intensive farming would like.

In this chapter, I explain how regulation of cell ag and plant-based foods will work in key markets, as well as the obstacles that stand in the way of the New Agrarian Revolution.

Regulation and lobbying can go hand in hand, as regulators of novel foods can sometimes be influenced by the depiction of cell ag or plant-based foods as 'Frankenfoods' that are somehow unnatural and carry hidden health risks. Most of the people who peddle such falsehoods are large farming companies, established food producers, or their representatives. It is nonetheless important to understand their concerns, and to advocate hard for the benefits of these novel foods and products.

The principal avenues of attack on cell ag and plant-based foods are: that they are unnatural and unhealthy; that the environmental harm of conventional farming is exaggerated; that livelihoods and traditions are at stake; that topsoil erosion would occur without foraging animals; and that consumers want the 'normal' products and won't accept the new.

All of this can be countered, but their lobbying is an important speed bump that needs to be flattened if the new industry is to succeed rapidly. And succeed it must.

The latest figures are not readily available, but in the USA in 2014, the farming industry spent US $10.8 million in contributions to political campaigns and another US $6.9 million in lobbying the federal government. The US meat business is as big as the entire GDP of Hungary and it often sponsors self-serving research, rather like the tobacco industry used to. In the US Senate, there is already a bill for consideration sponsored by Senators Mike Enzi (Republican, Wyoming) and Jon Tester (Democrat, Montana), known as the Enzi-Tester Bill (or the Food Safety Modernization for Innovative Technologies Act). The bill is designed to ensure transparency in any new foods using animal cell-culture technology.

'Americans shouldn't have to guess what they are buying at the grocery store checkout line,' Tester has said. 'If cell-based meat is sold next to real Montana beef at the store, the labelling should be clear to consumers so that folks can make informed choices about what they're feeding their families.' The use of 'folks' should not be confused with being nice to the new industry. It is a laying down of the gauntlet to upstarts seeking to undermine the farms of Montana and Wyoming.

Although every sector of the agricultural industry has its resistance brigades lined up against the New Agrarian Revolution, the main lobbyists against progress are the producers of conventional meat. The aim of these lobbyists and of their allies is to gag the budding agrarian revolution – so called 'ag-gag' rules and laws.

In the US, the National Cattlemen's Beef Association, the National Chicken Council, the National Pork Producers Council, the Texas Cattle Feeder Association, the Livestock Marketing Association, and the United States Cattlemen's Association (referred to in Washington collectively as "the barnyard") are particularly powerful, even if they sound benignly Monty Pythonesque.

These lobby groups most certainly are not benign and they spend a large amount of money pleading to get their way, which can include hindering the proliferation of what they call the 'fake foods' industry. They will not even surrender the term 'meat'. As an example, in the two years leading up to the new 'Dietary Guidelines' advice published by the US Government in 2015, they spent US $4.5 million collectively on trying to shape those guidelines to reflect their views.

In 2018, the US Cattlemen's Association filed a petition to one of the two key national food regulatory bodies, the US Department of Agriculture (USDA), asking it to make sure that consumers were properly informed of the difference between beef products derived from cattle and those created by cell ag.

Mark Post, co-founder of Mosa Meat and regarded as the living godfather of cell cultured meat, has used a Dutch word – *achterhoedegevecht* – in regard to this and to other efforts of the powerful lobby groups. This word translates roughly as 'futile rear-guard action', as the tide of progress and necessity overwhelms the old guard, rather like the horse and trap lobby was overwhelmed by the rise of the automobile more than a century ago. Mark points to the remarkable rise in alternative milks in the past 10 years, despite considerable opposition particularly on labelling, as an example of how the currents are changing in favour of the new industries, and I think that he is right.

However, an analysis of the lobby groups reveals that they are financially powerful and well-connected. In the US, one of the most important markets at the moment (just behind Europe), for example, the National Cattlemen's Beef Association apparently has annual subscription and other income of US $60 million, and they are always trying to shape food policy. Because of the way that rural states are represented in the Senate, the farming lobby is promoted more highly in government circles than the number of people involved in the industry or its share of GDP might normally command. Senators Enzi and Tester accordingly represent just 0.5 per cent of the US population, but constitute two per cent of the Senate.

The major 'meatpacking' (a euphemism for slaughtering) companies in the US, such as JBS USA Holdings Inc. (with a listed Brazilian parent), Tyson Foods, Cargill, Smithfield, Hormel, and the National Beef Packing Company, often work with the cattlemen groups to lobby for the interests of their industry. As an example, the 'checkoff' system, devised by the National Cattlemen's Association and by the National Pork Council, and endorsed by the US Government, is used by Tyson amongst others to promote the idea that they pursue 'humane handling' of animals, through a process of levying dues on producers to lobby for their industries. This 'checkoff' system applies throughout the farmed animal business and egg production in the US. In a sense, the conventional farm lobby is a bit like the gun lobby – powerful and well-organised in the face of general opposition from the public to the practices they are seeking to maintain.

Others, of course, beg to differ as to what constitutes 'humane handling'. People for the Ethical Treatment of Animals (PETA) has bought shares in the major meatpacking and production companies to agitate against their production methods. PETA's advocacy has been stepped up during the pandemic, with so many slaughterhouse workers infected with Covid-19 and many dying due to the cold and cramped conditions in which they work. The activist group intends to attend Annual Meetings and to lobby companies to 'pack' only vegan meats.

Because many of the big food producers (as opposed to the meatpackers) are moving into the clean meat space – both as investors and manufacturers – they do not appear to be quite as vocal in their support for the US conventional meat industry as they once were. These food producers just want to sell products and have no particular allegiance to a conventional beef burger versus a cell ag or plant-based one. Their objective is to follow and shape consumer tastes and as a result their devotion to conventional meat is diminishing. And it is the same with the major fast food and restaurant chains, many of which now offer vegan meat options. This list includes McDonald's, Carl's Jr. and Denny's, which sell Beyond Meat; Burger King which sells Impossible Burger; and, in the UK, the large bakery chain Greggs, which supplies Quorn-filled sausage rolls to the masses.

In addition, the USDA is not just a regulatory body – it also seeks to promote the US farming industry and its international exports. This is evident in the current discussions around a UK-US trade deal, where US standards, including, for instance, the washing of chickens in chlorine, are the subject of intense debate in the UK. The USDA wants to promote US farm exports, as well as to protect the interests of incumbents.

The resistance to the inexorable march of meat alternatives is undoubtedly strong, especially in the US. Luckily, it is not as successful as might have been imagined, given the lobbying power of the farmers. The meat industry recently tried to outlaw the term 'veggie burger' in a federal court in the US, but the attempt was thrown out. In addition, a bill that would have required tighter packaging and labelling rules for clean meats, was rejected by the Virginia state legislature. Lawmakers received a letter from the National Grocers Association, the Grocery Manufacturers Association and the Plant-Based Foods Association saying that 'new and unfamiliar packaging would only confuse shoppers and frustrate retailers at a time when demand for such options is at an all-time high'.

Washington State has gone one step further than the others by trying to ban the sale of cultivated meat, but a bill to enforce this has not yet come up for a vote.

In Arkansas, Tofurky (trademark of Turtle Island Foods) appealed and managed to overturn a law which would have imposed fines for any label that used meat terms to describe plant-based foods. The Good Food Institute was instrumental in this legal success and based their argument on enforcing the First Amendment right to freedom of speech, citing the fact that edible parts of nuts and fruit are often referred to as 'meat'. In addition, no consumers had complained to the state about 'being confused' or had requested that plant-based companies go out of their way to emphasise that their products are different from conventional meat.

There is no real coherent strategy being employed by the resistors of change. As an example, and in contrast to the restrictive rear-guard legislation being proposed in rural states, the North American Meat Association actually wants lab-cultured meat to be referred to as 'meat' so that it cannot escape the regulations that conventional meat does. This is what I would call a 'turkeys-voting-for-Christmas' strategy.

The conventional meat industry is in some cases taking the view that if you can't beat 'em, you might as well join 'em. So, Tyson was an early investor in Beyond Meat (unwisely selling its equity pre-IPO!) and has also, alongside Cargill, invested in cell ag Memphis Meats.

There are, of course, precedents for the meat lobby's type of Agro-Luddism, notably the butter versus margarine 'war' of 150 years ago. Margarine was first introduced in the 1870s and was a shelf-stable and cheap alternative to butter. It still is.

Then, as now, the rural lobby swung into action. States producing dairy, such as New York, Ohio and Pennsylvania actually banned margarine, and Congress imposed a tax on the stuff. Over time, it did not work, and in total margarine and spreadable fats have a roughly 50 per cent share of the market in the US, with butter enjoying the other half. Neither is particularly good for you.

Skip forward a few generations, and the same resistance to change recurs. Unilever went after Hampton Creek (the predecessor to JUST) in 2014, claiming that Hampton could not call its product Just Mayo because the Food and Drug Association (FDA) guidelines specified eggs as a key component of mayonnaise.

Unilever wisely dropped the suit and is now an active proponent of plant-based foods.

The same thing has happened in dairy, with conventional milk producers arguing against plant-based milks, such as almond or soy milks, being called 'milk', despite the fact that they have been so described since the 1980s.

The USDA regulates meat and the meat industry is vocal in trying to entrust it with sole responsibility for inspecting cultivated products, presumably because it is not familiar with biotech. At the moment the FDA shares regulatory oversight with the USDA for cell ag foods.

Politicians have, naturally, become involved in this debate between farming lobbies and the disruptors of the conventional meat industry. Ted Cruz, a right-wing Republican senator who is particularly negative on vegan food, takes one side, and opponents such as 2020 presidential nominee candidate Beto O'Rourke, who unsuccessfully ran for Cruz's seat in Texas in 2018, take the opposite stance.

Rural states, where animal farming is concentrated, are likely to continue to try to hinder the cell ag and plant-based meat and dairy initiatives, though their chances are slim over the long term. The encroachment of milk alternatives in Europe, soon followed by dairy and egg alternatives, shows the likely trajectory for the meat industry worldwide – one of slow decline and an eventual demise. European Livestock Voice, an EU-based advocacy group for conventional meat producers, says that there is a need 'for detailed and transparent life cycle assessment of real cultured meat production systems'. It adds, based on currently available data, cultured production 'offers no environmental advantage compared to real meat'.

*In vitro* meat, they say, 'cannot be considered as a short-term alternative as it will have to first face the long and challenging process of consumer acceptance'. My riposte to this nonsense is: 'they would say that, would they not?'

But it is true that consumer acceptance will be a big part of the future success or otherwise of plant-based and cell ag foods. A key factor in this acceptance will be using the right language to describe these novel products. Our language must be as nuanced as that used by conventional meat producers; for instance, no one talks of coagulated mother's milk, which is what cheese is, nor do they substitute the word lamb for sheep carcass.

Another European organisation, COPA-COGECA, representing farmers and agri-cooperatives, has said that a reduction in livestock production in the EU would 'have consequences that are currently forgotten in the public debate around meat alternatives. Who will take care of pastureland and mountain territories? Who will accept the relocation of our proteins productions [*sic*] in countries that do not comply with EU standards? How will we prevent rural exodus? The bright new world promised by *in vitro* promoters might not be the one expected by consumers.'

The European resistance brigades seem much less well-organised and rather sappy in comparison to their American cousins, which is the reason that the first cell-cultured meats might appear on European plates. Indeed, an attempt by lobbyists for meat producers to forbid alternative meat producers to use words such as "sausages" or "burgers" in descriptions of their foods was voted down in late 2020 by the European Parliament. There is also internal pressure within European states to cut down on meat consumption for environmental concerns. The Danish finance minister has set out plans to ban meat in all public canteens, including army barracks, for two days per week. There have also recently been calls for a climate tax to be imposed on foods such as red meat and dairy from the UK Health Alliance on Climate Change (UKHACC), which includes 10 Royal Colleges of medicine and nursing, the British Medical Association, and the Lancet.

The Lancet Planetary Health Journal has recently predicted that 2030 will be the peak year for worldwide conventional meat consumption, and it is a fact that, on a global scale, average meat consumption per capita has almost doubled since 1961. Each person consumed around 43 kg of meat in 2014 and 47 kg in 2017, according to UN data. However, over the past decade plant-based foods have been growing in sales at five times the rate of conventional foods. In the year ending in 2019, US retail sales of plant-based foods grew by 11 per cent compared to just two per cent for the retail food market overall.

Even the federal government is beginning to help the cell ag industry – a little bit. After conversations with the Good Food Institute and an early grant of US $250,000 from GFI to UC Davis in California for cultivated meat research, the National Science Foundation, funded by the US government, also made a US $3.5 million grant to the university. This is the first ever help from the US government for the industry – a big deal.

Meanwhile, the conventional meat industry faces more direct and aggressive tactics from animal and climate change activists, particularly in the US, which is the main battlefield for the meat producers versus the good guys.

An organisation called Direct Action Everywhere (DxE), a kind of animal counterpart to Extinction Rebellion, the climate change group, does what it says on the tin. Its notorious co-founder, Wayne Hsiung is currently facing up to 60 years in a US prison, after having visited a pig factory farm owned by Smithfield Foods in 2017 and 'liberating' some piglets, as well as allegedly causing damage. The group termed this Operation Deathstar. DxE wants to expose the reality of factory farming – to break consumers' typically nostalgic and erroneous view of how animals live on farms. It is not a chocolate box picture of bucolic contentment.

Most negatively for Smithfield, which tried to get Wayne to apologise for entering and exposing what he describes as a dystopian kind of place, full of suffering, is the attention he and his kind have drawn to the cruelties involved in factory farming.

Wayne rejected a deal with Smithfield, which is now pursuing a trial against him. No doubt the footage taken in the pig sheds as well as drone images of the facility will be highlighted during any proceedings, hopefully accelerating the demise of the conventional meat industry. Unfortunately, Wayne may pay a heavy price for being so committed to the cause. His defence, which will involve jurors using VR headsets, watching the films he and his colleagues have assembled, will represent a landmark for the battle between established producers and the advocates of a new form of farming.

The particular footage of Operation Deathstar shows the intrusion into the facility by Wayne and others. The video is harrowing and saddening. It was published by the *New York Times* and I hope it will be influential in getting Wayne out of his predicament.

The pushback from the industry was predictable, with Smithfield Foods accusing DxE and Wayne of doctoring footage; it also commissioned an audit from a third-party which suggested no animal cruelty had taken place at the facility in question. I would like to make a comment here – but better not!

The industry has mobilised further forces in its battle to prevent the onslaught of vegan foods. There are the subtle and not-so-subtle allegations that the animal rights activists are left-wing radicals intent on breaking the existing capitalist system – and are therefore not credible. Also, there are the claims that the activists' agenda is being pushed by the food multinationals, such as Nestlé, which apparently promote veganism as they can generate huge profits by producing plant-based meats, in contrast to the paltry ones available on conventional meats. Additionally, the description of the movement as 'woke consumerism' is deliberately pejorative, trying to conflate the goals of most of us to reduce emissions, abolish animal cruelty where possible, and to upgrade the quality of the foods we put in our bodies, with anti-capitalism.

The fact that George Monbiot and Chris Packham in the UK, for example, are left-leaning in their politics does not mean that they are not correct on the central issue at hand. The world needs to change the way it farms animals and other foodstuffs, as well as the way that many materials are created. Indeed, right wingers are just as likely as left-leaning people to be 'woke' when it comes to issues surrounding intensive farming – which is a good thing.

There is a valid point to be made that animals, or at least their waste materials, are indeed valuable to the replenishment of topsoil in farms, but there are ways of replenishing the soil without recourse to industrial-scale farming. In addition, about 50 per cent of topsoil erosion is caused by animal farming itself. As Ethan Brown of Beyond said to me in his interview, 'plants grown to be used as animal feed are much less valuable than plants that grow for human consumption', and eventually livestock farmers will understand this, because the economics of livestock farming are only going to get worse.

If there were a lot fewer grazing animals, feed/decaying matter (for instance, hay, straw and vegetable compost) would act as soil replenishers rather than being fed to animals. A clear distinction needs to be drawn between animals fed on feedlots that never go outside, and the much smaller number of animals that graze outside. Grass-fed cows and pigs that feed on food waste will likely continue to have a role in the food chain. And there is plenty of waste in the food chain, a large part of which will be eliminated by the New Agrarian Revolution, where foods will have longer shelf lives and factory-to-plate waste will be considerably reduced.

Boston Consulting Group estimates that the amount of food wasted around the world will rise by a third before the year 2030, to 2.1 billion tonnes. The USDA believes that up to 30 or 40 per cent of the US food supply is wasted in an average year. Worldwide, food worth about US $1.2 trillion is wasted EVERY YEAR.

The industrialisation of US farming, with a low regard for animal welfare and the use of multiple chemicals, antibiotics, and fertilisers, worked well for generations but it has run its course. US exports of such food have boomed, particularly to less developed countries, which are increasingly avid consumers of protein. The US enjoys a regular surplus on food year after year, which was worth about US $6 billion in 2019.

The protection of that surplus takes many forms: denial of the environmental impact of industrial farming, lobbying to hinder the new alternatives (particularly to meat, poultry, fish and dairy), and efforts to 'dress up' the industry to make it look more benign than it is.

One example of a wolf dressed up in sheep's clothing, in the sense that he promotes the continued farming of animals, albeit in an organic way, is Allan Savory. Allan is an octogenarian, ecologist, and TED Talk star – and he preaches the idea that pasture can be made more diverse, more productive and that more grasses will grow if tight-knit groups of roaming livestock are used for that purpose.

If ruminants are allowed to chomp away, without the fields on which they graze normally being 'rested' from time to time, Allan thinks a diversity of healthy grasses will grow, replenishing the soil and capturing carbon. So, Allan is a hybrid good guy, in the sense that he advocates cattle being taken off feedlots and put out to a specific type of pasture (which is less cruel). But of course, say opponents like George Monbiot and *Slate* journalist James McWilliams, all he is doing is allowing the continued raising of animals for food, when much worthier alternatives are becoming readily available.

Environmental sceptic Bjorn Lomborg (who obviously does not pay much attention to the wildfires raging around the world) believes that substituting meat for vegetables and plants would only reduce carbon emissions by about two per cent, against the received wisdom of about 15 per cent (underlined by no less of an organisation than the FAO). He justifies this laughable figure on the grounds that plants would have to be grown in greater numbers to satisfy human consumption; but he doesn't properly take into account the fact that much of plant production (as much as 36 per cent) goes to feed animals, which are notoriously poor at converting plants into protein in the form of their meat. One third of the world's cultivated land is used to produce one billion tonnes of fodder a year for feeding animals. These crops are principally soy and maize. Additionally, about a quarter of all globally available freshwater is used for livestock farming. In fact, a well-recognised study (Pimentel, 2003) demonstrated that a kilo of animal protein absorbs more than 100 times the amount of water used to produce one kilo of grain. In the case of beef, it takes about 15,000 litres of water for one kilo of cattle meat.

Vast amounts of often harmful chemicals and fertilisers are used in the production of this fodder, and large swathes of forest are destroyed in the race to produce more. The global fertiliser market was valued at US $156 billion in 2019 with Asia Pacific accounting for about 60 per cent of the global total.

Farmers, to be fair, are in many cases aware of the negative environmental impact of their profession and some are doing something about it. For instance, in a small minority of cases, farmers in the US and Europe are trialling the feeding of cows on a type of seaweed to lower methane emissions. They are also trialling anti-methane vaccines and employing selective breeding to raise cows which do not belch as much methane, which is about 30 times worse for the environment than carbon dioxide. In addition, Dutch biotech firm DSM has created a methane-inhibiting molecule called 3-NOP, which can supposedly reduce emissions per cow by about a third.

There is also an argument which is made by the Resistance that eating plant-based foods is not necessarily any healthier for people than eating animals, and there are some instances of that being true. However, this is generally not the case and it certainly does not apply to cell ag foods.

Ethan Brown of Beyond, for instance, told me that the next iteration of the Beyond Meat burger would have a lot less fat and carbohydrates, and already companies like Meatless Farm play up the 'healthiness' of their plant-based foods.

But the reality is that all plant-based foods can be *made* healthier, and indeed often are, whereas conventionally farmed meat is what it is. Generally raised on feedlots on corn and soya, this is both bad for the environment and the unfortunate animals and fish that are often dosed with antibiotics and hormones and treated pretty badly.

The 'relative healthiness' argument just will not fly, as increasingly the plant-based foods, which were once highly processed, are engineered into something much, much better.

And they do not have a high bar to achieve this. In the estimation of the United States Centers for Disease Control and Prevention, one sixth of Americans will get sick every year from food poisoning, with about one in 28 people in the UK also succumbing. These cases are mostly from salmonella and campylobacter.

The other old argument, that meat is central to stature, skeletal strength and IQ, can be debunked as plant-based meats can, and in many cases do, provide all the central nutrients of meat – and more. The idea that vegetarians and vegans have to be pasty, spotty, and unhealthy is an outdated one.

And, of course, cell ag foods will provide the ultimately healthy replicas of the purest and best meat, without harmful additives and environmental effects. They will have everything that an animal provides, except that they will not come wrapped in a living skin and body.

Our world does not have much time to slow down climate change, to dismantle the barbaric way in which many animals are farmed, and to stop deforestation in the pursuit of growing crops for protein production via animals.

Philanthropist and successful British entrepreneur Jeremy Coller, whom I have met, has in recent years devoted himself to the cause of eliminating animal suffering. Jeremy is not just a passionate advocate of clean foods; he is also vegan and a particularly canny judge of good investments in the space. He makes these investments through CPT Capital, the venture arm of his family office. CPT has invested in many of my top picks in this space and recently led the US $91 million round into Geltor, as well as leading a small round for Better Dairy, the UK startup, whose enthusiastic and approachable CEO, Jevan Nagarajah, I have spoken to.

Jeremy's foundation and his experienced team also launched the Coller FAIRR (Farm Animal Investment Risk and Return) Protein Producer Index in 2015, which is described as the world's only comprehensive assessment of global meat, dairy, and fish farming companies on material Environmental Social and Governance (ESG) risks. ESG is increasingly a governing principle of major investors around the world. FAIRR has identified that two in five of the global food giants have teams developing plant-based alternatives to meat and dairy, and 475 major food retailers in the world sell plant-based meat alternatives on the meat-aisle.

Investors accounting for US $23 trillion under management (which is more than the size of the whole US economy) are members of this initiative, which reviews and monitors over 60 global companies to understand how resilient they are to key risks. FAIRR organises events and produces in-depth reports on such things as antibiotic overuse in farming.

Nestlé, one of the largest food giants, has announced plans to build a US $100 million plant-based food plant in China to grow its plant-based sales in the world's most populous market. Unilever, another giant, updated its 'Force for Good' strategy in 2019 to sell more plant-based foods as part of a consumer push towards *better for me and the planet*. 'Today's investors have the opportunity to simultaneously deliver long-term growth and help preserve natural resources for future generations', according to UBS, the investment bank.

Another initiative, already alluded to, designed to support and advocate for the nascent cell ag industry is the Washington DC-based Alliance for Meat, Poultry and Seafood Innovation (AMPS Innovation); so far comprised of BlueNalu, Memphis Meats, JUST, Finless Foods, Fork & Goode, Artemys Foods, and New Age Meats. AMPS Innovation says it is working with the FDA and USDA to demystify what cell-based meat actually is and how it should be approached. 'We think that the USDA and the FDA are really doing an awesome job,' says Mike Selden, CEO and co-founder of Finless Foods, mentioned earlier. 'We commend the FDA and USDA for the work they have already done... We look forward to seeing additional details to establish a clear, predictable, efficient, and risk-based regulatory path to market for cell-based/cultured products.'

An area of regulatory contention is, of course, the whole field of GMO (genetically modified organisms) as well as gene editing, likely using CRISPR techniques. GMO plants or processes are regarded with suspicion by the European Union, and it appears probable that they will look at gene-edited plants or meats in a similarly negative light.

Indeed, a court in the EU decided in 2019 that Cavendish bananas, modified by gene editing techniques to build resilience against disease, would have to pass the same tests as conventionally genetically modified (GMO) plants that are altered as to contain foreign DNA. In practice, this is such a high bar that European imports of Cavendish bananas, which account for almost a third of global Cavendish imports, will be under threat. Cavendish, as mentioned earlier, is being threatened by disease and needs to be reengineered to provide resilience *(see Tropic Biosciences, Chapter 3 p.160)*. This is unlikely to happen unless the EU's resistance to anything with the word 'gene' in it is changed. The EU has allowed a couple of minor GMO strains to be sold in its territory. MON 810 maize from Monsanto was authorised for cultivation in 1998, but this authorisation has now expired and awaits renewal. There is also a potato starch GMO from BASF, which was licensed in 2010.

Gene editing will, however, be important especially as the science of artificially creating genetic material becomes more sophisticated. Gene editing dates back to 1973 and the discovery of 'recombinant DNA' technology, originally used by biotech, but finding its way into genetically modified (GM) crops in the 1990s. The development of CRISPR (clustered regularly interspaced short palindromic repeats) and its derivatives in the 2010s has now allowed scientists a way of making precise changes in specific genes.

Unfortunately, gene editing is grouped into the same category as the shunned GMOs in Europe, even though gene editing usually alters existing genes rather than adding foreign DNA to a plant.

A GM animal, in the form of an Atlantic salmon called AquAdvantage, is the only one licensed anywhere, where two genes have been added to make the fish grow faster and larger. It is only on sale in Canada and is produced by a company called AquaBounty Technologies.

The European Food Safety Authority has a system called the Novel Food Regulation, which it will be mandatory for almost all cell ag products to conform to. This will involve a process of around 18 months of scrutiny and review for a product to get onto the European market. (See broader description below).

The Europeans seem tougher on labelling than the Americans, notwithstanding the best efforts of the various cattlemen's organisations and elements of the US Senate. For instance, with one or two exceptions ('coconut milk' in the UK and 'lait d'amande' in

France) using the word 'milk' in association with plant-based 'milks' is not allowed. This does not seem to have deterred uptake of such brands as Oatly or Alpro, however, as consumers are now fully aware of the plant alternatives to cow's milk.

The differing – and changing – rules on food regulation are reflective of individual countries' vested interests, as well as differing degrees of caution in regard to foodstuffs and human health.

# REGULATION – COUNTRY BY COUNTRY

Regulation of the nascent New Agrarian companies varies according to country and type of food. Plant-based foods generally face an easier path to both market acceptance and regulatory approval, although any that contain GMO ingredients or gene-edited components will likely be excluded from the key European market.

Plant-based foods and foods made by fermentation, typically contain what the FDA in the US calls GRAS (Generally Recognised As Safe) components. Foods that are produced by microbial or other forms of fermentation, such as the latest generation of alternative milks and cheeses, face a similar path to regulatory approval and to consumer acceptance.

Cell ag products not designed for human consumption, such as leather or cotton, should face minimal, if any, regulatory scrutiny, and a warm welcome from the consumer.

Companies producing foods by cellular means face the highest hurdles of all, because of the perception – encouraged by the lobbying Agro-Luddites – that their products are somehow 'Frankenfoods', which will undoubtedly be reflected in the extra scrutiny from regulators in most parts of the world.

The best companies in this area, however, are well aware of this and are already engaged with key regulators to overcome doubts and issues before they engage in mass scale production and sales. BlueNalu, Mosa, Meatable, and Memphis are good examples of companies doing just this. BlueNalu will only have to cooperate with the FDA to regulate its cell-based seafood, in a process that takes 6 months. BlueNalu intends to have products on the market in the second half of 2021.

Funnily enough, while all cell-based seafood is exclusively regulated by the FDA there is one exception – catfish, which I never liked anyway! This is because the Catfish Farmers of the US, the trade association, asked to be more stringently regulated to stymie the less salubrious production methods of their Vietnamese rivals, who farm pangasius, an equivalent product.

The regulation of fish has long been within the purview of the FDA alone. Meat, poultry and eggs are under the joint scrutiny of the USDA and FDA, since it is a tenet of US regulation that meat should be under continuous supervision, and that fish do not require such in-depth attention.

It should also be noted that the fishing industry – even though it employs 1.2 million people in the US – is not nearly as well-organised as the meat industry, making it easier for the producers of cell ag food, like BlueNalu and Wildtype, to get to market faster.

There is considerable speculation as to which jurisdictions will be first to grant licences to cell ag firms, with Singapore, Israel, China, and the US the leading candidates to allow early entry of cultivated foods to their respective markets. Josh Tetrick of JUST, for example, thinks that Singapore will be the first jurisdiction to allow cell ag products to be sold, because of their huge concern for food safety and security. He is also enamoured of the Novel Foods Regulation of the European Food Safety Agency (EFSA – see below).

The Good Food Institute has teams focused on cultivated meat regulatory approval in India, Israel, Brazil, Europe, and Asia Pacific. It reports good progress everywhere because, explains GFI's Bruce Friedrich, cultivated meat solves problems that governments care about (e.g., antimicrobial resistance, climate change, and so on). GFI's scientists and policy experts are even starting or joining trade groups, and are working with the government of Singapore on a model food safety protocol for cultivated meat that can be used around the world.

Chris Bryant, Director of Social Science at the Cellular Agriculture Society, a charity aimed at popularising cellular meat, has said that cellular meat will 'take off' this decade, and that cell-based meats could be on the market in Europe as early as 2022.

Regulators and nations are facing individual issues when it comes to approving these novel foods. Those with established farming communities with strong voices, and possibly export surpluses on food products, such as the US, Australia, New Zealand and Brazil, face strong lobbying pressure as well. Countries such as Singapore and the main Middle Eastern countries face opposite pressures – they are almost totally dependent on imports for food, and would love to find ways of growing protein at home, so they urgently need to embrace the new industry.

Countries in Europe are somewhere in between: GMO-related products are already effectively disallowed by a hugely complex approval process in most European countries, and some of these countries are major agricultural exporters in their own right; notably France, Italy, Spain, Denmark, and the Netherlands.

As a result, these countries may be less inclined to support the widespread sale of novel foods. Countries such as the UK, which depends on imports for about half of its food supply and has a pressing need to develop new high-tech industries to transition to post-Brexit sources of trade, could well be leaders in the space in due course. It is interesting that an industry that was formerly dominated by Silicon Valley is now spreading its wings around the world, with many leading plant-based companies based in the UK, and Mosa Meat in the Netherlands.

## USA

On 7 March 2019, it was decided that the FDA would oversee cultivated meat production up to the point of harvest, while the USDA will oversee the production of the product, including labelling and marketing. The FDA regulates cell-based seafood on its own, which is a positive for companies such as BlueNalu and Wildtype.

The chief concern of the 2019 agreement is to ensure that clean meat products on the market are 'safe, wholesome and unadulterated'. Plant-based foods are regulated by the FDA, including those like the Impossible burger, which contains GMO derived components. Generally, this is not a difficult process to navigate.

In terms of food produced by fermentation, or a variation thereof, the FDA have so far approved it as GRAS, as it has never found any harmful effects from a fermented food (in contrast to the EU – see below). Fermentation has been around for millennia and was originally used to stabilise foods to preserve perishable produce. Now, the technology is used far and wide (particularly in Asia) to add organoleptic (taste, texture, smell) attributes to food, as well as to add functionality (e.g. with probiotics).

On the following pages you will find an interesting table outlining the path to market for clean foods, offering comparisons on the regulatory approaches of the USA and the EU.

| | FDA ('PRE-HARVEST') | EU |
|---|---|---|
| **1.** | Pre-market consultation to evaluate production materials & processes | No formal pre-market consultation procedure in EU Novel Foods (NF) framework, except the optional consultation at Member State level in case of doubt whether the product qualifies as a Novel Food (which is clear in the case of clean meat) |
| **2.** | Oversee cell collection and quality of cell banks | Oversight of preparatory production steps, as well as registration of a company as a food business operator (FBO) will be done at Member State level. In the Netherlands, FBOs working with products from animal origin, require a so-called recognition (*'erkenning'*). This is a more detailed procedure (average term: 8 weeks) than the mere registration of a FBO (average term: few days). |
| **3.** | Oversee production process until harvest | |
| **4.** | Ensure companies comply with FDA requirements: facility registration, cGMP and other applicable food legislation | |
| **5.** | Where needed: issuing regulations or guidance or additional requirements re. # (2) and (3) to ensure that biological materials exiting the culturing process are safe (FFDCA) | EU Hygiene regulation targeting food of animal origin (853/2004) to apply and potentially national legislation as well. In the NL, the Commodities Act Decrees on hygiene and on the preparation and packaging of foodstuffs are applicable. Additional requirements ('conditions of use') may also be included in individual Novel Food authorisations. |

| | USDA ('POST-HARVEST') | EU |
|---|---|---|
| **6.** | Inspections and enforcement directed at safety of cell banks and culturing facilities | Inspections and enforcement are done at Member State level. In the Netherlands the responsible entity is the Dutch Food Safety Authority. |
| **7.** | Determine whether harvested cells are eligible to be processed in meat or poultry products | The NF-framework requires FBOs, in their application for market authorisation, to specify the source of the product, its production process and typical compositional features. No additional eligibility test upon cell harvest prior to production of food products. |
| **8.** | Require each clean meat company to obtain a so-called grant of inspection | Not required under EU legal framework. Registration (or recognition) with the competent Food Safety Authority provides the authority with the legal basis for inspection. Obviously, a Novel Food authorisation must also be obtained before placing the product on the market. |
| **9.** | Conduct inspections in establishments where cells cultured from livestock and poultry are harvested, processed, packaged or labeled to ensure that the resulting products are safe, unadulterated, wholesome and properly labeled. | Inspections will be executed at a Member State level, based on the Official Controls Regulation 854/2004 targeting products of animal origin for human consumption *inter alia*. |
| **10.** | Pre-approval of labeling of clean meat products and inspection thereof | No pre-approval of product labels under EU NF-framework. It is the responsibility of the FBO himself to comply with applicable labeling legislation, such as the Food Information to Consumers Regulation 1169/2011. |

**11.** Where needed: develop additional requirements to ensure the safety and accurate labelling of clean meat products

Safety and Labeling provisions already in place at EU level. These are embodied in the General Food Law Regulation 178/2002 and the Food Information to Consumers Regulation 1169/2011 respectively. Furthermore, specific labeling requirements may be included in Novel Food authorisations. Also, post-market monitoring requirements may be imposed. In any event, FBOs should inform the Commission of any new relevant information regarding the safety of the NF they have placed on the market.

**12.** Enforcement actions re. adulterated or misbranded food products

See comment to #6. Competitors, consumers and watchdog organisations may also bring cases regarding misleading food information before self-regulatory bodies. From example, unpermitted references to 'meat' could be a topic of such cases.

## BOTH FDA AND USDA

**13.** Each entity to cooperate with the other upon transfer or regulatory oversight at harvest

**14.** Each party to notify the other if it identifies objectionable conditions resulting in adulterated/misbranded clean meat products

*Reproduced courtesy of Hill Dickinson LLP.*

# EUROPEAN UNION - EUROPEAN FOOD SAFETY AUTHORITY

The General Food Law Regulation in the European Union (EC No. 178/2002) established the European Food Safety Authority (EFSA) and laid down the procedures in matters of food safety.

New food types, such as cell ag foods, fall under the Novel Food Regulation regime, which was revamped in 2018. This regime also includes the licensing of certain fermented foods, which escape serious regulation in the US. Increased European regulation of fermented foods arose as a result of the death of a patient from the ingestion of Japanese *Bacillus natto*, introduced into soybeans. At the time, the patient was on anti-hypertensive drugs, including low-dose aspirin for blood thinning.

The Novel Food Regulation is the path by which companies such as Mosa Meat hope to get their products on the European market. 'Novel food' is defined as food that had not been consumed to a significant degree by humans in the EU before 15 May 1997, when the first Regulation on novel food came into force. Types of food falling under the regime include krill, chia seeds, noni juice, and UV-treated foods.

Novel Foods must be safe for consumers, properly labelled and must satisfy certain requirements to composition (e.g. physiochemical, biochemical, and microbiological characteristics). In the case of cell ag foods, one of the key issues will be how many components of the growth media remain in the finished product.

Submission of applications is free, but applicants have to carry out all the relevant studies at their own expense. One issue with this regulatory regime is that it requires total transparency, which in some cases makes it difficult for companies that are relying on trade secrets rather than patents for their production process. They would be forced to reveal these secrets, which may well be a hindrance to some companies exploiting the European markets.

## UK

The Food Standards Agency (FSA) is responsible for food safety and food hygiene in England, Wales, and Northern Ireland. It works with local authorities to enforce food safety regulations and its staff work in meat plants to check standards are being met. The FSA at the moment fully adopts the regulations of the EFSA, but that is likely to change post-Brexit, in January 2021.

# ASIA

Asian rules on food are divergent, and sometimes key off US rules, but are generally country-specific.

# MOO'S LAW

### SINGAPORE
For some observers, Singapore is amongst the most enlightened of all nations in the food space; recognising the need for alternative proteins, especially given its precarious position as a country almost totally dependent on food imports. The Singapore Food Agency (SFA) is actively formulating a framework for regulating cell-based meat production, and the city state is home to a number of startups in the cell ag space, notably Shiok Meats and TurtleTree Labs. Turnaround time for the evaluation of novel foods in Singapore is estimated at between three and six months, which is remarkably fast compared to other jurisdictions.

### JAPAN
It is not entirely clear what regulatory regime the cell ag and novel food manufacturers will face in Japan, where vested interests of local farmers are of serious import in food trade. Japanese people are amongst the most voracious consumers of fish in the world, amounting to about 33 kg per head per annum, although this figure has been falling slightly as a more Westernised diet is adopted.

IntegriCulture, the local champion in the cell ag space, with a likely launch of a foie gras product in 2021 (not a product usually associated with Japan!), is supported by the Japanese government, so it is possible that the country could be engaging in a positive way with the nascent industry.

### HONG KONG
Apparently, according to Carrie Chan of Avant Meats, the HK startup covered in Chapter 3, Hong Kong only has very basic food standards, so is unlikely to be at the forefront of approving cell ag products.

### CHINA
As the most populous nation on Earth, China will be a very important market for the New Agrarian companies, some of which are home-grown. In September 2019, industry leaders, government members and lobbyists met in Beijing to discuss labelling and regulatory regime considerations for plant-based and cell-ag meats.

It is rumoured that China has already signed deals with Israeli companies, including SuperMeat and Future Meat Technologies to import cultivated meats. There is as yet no regulatory framework for these types of foods, but as the world has seen time and time again, once China decides to do something, it will do it quickly. This is especially a priority given the unsafe element of a lot of Chinese intensive farming, and of course, the effects of the infamous wildlife trade.

### MIDDLE EAST
Middle Eastern countries face a unique challenge because of the near absence of any

agriculture in many countries, due to their landscape, aridity and climate. Although the regulatory frameworks for the region have not yet been established, I know from personal experience that this region will be one of the most promising for cell ag companies and that a large number of joint ventures will be established to situate production near the point of consumption.

## INDIA

Food Safety and Standards Authority of India (FSSAI) is an autonomous body established under the Ministry of Health and Family Welfare and, as yet, no regulatory regime has been established for the type of company that we are interested in.

## AUSTRALIA AND NEW ZEALAND

In Australia, food standards in the Food Standards Code are law and are enforced by the States and Territories, under their own laws. The Department of Agriculture, Water and the Environment (DAWE) is responsible for enforcing food regulations at the border in relation to imported food. In New Zealand, an extra step is required to put the joint food standards into law.

# TAXATION

It is also worth noting that, in some countries at least, climate change is likely to produce a 'meat tax', and no doubt that will be driven in part by governments' insatiable desire to raise more money.

The introduction of a 'livestock levy' was mooted in the 2016 Paris Agreement on climate change.

Politicians in Germany have recently been raising the issue with regularity. A Dutch-based advocacy group, the True Animal Protein Price Coalition (TAPP) has said that a tax on beef, pork and chicken could see up to a 70 per cent drop in meat-eating in Europe by 2030.

Some countries or regions have already successfully introduced sugar taxes to cut obesity and associated diseases. Notably, Chile has enjoyed considerable success with its own equivalent tax, with a significant reduction in sugary food sales as a result.

Brazil, the world's second largest beef producer, has done the opposite: high import taxes designed to protect Brazilian industry have limited the ability of alternative protein companies to gain ground there.

# COMPANIES AND INVESTMENT

---

**T**HE NEW AGRARIAN REVOLUTION IS HAPPENING NOW, AND AS WITH EVERY NEW PROMISING INDUSTRY, THERE WILL BE PLENTY OF PUBLIC COMPANIES TO CHOOSE FROM IN DUE COURSE. AT THE MOMENT, HOWEVER, THE PICKINGS ON THE PUBLIC MARKETS ARE FEW AND FAR BETWEEN, BECAUSE MOST OF THE PROMISING COMPANIES ARE SEQUENCING THROUGH THEIR VARIOUS PRE-IPO LISTING ROUNDS OF FUNDING.

These rounds start with a founders' round, then go onto a seed round, followed by a number of alphabetically named 'Series' rounds (Series A, Series B, etc.), and are typical of angel- and venture capital-funded companies.

This book contains a list of all of the promising and not-so-promising companies involved in the cell ag, plant-based, alt-materials, and picks and shovels companies, rated by myself and my investment colleagues, Anthony Chow and Laura Turner.

Many of these companies are rated on the basis of our perception of quality of management, business plan, the competitive landscape for their products, and valuation, which generally is referenced either to open rounds of financing or our expectation of valuation at the next round.

The few available listed companies are rated also, although I recommend that investors do not buy the shares of 'traditional' food producers on the basis of any exposure to 'new' food or materials companies, or to their own-brand plant-based foods, as the impact of these will generally be very diluted in the context of the sheer size of these companies. There are a few investable companies that are already public, including the excellent Beyond Meat, and Sartorius in picks and shovels. But generally speaking, investors must either find a way of investing directly, or wait for IPOs to come along, or invest in a collective vehicle.

In a bit more detail:

1.  Wait for promising cell ag and cell-material companies, as well as picks and shovel companies, to go public. I would recommend that anyone who is interested in participating in the IPOs of any of these companies contact them directly and put themselves on relevant mailing lists.

2.  Investors who have a bit more to spend (and by this I would suggest US $100,000 per company) might put themselves forwards as candidates to invest in whatever the next

round of funding a company is contemplating, and contact the company directly.

3. Invest in an investment vehicle that covers the area. At the moment, the only vehicle I know of for retail investors to gain direct exposure to cell ag is Agronomics, in which I have a major interest. However, I expect such vehicles to multiply as the New Agrarian Revolution gathers pace, and the website will be updated accordingly as they appear.

4. There will be some standalone successes, including Beyond Meat and Impossible in plant-based foods, and several cell ag companies in seafood, meat, and materials, but most companies will either:

**Fold.** There will be increasing competition throughout the sector, and marginal players with inadequate management, poor IP, poor execution, or thin balance sheets will likely go bust. This is the way of the capitalist world and is a reason why investors should be diversified, do deep homework or place their investments in the sector with experienced teams.

**Sold.** Many existing food companies or materials companies will want to, and indeed in some cases are actively doing so, get in on the revolution that is underway. They will open their cheque books, and in my opinion, most of the good quality companies (see my ratings for this) will be bought in the next five years or so. This is where exceptional returns can be made.

**Bold.** Companies that are daring enough not to sell out, with the vision to build brands and distribution and raise significant sums, are likely to grow into large enterprises in their own right. Beyond is a good example, but likely JUST, Mosa Meat, BlueNalu, Memphis Meats, Meatable and VitroLabs will be in this category, along with some others. This requires bold entrepreneurship and high-quality backers.

So let's move on to the BEST company list – based on my opinion and the opinion of my colleagues and experts I have spoken to. It is a list of those companies that represent the crème de la crème of the industry. Think of this as a fantasy football team of what an IDEAL portfolio of New Agrarian Revolution companies looks like. These companies are also selected as the ones most likely to IPO in the near future, and therefore could be viable stock picks in the years to come. Beyond Meat (NASDAQ: BYND), is currently the only publicly-available company on this list, but there is no reason why Impossible Foods, The Meatless Farm, The Not Company or the LIVEKINDLY Collective could not shoot for an IPO in the next couple of years.

# TOP 25 COMPANIES LIST

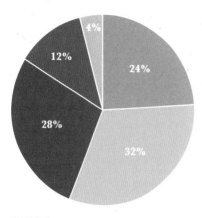
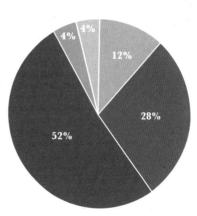

**SECTOR**

- ▨ FERMENTATION
- ▨ CELL-BASED
- ■ PLANT-BASED
- ■ MATERIALS
- ▨ PICKS & SHOVELS

**LOCATION**

- ▨ ISRAEL
- ■ USA
- ▨ ASIA
- ■ EUROPE
- ▨ LATIN AMERICA

| COMPANY NAME | SECTOR | LOCATION |
|---|---|---|
| ALEPH FARMS | CULTIVATED MEAT | ISRAEL |
| BEYOND MEAT | PLANT-BASED | USA |
| BLUENALU | CULTIVATED SEAFOOD | USA |
| BOLT THREADS | MATERIALS | USA |
| CLARA FOODS | FERMENTATION | USA |
| FUTURE MEAT TECHNOLOGIES | CULTIVATED MEAT | ISRAEL |
| GALY | MATERIALS | USA |
| GELTOR | FERMENTATION | USA |
| GREEN MONDAY | PLANT-BASED | ASIA |
| IMPOSSIBLE FOODS | PLANT-BASED | USA |
| LEGENDAIRY FOODS | FERMENTATION | EUROPE |
| MEATABLE | CULTIVATED MEAT | EUROPE |
| MEMPHIS MEATS | CULTIVATED MEAT | USA |
| MILLIPORE SIGMA | PICKS & SHOVELS | USA |
| MOSA MEAT | CULTIVATED MEAT | EUROPE |
| MOTIF FOODWORKS | FERMENTATION | USA |
| OATLY | PLANT-BASED | EUROPE |
| PERFECT DAY | FERMENTATION | USA |
| SOLAR FOODS | FERMENTATION | EUROPE |
| SUPERMEAT | CULTIVATED MEAT | ISRAEL |
| THE LIVEKINDLY COLLECTIVE | PLANT-BASED | EUROPE |
| THE MEATLESS FARM | PLANT-BASED | EUROPE |
| THE NOT COMPANY | PLANT-BASED | LATIN AMERICA |
| VITROLABS | MATERIALS | USA |
| WILDTYPE | CULTIVATED SEAFOOD | USA |

# CELL CULTURE

## ALEPH FARMS

**Main Product:** Beef
**Founded:** 2016, Israel
**Founders:** Didier Toubia, Shulamit Levenberg
**Website:** www.aleph-farms.com

Aleph is focussing on cultivating bovine meat. They are notable for being the first company to grow meat in space. To achieve this, they utilised technology developed by 3D Bioprinting Solutions to assemble a small-scale muscle tissue in micro-gravity conditions. Interestingly, they are stressing the key ability of the clean meat industry to offer transparency for the first time in our food supply chains. To this end, they have recently opened a visitor centre so that consumers might finally have a confident answer to the question: 'do you really know where your food comes from?'

Aleph has a strong team behind it with its founders emerging from the biomedical sector. VP Dr. Neta Lavon, former COO of Kadistem, is an expert in stem cell applications, and CSO Professor Shulamit Levenberg's discoveries in the vascularisation of stem cell-derived tissue constructs have made a significant impact on the field. CEO Didier Toubia previously co-founded IceCure, which went public in 2010 and oversaw the sale of NLR Spine to SeaSpine in 2016. He was trained as a food engineer and biologist at AgroSup.

Their recent Series A funding round raised US $12 million, contributing to their total raise of US $14.4 million to date.

*Further details of the company's activities are featured in Chapter 1, p.30, and Chapter 3, p.133.*

## ARTEMYS FOOD

# ΛRTEMYS
# FOODS

**Main Product:** Beef
**Founded:** 2019, Bay Area, California, USA
**Founders:** Joshua March, Jessica Krieger
**Website:** www.artemysfoods.com

Artemys is a startup working on cultivated meat. In July 2020, they emerged from stealth mode and revealed details of their plan. They will focus on hybrid products that combine cultivated meat with plant-based ingredients to reduce costs and improve texture.

# AVANT MEATS

**Main Product:** Fish maw
**Founded:** 2018, Hong Kong
**Founders:** Carrie Chan, Mario Chin
**Website:** www.avantmeats.com

Avant Meats is a startup working on cultivated seafood beginning with fish maw, which is a delicacy in Asia. They began their focus on fish maw to capitalise on local Asian food habits. Believing that the biggest hurdle to commercialisation is the production cost, they decided that developing a product which required a simple structure with only one cell type would be a quicker route to price parity than with cheaper and harder-to-produce meats such as chicken and pork. They have already developed the cell lines for croaker, which is known for its better-quality fish maw, and are hoping to produce this at a new pilot facility next year. In order to get the texture correct – an important aspect of Chinese cuisine – they have developed an in-house plant-based scaffold. They also have a fish fillet scaffold in formulation and are currently exploring different plant-based materials with which to create it.

Carrie and Mario have chosen a B2B model for Avant in order to save time on marketing and consumer branding, which can slow the path to profitability. It also means that they can focus more on developing their technology without distraction. They hope to get their first product on the market by the end of 2021 or the start of 2022. To date they have raised US $1 million in seed funding.

*Further details of the company's activities are featured in Chapter 3, p.146.*

# BIOTECH FOODS

**Bio.Tech. Foods.**

**Main Product:** Pork
**Founded:** 2017, Spain
**Founders:** Mercedes Vila Juarez, Iñigo Charola
**Website:** www.biotech-foods.com

Biotech Foods is working on cultivated pork meat, which will be sold under the brand name Ethicameat. They recently conducted a consumer survey of the Spanish market, which found that 41 per cent of those surveyed would eat cultured meat outright, with 26.6 per cent stating that they didn't know.

In March 2019, Biotech Foods completed a seed round of EUR 2.2 million, bringing total funds raised to EUR 2.5 million.

## BIOFOOD SYSTEMS

**Main Product:** Beef
**Founded:** 2018, Israel
**Founders:** Yohai Ben Zikiri, Arturo Geifman
**Website:** www.biofood-systems.com

BioFood Systems are working on cultivated and plant-based beef products. Their founders have been in the meat industry for more than 30 years, and hope to put plant-based meat products to market and use those revenues to finance their cultivated meat project. They hope to finish their R&D phase for plant-based meatball and burger products by late 2020.

Their financials are undisclosed.

## BLUENALU

**Main Product:** Seafood
**Founded:** 2017, California, USA
**Founders:** Lou Cooperhouse, Chris Dammann
**Website:** www.bluenalu.com

BlueNalu is an exciting company focussing its attention on becoming the global leader in cellular aquaculture. It has devised a path to the mass market which first focuses on the more obscure fish, such as bluefin, tuna, mahi mahi and yellowtail amberjack, in order to achieve price parity with those more exclusive fish before using their platform technology to go on to produce any fish in the future at large scale. BlueNalu has developed processes which eliminate the need for foetal bovine serum, one of the biggest obstacles for cultivated meat companies in ensuring their products are 100 per cent animal-free and therefore suitable for the vegan market.

BlueNalu's competitors have not yet been able to produce whole-muscle fish which could be prepared with a similar level of variety. In December 2019 BlueNalu demonstrated their cultivated yellowtail amberjack fish and the various ways in which it could be cooked, just like traditionally-farmed fish. They were able to present the fish as medallions atop a bisque of roasted squash, and in an acidified form in a kimchi recipe. The taste test also had their yellowtail battered and deep fried, as well as prepared in a poke bowl, demonstrating the quality of the product and opportunities for chefs to create versatile dishes in the exact same way without contributing to the scourge of overfishing, which has halved populations of marine species since 1970. It is an exciting move beyond the fish-flakes-in-fish-cakes which a number of other companies have so far produced.

I am confident that BlueNalu has an impressive team behind it and an ambitious vision already in the works. CTO Chris Dammann is a scientific expert in cell biology, tissue culture and genomics, with extensive experience in intellectual property, having previously founded a consulting firm that advised companies on innovation management in the biosciences sector. CEO Lou Cooperhouse has worked in the food industry for 35 years and is widely recognised as a leading global authority in food business innovation and technology commercialisation. He is a key leader in this space.

They aim to have BlueNalu products sold in the next two to three years and have released schematics of its future large-scale food facilities, including 150,000 square feet facility to produce 18 million pounds of seafood products per year.

BlueNalu secured US $4.5 million in 2018 from a global assortment of investors. In a recent Series A round of funding, they managed to raise an impressive US $20 million from investors including Griffith Foods, Nutreco, Pulmuone, Rich Product Ventures, Agronomics and Sumitomo Corporation of Americas. They have raised a total of US $24.5 million.

*Further details of the company's activities are featured in Chapter 3, p.138.*

# CELL FARM FOOD TECH

| | |
|---|---|
| **Main Product:** | Beef |
| **Founded:** | 2019, Argentina |
| **Founders:** | Sofia Giampaoli |
| **Website:** | www.cellfarmfoodtech.com |

This is Latin America's first cultured meat startup. They want to be the world's provider of stem cell lines that the emerging clean meat industry will be able to rely on. They are seeking to develop serum-free culture media and a way to standardise a biotechnological process to produce meat from animal stem cells; avoiding raising cattle and other livestock animals. Cell Farm Food Tech possesses a proprietary stem cell bank with the best Argentine bovine genetics, which they can use to upscale cultured meat production and draw down costs. They are taking a B2B approach.

Cell Farm Food Tech has raised a US $200k seed.

## CLEARMEAT

**Main Product:** Chicken
**Founded:** 2019, India
**Founders:** Pawan Dhar, Siddharth Manvati
**Website:** www.clearmeat.com

ClearMeat is India's first cell-based meat company. They aim to bring cultivated minced chicken products tailor-made for the Indian market, in order to accelerate clean meat adoption in India. ClearMeat is focusing on minced meat because it is the easiest product which does not require intensive R&D and so can go to market much quicker.

The company is taking both a B2B and B2C approach and has already received interest from B2B chains in Israel, Turkey, and India.

Their finances are currently undisclosed.

## CUBIQ FOODS

# CUBIQ
## FOODS
Smart fat solutions

**Main Product:** Fat
**Founded:** 2018, Spain
**Founders:** Andrés Montefeltro, Raquel Revilla
**Website:** www.cubiqfoods.com

Cubiq Foods is a startup working on cultivated fat. They are accelerating their production of Omega-3 fatty acids, and their technology could reduce the use of unhealthy trans fats and palm oil, the widely-used, versatile oil that is a major driver of deforestation. They hope to find applications for their products in baked goods, snacks and processed foods such as nuggets, as well as in meat substitutes.

In 2019, Cubiq raised US $13.6 million. In May 2020 it received EUR 5 million from Blue Horizon Ventures for a 35 per cent stake in the Company, alongside Moira Capital Partners.

## FINLESS FOODS

**Main Product:** Seafood
**Founded:** 2016, California, USA
**Founders:** Mike Selden, Brian Wyrwas
**Website:** www.finlessfoods.com

Finless Foods is currently cultivating a dozen cell lines for different species of fish, including bluefin tuna, which CEO Mike Selden believes will be the key to the huge Japanese cuisine market. The company claims to have drastically reduced the cost per pound of their tuna line, from US $19,000 to US $4,000, and is hoping to bring it down to US $20 per pound by 2025.

In 2019, the company partnered with Russian 3D Bioprinting Solutions to print a small fish-like mass in space, on the International Space Station.

Finless Foods received initial funding of US $3.5 million in a seed round from investors including Draper Associates and Babel Ventures.

*Further details of the company's activities are featured in Chapter 3, p.146.*

# FORK & GOODE     FORK&GOODE

**Main Product:** Pork
**Founded:** 2018, New York, USA
**Founders:** Niyati Gupta, Gabor Forgacs
**Website:** www.forkandgoode.com

Fork & Goode is a spin-off startup from Modern Meadow *(see Chapter 3, p.148, and Chapter 5, p.259)* and is working on cultivated pork meat. They have a strong team behind them, experienced in building biotech companies. CEO Niyati Gupta, Harvard MBA and McKinsey alum, previously launched a food brand. Chief Scientific Officer Gabor Forgacs, a former academic, co-founded Modern Meadow and Organova with his brother Andras Forgacs, who serves as director. The board is rounded off by Anthony Atala, founding director of the Wake Forest Institute of Regenerative Medicine and author of over 500 academic articles. The team at Fork & Goode show the potential crossover between modern agriculture and modern cellular technology in medicine.

They raised US $3.54 million in seed funding in 2019, with participation from Firstminute Capital.

# FUTURE MEAT TECHNOLOGIES   FUTURE MEAT

**Main Product:** Chicken, beef, lamb and pork
**Founded:** 2018, Israel
**Founders:** Rom Kshuk, Yaakov Nahmias
**Website:** www.future-meat.com

This startup is working on cultivated meat, focused on fat production using fibroblasts. Future Meat Technologies has developed a species-agnostic technology platform, meaning that they can cultivate any type of animal meat using their technology. Future Meat Technologies is aiming to supply its cultivated fat B2B to create products integrated with plant-based protein and gain early market traction.

Future Meat raised US $14 million in a Series A funding round in 2019, in order to build a production plant. This was the second largest investment round in cultured meat to date, bringing their funding total to US $16.5 million. A substantial Series B funding round will be required in 2021. Their most recent funding round was led by S2G Ventures, who were involved in Beyond Meat's IPO, along with Emerald Technology Ventures. They were joined by Manta Ray Ventures, a UK venture capital firm, Bits x Bites, a Chinese food tech VC, and Henry Soesanto, the CEO of Monde Nissin. In 2018 they also received investment from Tyson Foods.

*Further details of the company's activities are featured in Chapter 3, p.99.*

## GOURMEY

**GOURMEY**
PARIS

| | |
|---|---|
| **Main Product:** | Foie gras |
| **Founded:** | 2019, France |
| **Founders:** | Nicolas Morin-Forest, Antoine Davydoff, Victor Sayous |
| **Website:** | www.gourmey.com |

GOURMEY are working on cultivated foie gras and are aiming to launch their product by 2022 or 2023. They extract cells from a freshly-laid duck egg and grow them in a cultivator. They have plans to advance to several other types of meat in the future.

GOURMEY has raised US $2 million in seed funding, with support from the European Union and French government.

*Further details of their activities are outlined in Chapter 3, p.123.*

## HIGHER STEAKS

**Hs**
**Higher Steaks**

| | |
|---|---|
| **Main Product:** | Pork |
| **Founded:** | 2017, London, United Kingdom |
| **Founders:** | Benjamina Bollag |
| **Website:** | www.highersteaks.com |

Higher Steaks is working on cultivated meat. They chose to start with pork because of the research and money available in the field, and the potential to adapt any breakthroughs to other meat types. Pork also avoids the added complication of developing the taste of blood associated with beef. They have produced their first hybrid products in the form of bacon strips (70 per cent plant-based, 30 per cent cultured) and pork belly (50 per cent plant-based, 50 per cent cultured). They hope to reach the consumer market in 2022 or 2023.

Higher Steaks have raised US $200k.

## HOXTON FARMS

**HOXTON FARMS**
cultivating the revolution

| | |
|---|---|
| **Main Product:** | Fats |
| **Founded:** | 2020, London, UK |
| **Founders:** | Max Jamilly, Ed Steele |
| **Website:** | www.hoxtonfarms.com |

Hoxton Farms are aiming to become a lead player in the expanding fats and oils industry currently valued at US $350 billion globally. They have conducted taste tests on plant-based meat analogues, which demonstrated that the addition of just five to ten per cent purified fat drastically enhances the flavour and consumer satisfaction of the product. The company has a proprietary modelling and optimisation platform and is hoping to have a pilot facility running by 2022, after which rapid scaling can take place. Hoxton Farms have been talking to a number of plant-based meat and dairy companies about incorporating Hoxton Farm fats into their products. The founders believe that cultivated muscle does not really add any more by way of cooking times, texture or taste than plant-based analogues, but rather it is the fat that affects these key qualities.

In September 2020, Hoxton Farms were raising a US $1.5-2m seed round, to fund their initial R&D in preparation for establishing a pilot production facility.

## INNOCENT MEAT

| | |
|---|---|
| **Main Product:** | Beef |
| **Founded:** | 2018, Germany |
| **Founders:** | Laura Gertenbach, Philipp Wolters |
| **Website:** | www.innocent-meat.com |

Innocent Meat is Germany's first cultivated meat startup. They are using a pioneering bioreactor and process design to effectively reduce the volume of cell media used in manufacturing.

## INTEGRICULTURE

**Main Product:** Foie gras and CulNet technology platform
**Founded:** 2015, Japan
**Founders:** Yuki Hanyu
**Website:** www.integriculture.jp

IntegriCulture are working on cultivated meat, starting with foie gras and leading an open-source movement. Their patented *CulNet System* can culture cells at four to five orders of magnitude less expense in order to overcome what are currently prohibitive costs in the culturing of cells. Because of the versatility of this platform, IntegriCulture believes it makes an ideal general platform for clients producing foods, supplements, cosmetics, and pharmaceuticals. They are funded by the Japanese government. They plan to build their production site in 2020, to launch their foie gras in 2021. They will release processed meat in 2023, and steak in 2025.

IntegriCulture raised US $7.4 million in Series A funding in May 2020, bringing total funds raised to US $10.4 million. In September 2020 they received a further US $2.2 million as a grant from the Japanese government.

*Further details of the company's activities are featured in Chapter 3, p.167.*

## EAT JUST

**Main Product:** Cultivated chicken, beef and plant-based liquid egg
**Founded:** 2011, California, USA
**Founders:** Josh Tetrick, Josh Balk
**Website:** www.ju.st

JUST gained prominence as the creator of the highly successful plant-based egg substitute made with mung beans. More recently, co-founder Josh Tetrick has been promoting their exploration of cultivated meats. They are working on the production of cultivated chicken with ambitions to add a range of proteins including Wagyu beef, to their existing line-up of plant-based vegan foods, and are now scaling in a 1,000 litre bioreactor.

JUST has raised US $300 million in total and is valued at US $1.2 billion.

*Further details of the company's activities are featured in Chapter 3, p.119.*

## LAB FARM FOODS

| | |
|---|---|
| **Main Product:** | Beef |
| **Founded:** | 2019, New York, USA |
| **Founders:** | Dave Schnettler, Tiziano Barberi |
| **Website:** | www.labfarmfoods.com |

Lab Farm Foods are working on cultivated beef. They are a part of Merck KGaA Accelerator as one of the two first cellular agriculture companies, and members of NYU Longone's Biolabs Incubator.

Their financials are currently undisclosed.

## MEATABLE

| | |
|---|---|
| **Main Product:** | Pork and beef |
| **Founded:** | 2018, Netherlands |
| **Founders:** | Krijn de Nood, Daan Luining and Mark Kotter |
| **Website:** | www.meatable.com |

Meatable is developing a unique technology based on induced pluripotent stem cells (iPSCs) derived from discarded animal umbilical cords. The technology, developed with Roger Pedersen, a Cambridge University-based stem cell biologist, as well as with Mark Kotter, a neurosurgical clinician also based in Cambridge, is called OPTi-OX cell reprogramming and will enable them to redirect notoriously tricky iPSCs into the desired muscle and fat cells within five days. This will offer a 25-fold improvement on the standard economics of cellular agriculture.

Meatable has raised a total of US $17 million from backers such as Blue Yard Capital, Atlantic Food Labs, Backed, and Agronomics.

*Further details of the company's activities are featured in Chapter 3, p.132.*

## MEAT TECH 3D

| | |
|---|---|
| **Main Product:** | 3D printed meat |
| **Founded:** | 2019, Israel |
| **Founders:** | Sharon Fima |
| **Website:** | www.meatech3d.com |

# MOO'S LAW

Meat Tech 3D has developed 3D printing technology to make meat from cells retrieved from an animal's umbilical cord. Once 3D printed, the cells are placed in incubators to mature and grow, helping to create the foundations for a true cut of meat rather than simply a 'patty' of muscle fibres.

Notable people involved include the serial entrepreneur Professor Shlomo Magdassi of the Hebrew University and Danny Ayalon, former Israeli Ambassador to the United States.

They were established with US $2 million seed in 2019 and now trade on the Tel Aviv Stock Exchange, having merged with Ophectra Real Estate and Investments in October 2019. They have recently completed a US $5.8 million funding round with investment from Rami Levy, the Israeli supermarket magnate, Adom, an Israeli meat importer, and American investors. Now it looks like Meat Tech is headed for the NASDAQ.

## MEMPHIS MEATS

**Main Product:** Beef, chicken, duck
**Founded:** 2015, California, USA
**Founders:** Uma Valeti, Nicholas Genovese, Will Clem
**Website:** www.memphismeats.com

This company's ambitious goal of feeding 10 billion people by 2050 while offering consumers a range of additional choices in meat, poultry and seafood is matched by the scale of investment that has recently been made in it.

Memphis Meats have produced many of the world's breakthroughs in cell-based meat; creating the first beef meatball in 2016 and the world's first chicken and duck in 2017, and having developed a method to cultivate meat which does not require foetal bovine serum.

Founded by cell biologist Nicolas Genovese, PhD, and Uma Valeti, MD, who was a heart surgeon before moving into this space, the team has drawn the attention of Kimbal Musk, Bill Gates, and Richard Branson. They also have the support of investors such as SoftBank Group, Temasek, Norwest, and Threshold Ventures as well as food industry leaders Cargill and Tyson. An investment from Tyson, one of the world's largest meat producers, demonstrates the interest traditional food companies have in keeping ahead of technological innovation within the food industry so as not to lose their market share.

Their recent US $161 million funding round, in early 2020, roughly doubled the amount of money in the sector overall, making them a powerhouse in the cultivated meats industry and thus one of the most important companies which investors should be watching. To take the product to the mass market, they have plans to bring a factory into operation, which will begin producing prototypes of its products for the public. It could take between 18 months and two years for this factory to become viable, and it represents a significant leap towards commercialisation.

Memphis Meats' US $161 million Series B raise brought their total funds to over US $180 million.

*Further details of their activities are outlined in Chapter 3, p.130.*

## MIRAI FOODS

**Main Product:** Beef
**Founded:** 2019, Switzerland
**Founders:** Christoph Mayr, Suman kumar Das
**Website:** www.miraifoods.com

Mirai Foods is developing cultured meat beginning with minced beef, with plans to expand into other types of protein. They want to be a leading household brand for cultivated meat by 2030, and as such will cover the entire value chain, including marketing and distribution. In 2020 Mirai Foods conducted a well-received event for prospective investors to taste their cultivated beef – the first time cultivated meat had been both grown and tasted in Switzerland. They are eventually looking to explore different kinds of species outside of beef and poultry, and have strong proprietary knowledge on which they intend to file patents.

Co-founder Christoph Mayr previously built the Korean business of Delivery Hero (Yogiyo) as COO, and exited in 2017 via an IPO. Suman kumar Das has experience surrounding muscle stem cell physiology and cell metabolism, having spent seven years at Novartis in Switzerland.

Their finances are undisclosed, but they have told me that they are currently raising a seed round.

## MISSION BARNS

**Main Product:** Duck and pork fat
**Founded:** 2018, Bay Area, California, USA
**Founders:** Eitan Fischer, David Bowman
**Website:** www.missionbarns.com

Mission Barns is focussed on creating animal fats, namely duck and pork fat. The co-founders decided to take up the challenge of producing fats because they saw that the fat substitutes traditionally used in the food industry – coconut and palm oil – can be both bad for the environment and inadequate replicates of the real thing, lacking the juiciness and texture of animal fats.

They have thus far produced both duck and pork fat, and have created a hybrid plant-based bacon with 20 per cent cultivated pork fat.

They are looking to partner with existing food producers and cosmetic producers and have raised a total of US $6 million, with hopes to close a further round of US $20 million by the end of 2020.

*Further details of their activities are outlined in Chapter 3, p.134.*

## MOSA MEAT

**Main Product:** Beef
**Founded:** 2015, Netherlands
**Founders:** Mark Post, Peter Verstrate
**Website:** www.mosameat.com

Mosa Meat was one of the first companies established in the cultivated meat space thanks to its pioneering founder, Mark Post. Post, whose academic research at Maastricht University was funded by Sergey Brin, developed the first cultivated meat burger in 2013, which cost around US $250k, making him widely regarded as the 'father of cultured meat'.

Post's background is in medicine, working as a doctor and researcher on tissue engineering for vascular grafts. He has been an assistant professor in medicine at Harvard, associate professor at Dartmouth, and Professor of Angiogenesis in Tissue Engineering at the Technical University in Eindhoven. His research at Maastricht demonstrated the way myosatellite cells could be taken and proliferated in growth medium inside a bioreactor where they would differentiate, without any genetic modification, to form myotubes, which form the shape of muscle fibres when placed into a structured gel. It was this research that effectively kickstarted the cultivated meat industry.

Mosa Meat has since been focussed on scalability, with the hope to get their first products on the market in the next three to four years. In 2018, they raised US $8.8 million from M Ventures and leading Swiss meat manufacturer Bell Food Group. More recently, in January 2020 they announced a strategic partnership with Nutreco, a global supplier of animal nutrition and aquafeed, and Lowercarbon Capital, a fund led by Chris Sacca that invests in planet-healing technologies.

In September 2020 they raised a further US $55 million in a round led by Blue Horizon Ventures, with participation from Agronomics.

Mosa Meat has raised over US $64 million in funding, making it one of the best capitalised companies in the sector.

*Further details of the company's activities are featured in Chapter 3, p.124.*

## MZANSI MEATS

**Main Product:** Antelope, Beef
**Founded:** 2020, South Africa
**Founders:** Brett Thompson
**Website:** mzansimeat.co

Mzansi is currently in the early stages of research and development, with cell lines from a few different species harvested and banked. They are working on proliferation protocols for antelope and bovine myoblasts and adipocytes, and are hoping to have their cultivated cell lines available for sale to other cell ag companies by the end of 2020. They will register the processes and methodologies they have been developing in the lab as IP at the end of 2020.

Mzansi Meats has received pre-seed angel investment from Ryan Bethencourt and are in discussions with several other venture capital funds regarding an upcoming raise.

## NEW AGE MEATS

**NEW AGE MEATS**

**Main Product:** Pork
**Founded:** 2017, Bay Area, California, USA
**Founders:** Brian Spears
**Website:** www.newagemeats.com

New Age Meats presented the world's first cultivated pork sausage at a taste testing in 2018. Since then, they have been focussed on developing a highly-automated bioprocess with a novel bioreactor design created in-house.

In January 2020 they raised US $2.7 million in seed funding in a round led by ff Venture Capital, with support from Agronomics, followed by a US $2 million seed extension in July 2020, bringing their total financing up to US $5 million to date.

*Mentioned in Chapter 3, p.132.*

## PEACE OF MEAT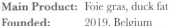

**Main Product:** Foie gras, duck fat
**Founded:** 2019, Belgium
**Founders:** Dirk von Heinrichshorst, David Brandes, Eva Sommer
**Website:** www.peace-of-meat.com

Peace of Meat is focussed on developing duck fat and foie gras. They have collaborated with KU Leuven, the University of Lyon and Reutlingen University to create a consortium for the development of their products.

They raised EUR 900k in pre-seed funding and were awarded a EUR 3.6 million grant from Flanders Innovation and Entrepreneurship (VLAIO). Meat Tech has invested EUR 1 million in Peace of Meat, part of a plan for a full acquisition of the company.

*Mentioned in Chapter 3, p.123.*

## SHIOK MEATS

**Main Product:** Shrimp
**Founded:** 2018, Singapore
**Founders:** Dr Sandhya Sriram, Dr Ka Yi Ling
**Website:** www.shiokmeats.com

Shiok means fantastic and delicious in Singaporean and Malay slang. They are the first cultivated meat company in Singapore and south-east Asia. Shiok are developing shrimp, and carried out the first tasting of their siu mai shrimp dumplings in April 2019. By the end of 2020 the Shiok team wants to cut the cost of producing one kilogram of shrimp meat from US $5,000 to US $50 both by signing a low cost deal for the nutrients needed to grow the cells and by working on scale. Shiok Meats intends to launch in the Singaporean market, following regulatory approval from the Singapore Food Agency (SFA), in 2022.

Their lead investor is Henry Soesanto, the CEO of Monde Nissin, the Filipino company which purchased Quorn Foods in 2015. Shiok Meats has received US $4.7 million in seed funding, including support from Y Combinator, Agronomics and VegInvest. In September 2020, Shiok Meats closed a US $12.6 million Series A financing round led by Aqua-Spark. This brings their total funds raised to US $20.4 million.

*Further details of their activities are outlined in Chapter 3, p.144.*

# SUPERMEAT

| | |
|---|---|
| **Main Product:** | Chicken |
| **Founded:** | 2015, Israel |
| **Founders:** | Ido Savir, Koby Barak, Shir Friedman |
| **Website:** | www.supermeat.com |

SuperMeat is working on 'meal-ready' cultivated chicken, and recently revealed their test restaurant, situated in Tel Aviv, Israel, and named 'The Chicken'. This makes SuperMeat the first cultivated meat company to offer a restaurant experience where customers can try its cultivated chicken. They had a US $3 million seed round in 2018 and have raised US $4.2 million so far (including crowdfunding from Indiegogo). Notable investors include PHW Group, Stray Dog Capital, and New Crop Capital.

# VOW

| | |
|---|---|
| **Main Product:** | Kangaroo |
| **Founded:** | 2019, Australia |
| **Founders:** | George Peppou, Tim Noakesmith |
| **Website:** | www.vowfood.com |

Vow saw the opportunity to bring new, more exotic, foods to the market; blending multiple cell types to create better flavours, textures or nutritional profiles, from both domesticated and undomesticated species. They are working on kangaroo, goat, alpaca, lamb, rabbit, pork, and prawns. Mid 2020, Vow showcased its preliminary prototype products, including a kangaroo dumpling. Their financials are currently undisclosed.

# WILDTYPE

| | |
|---|---|
| **Main Product:** | Salmon |
| **Founded:** | 2016, Bay Area, California, USA |
| **Founders:** | Justin Kolbeck, Aryé Elfenbein |
| **Website:** | www.thewildtype.com |

After beginning to explore cultivated meat with foie gras, Wildtype moved on to salmon due to the size of the market and the pressing need to address fish stock depletion. Seafood is the number one source of protein around the world, and salmon is the most consumed finfish in the US and second most consumed seafood after shrimp. Their salmon sushi rolls currently cost US $200 to produce, but they want to reduce that to US $5.

Their most recent funding round was led by CRV with the lead of their seed round, Spark Capital, also participating alongside Root Ventures and other existing investors. This Series A raise of US $12.5 million closed in October 2019, contributing to a total raise of US $20 million which, among other things, has enabled their co-founder and CEO, Justin Kolbeck to assemble an impressive team of 18 full-time employees (including 16 scientists, mostly PhDs and postdocs).

Wildtype was originally hoping to rely on a B2B2C model, whereby restaurants (where two-thirds of salmon is consumed in the US) would be supplied first, in order to shape consumers' experience of the product. However, it is reviewing its commercialisation strategy in the wake of Covid-19. Justin is keen to explore numerous avenues to get cultivated products to consumers.

*Further details of their activities are outlined in Chapter 3, p.144.*

# CELL CULTURE GROWTH MEDIA

## BACK OF THE YARDS ALGAE SCIENCES

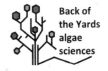

| | |
|---|---|
| **Main Product:** | Media, plant-based foods |
| **Founded:** | 2018, Illinois, USA |
| **Founders:** | Leonard Lerer |
| **Website:** | www.algaesciences.com |

Back of the Yards Algae Sciences (BYAS) develops sustainable algal ingredients for application in foods, beverages, and the general and cellular agriculture industries. They are developing algae-based cell culture media and are also producing high protein plant-based ingredients, novel organic biostimulants used in vertical farming, and natural blue food colourant. They have three top-tier R&D laboratories: Circular Economy, a Cellular Agriculture Lab (CECA) to develop cell culture technology; Algae-Digester Lab; and a Food Innovation-Bioreactor Lab with a test kitchen to work on the 'to plate' end of cellular agriculture.

They have told us that their products are in late-stage development in their pilot production facilities in Chicago. Their main ingredients, natural blue colourant and algal powders for sustainable plant-based meats, will be commercialised later in 2020, when BYAS' plant in Utah comes on-stream. They have received early stage investment from GROW and Kickstart accelerators, amongst others, and are currently preparing for their first major fundraising round. BYAS has a patent pending for their ocre technology and applications, with a number of provisional patents in the works for 2020.

*Further details of their activities are outlined in Chapter 3, p.166.*

# BIFTEK

**Main Product:** Media
**Founded:** 2018, Turkey
**Founders:** Can Akcali, Erdem Erikci
**Website:** www.biftek.co

Biftek is a startup developing serum-free cell culture media to tackle the prohibitive costs of using FBS (foetal bovine serum) to grow meat: FBS currently constitutes 80-90 per cent of the cost of meat cultivation. Professor Can Akcali previously worked as the professor in Bilkent University's Molecular Biology and Genetics Department and is currently the vice president of the Stem Cell Institute in Ankara. Dr Erikci received his PhD at the Max Planck Institute before co-founding tarla.io (an agronomy database) and iklim.co (a dangerous weather early-warning service).

The company has received US $200k in government grants and a further US $200k in pre-seed funding from Big Idea Ventures' acceleration program. In August 2020, Biftek raised US $400k in seed funding at a pre-money valuation of US $8 million, and will file their first patent in the second half of 2020.

# CULTURED BLOOD

**Main Product:** Blood
**Founded:** 2019, Netherlands
**Founders:** Robert ten Hoor
**Website:** www.culturedblood.com

Cultured Blood is a startup working on manufacturing cultivated blood for the meat industry. In order to combat the steep price of lab-culture medium, they will provide manufactured real blood to the cultured meat industry, which should also improve the flavour of the meat product. The flavour of the final product is influenced by the serum used, a fraction of which will remain inside the clean meat. The iron in red blood cells, however, gives meat its characteristic flavours, and so producing a blood as close to natural blood – including red blood cells – will result in a more favourable growth medium. Their finances are currently undisclosed.

*Further details of their activities are outlined in Chapter 3, p.166.*

## FUTURE FIELDS

**Main Product:** Media
**Founded:** 2017, Canada
**Founders:** Matt Anderson-Baron, Jalene Anderson-Baron, Lejjy Gafour
**Website:** www.futurefields.io

Future Fields create enabling technologies for the production of cultivated meats. They offer three services: co-design and IP development for those who have yet to define the key components that support the growth of their cell line in culture; custom growth media production and growth factor cocktails for those who have defined their cell line requirements but to whom cost, volume or components remain pain points; and cellular goods policy and advice for those new to the space. Future Fields successfully closed their seed funding round in June 2020 and are now shipping their cell growth media to companies globally.

*Further details of their activities are outlined in Chapter 3, p.166.*

## HEUROS

**Main Product:** Media
**Founded:** 2017, Australia
**Founders:** Nick Beaumont
**Website:** www.heuros.com

Heuros is a startup creating environmentally-sustainable and affordable growth media to enable cultivated meat companies to scale their production effectively. Their growth medium technology is as natural as possible, and so does not use genetic modification or recombinant proteins. Heuros media stimulates the growth of bird and mammal muscle cells, and they are also developing novel bioreactors for the large-scale production of cultivated meat. Heuros has recently completed a seed round of undisclosed size.

*Further details of their activities are outlined in Chapter 3, p.166.*

## LUYEF BIOTECHNOLOGIES

**Main Product:** Media
**Founded:** 2019, Chile
**Founders:** Kris Blanchard Tapia, Maria Soledad Gutiérrez, Randall Cossio
**Website:** www.luyef.com

Luyef Biotechnologies engage in B2B research & development to support the cultivated meat industry. The word Luyef means 'clean' in Mapudungun, the language of Mapuche people, and the company is creating a high-tech platform to produce cell-based meat, in order to bring a competitive product to market quickly.

Their finances are currently undisclosed.

## MULTUS MEDIA

**Main Product:** Media
**Founded:** 2019, London, UK
**Founders:** Kevin Pan, Cai Linton, Réka Trón.
**Website:** www.multus.media

The founders are a team of undergraduates out of Imperial Innovation Hub working on serum-free cell culture media to enable the cultivated meat industry. They use a machine-learning platform that takes a statistical approach to find the best ingredients to optimise their growth factor proteins and create an animal-free growth media for different specific cell types and tissues.

Given that protein components in growth media are typically very expensive and difficult to produce at scale, Multus Media's platform will be able to modify natural proteins to increase or enhance specific performance characteristics so they perform better at scale. Their use-based platform will increase yield and streamline downstream processing. Their final goal is to produce a media which will cost US $1 per litre. They plan to file patents to protect their IP in the near future.

Multus Media was granted US $250k as part of the IndieBio programme and has been supported through various grants and competitions. They are looking to undergo a funding round later in 2020.

*Mentioned in Chapter 3, p.166.*

## SCINORA

**Main Product:** Media
**Founded:** 2016, Germany
**Founders:** Beat Thalmann
**Website:** www.scinora.com

Scinora is a biotech startup dedicated to improving cell-based processes for biopharmaceutical production and analytics using animal-free media. They enable cultured meat production and cell-based assay development.

Scinora's finances are currently undisclosed.

*Mentioned in Chapter 3, p.166.*

# BIOREACTORS/3D CELL CULTURE SUPPORT

## APPLIKON BIOTECHNOLOGY

**Main Product:** Bioreactors
**Founded:** 1974, The Netherlands
**Website:** www.applikon-biotechnology.com

Applikon Biotechnology is a world leader in developing and supplying bioreactors for a range of uses, from pharmaceuticals to biochemicals and bioplastics for industrial biotechnology. They are supporting the CLEANMEAT project, initiated by Meatable to develop the world's first scalable method for production of cell-based meat. Applikon provides bioreactor systems to enable cell cultivation, with the company Noviocell providing scaffolds to provide texture and structure to the meat. Applikon has 160 employees and Mosa Meat intends to work with them for their pilot production plant.

In January 2020 Getinge acquired 100 per cent of the shares in Applikon Biotechnology, which has annual net sales of around 450 million Swedish krona (US $51 million). Getinge paid approximately SEK 840 million (US $95 million), with the possibility of a maximum earn-out of around SEK 630 million (US $71 million) if agreed earnings performance is achieved in 2020-2021.

## ATLAST FOOD CO

**Main Product:** Bioreactors
**Founded:** 2019, New York, USA
**Founders:** Eben Bayer, Gavin McIntyre, Steve Lomnes, Russell Hazen, Andy Bass, Alex Carlton
**Website:** www.atlastfood.co

Atlast Food Co is a spin-off from Ecovative *(mentioned on p.257 of this chapter)* working on mycelium scaffolds for plant-based and cultivated meat in order to make 'whole cuts' of meat. They have also created a meat-free bacon product from mycelium.

# BIOCELLION

| | |
|---|---|
| **Main Product:** | Biomodelling |
| **Founded:** | 2013, Washington, USA |
| **Founders:** | Simon Kahan |
| **Website:** | www.biocellion.com |

Biocellion runs computer simulations of living system behaviours so that life science companies can quickly and cheaply run experiments to gain insight into how well their products work before testing them in petri dishes or animals. They believe that their computer modelling will enable the cultivated meat industry to develop efficient processes to accelerate it into a mature industry years before it otherwise would.

Biocellion founded cmmc.org, one of the first LLCs they are planning to create, which brings together a community of stakeholders from academia and industry to solve problems. Simon Kahan has told us that, in order to accelerate the path of high-quality cultivated meat products to market, the industry must tackle the twin problems of growth media optimisation and bioreactor optimisation. The former is difficult to optimise with modelling at this stage because the industry has not yet settled on a media standard and remains incredibly proprietary. As such Biocellion is focussing all of their energy on the optimisation of bioreactors, which have typically been used to grow a small number of cells for the pharmaceutical industry, not the ever-larger numbers at the scale needed for cultivated meat. The main problem they are modelling to solve is the tension between the fact that cell cultures cannot tolerate gradients in nutrients and oxygen, but at the same time the cells are very delicate and cannot deal with mechanical stressors which come from moving the fluid faster to get the nutrients throughout the whole. Biocellion has received grants from the GFI and Merck KGaA to look into this specific problem.

For investors, the fact that Biocellion retains the IP for the processes derived from its modelling for licensing out makes them incredibly attractive. They will release IP for non-commercial use to help the academic community, and increase demand for their modelling and ensure that researchers are familiar with their platforms. They will also licence this out to commercial companies. Biocellion currently has a non-exclusive licensing agreement with Merck KGaA, whereby they get a discount in return for the funding they put into the project. They have been licensed at over 70 labs in 13 countries.

*Mentioned in Chapter 3, p.165.*

## BIOMIMETIC SOLUTIONS

**Main Product:** Bioreactors
**Founded:** 2017, London, UK
**Founders:** Alana Santos Benz, Lorena Viana Souza, Ana Elisa Antunes
**Website:** www.sosv.com

Biomimetic Solutions are a B2B startup working on 3D scaffolds for cultivated meat layering to improve processes and reduce costs for clean meat companies.

They have raised US $100k in funding over two rounds, with their most recent investors being SOSV and RebelBio.

## CELLTAINER BIOTECH BV

**Main Product:** Bioreactors
**Founded:** 2015, Netherlands
**Founders:** Nico Oosterhuis
**Website:** www.celltainer.com

Celltainer Biotech develops, builds and sells single-use bioreactors for cell culture and microbial fermentation based on a unique technology providing high gas/liquid mass transfer under low shear conditions. They have recently chosen ProAnalytics as their new representative for the Eastern USA and Canada. Dr. Nico Oosterhuis spoke at the fifth International Conference on Cultured Meat in Maastricht in October 2019 about bioreactor design for the cultured meat industry.

Celltainer Biotech recently announced a close cooperation with Mosa Meat (among others) to develop a scalable bioreactor platform for cultured meat applications. The company is also involved in designing larger-scale reactors for cultured meat production, based on a scale-down approach, and holds several patents on their rocking bioreactor technology.

The company's finances are undisclosed.

# CELLULAREVOLUTION

**Main Product:** Peptide coating technology, bioreactor design
**Founded:** 2019, Newcastle, UK
**Founders:** Leo Groenewegen, Martina Miotto, Che Connon
**Website:** www.cellularevolution.co.uk

A spin-out from Newcastle University, CellulaREvolution are attempting to move from traditional batch culture to a continuous culture system. Their peptide-based coating allows cultured cells to grow without the need for FBS and with a high proliferation rate. The philosophy behind their technology is that the closer it mimics nature, the better. CellulaREvolution achieves this by combining a dynamic coating with their bioreactor to create a continuous system of cell proliferation that also allows for media recycling.

Early calculations of their technology's footprint show that one of their bioreactors is equivalent to a football pitch of conventional bioreactors. Given that scalability is of central importance to the cultured meat industry, this preliminary data is exciting to see. Their product has implications for both cultured meat and cell therapy, where high quantities of cells are required. Overall, the benefits of continuous production coupled with CellulaREvolution's technology allows for the production of more cells, of higher quality and at lower costs.

They have received grants from various bodies, including Innovate UK, totalling £186k in 2019 and £90k in 2020, and raised an initial seed of £180k. As of July 2020, CellulaREvolution is conducting a large funding round aiming to raise £2.5 million. They will use this to move to a larger commercial facility in the Newcastle Biosphere, grow their team and complete prototype designs before advancing their product to market early 2021 to 2022. Their IP is currently protected by two patents, with plans to file additional patents later this year on specific technology.

*Further details of their activities are outlined in Chapter 3, p.166.*

# CELLULAR AGRICULTURE

Cellular
Agriculture

**Main Product:** Bioreactors (hollow fibres)
**Founded:** 2016, Llanelli, UK
**Founders:** Illtud Llyr Dunsford, Marianne Ellis
**Website:** www.cellularagriculture.co.uk

Cellular Agriculture Ltd was the first UK startup in the cell-based meat space. Cellular Agriculture has developed a scalable hollow fibre bioreactor that can be used to grow cultivated meat at high yields, and is looking to deliver scaled technology for multi-species cell-based meat technology.

In 2018 InnovateUK funding enabled Cellular Agriculture to develop their proof-of-concept bioreactor system, which became the first automated cultured meat system to be demonstrated publicly when it was displayed at the Nemo Science Museum, Amsterdam, in 2019.

CEO Illtud Llyr Dunsford has 300 years of agricultural history in his family. He established *Charcutier Ltd*, a specialty meat-processing business, in 2011 as a farm diversification project, winning the title of Best Food Producer in the UK from the BBC Food and Farming Awards in 2016. Director of R&D Dr Marianne Ellis is Head of the Department of Chemical Engineering at the University of Bath. As a Chartered Engineer with experience in bioprocessing for tissue engineering, she has previously commercialised technology in cell therapies from academia into Cellesce Ltd and seeks to emulate those successes at scale with Cellular Agriculture. She has recently authored a paper with Neil Stephens (see bibliography) surveying the state of UK cellular agriculture in academia, industry and advocacy.

They have partnerships with the universities of Bath, Reading, and Aberystwyth, as well as with Innovate UK, Charcutier, Clean + Cool, and Merck. Their finances are currently undisclosed.

## CORNING LIFE SCIENCES

**Main Product:** Biotech equipment
**Founded:** 1851, New York, USA
**Website:** www.corning.com

Corning Life Sciences manufactures Matrigel, a solubilised basement membrane preparation. This matrix is extracted from a certain mouse tumour and is rich in various growth factors. Corning Life Sciences also produces a wide range of other equipment for biotech. Corning is a multi-billion dollar company on the New York Stock Exchange.

## INCUVERS

**Main Product:** Incubators
**Founded:** 2018, Canada
**Founders:** Sebastian Hadjiantoniou, Andrew Pelling, Charles Cuerrier
**Website:** www.incuvers.com

Incuvers are working on cell incubators for cultivated meat and other applications. They specialise in incorporating monitoring capabilities into their incubators. For example, their Live Cell Imaging Incubator is the first of its kind to enable you to effectively track the status of your cell culture and store all of the information in the cloud. The company's finances are undisclosed.

# KERAFAST

**Main Product:** Reagents
**Founded:** 2010, Massachusetts, USA
**Founders:** Bill Emhiser
**Website:** www.kerafast.com

Kerafast provides an online platform for scientists to trade reagents. Rather than using the cumbersome Material Transfer Agreement system, scientists can request reagents through Kerafast's platform instead. The company assists the providing lab with shipping as well.

Kerafast has raised a total of US $3.9 million. Their Series A round raised US $3 million in 2012. In 2014, a debt financing round netted US $634k, and two convertible notes in early 2016 totalled US $250k.

*Mentioned in Chapter 2, p.64.*

# KUHNER SHAKER

**Main Product:** Large industrial shakers
**Founded:** 1949, Germany
**Founders:** Adolf Kühner
**Website:** www.kuhner.com

Kuhner Shaker was founded in 1949 in Riehen Basel by Adolf Kühner and now leads the world in quality and technology for shaking machines, which are needed for large industrial cultures to be grown. This picks and shovels technology will become increasingly important as the world begins to rely more and more on cultivated food.

# MATRIX MEATS

**Main Product:** Scaffolding
**Founded:** 2019, Ohio, USA
**Founders:** Flavio Lobato, Ross Kayuha, Eric Jenkusky
**Website:** www.matrixmeats.com

Matrix Meats have developed a nanofibre 3D scaffold that can be used by clean meat companies to significantly increase the volume of meat product per batch. They claim that their scaffold enhances the taste of cultured meat products by designing nano-fibres that deteriorate into natural chemicals such as lactic acid, which helps lend slaughtered meat its particular taste. The scaffold will mean that current procedures of growing cells and then joining them together in a 'patty' can be discarded in favour of whole 'steak-like' portions of meat. Matrix Meats has completed a seed round of undisclosed size.

*Mentioned in Chapter 3, p.167.*

## MERCK MILLIPORE

**Main Product:** Bioreactors
**Founded:** 2010, Massachusetts, USA
**Websites:** www.merckmillipore.com/GB/en, www.sigmaaldrich.com

Merck Millipore, a subsidiary of Merck KGaA, has a market capitalisation of US $14 billion. They make bioreactors up to 2,000L. Now known as MilliporeSigma, after merging with Merck's newly acquired Sigma Aldrich subsidiary.

## OSPIN

**Main Product:** Modular bioprocessing
**Founded:** 2014, Germany
**Founders:** Jan Saam
**Website:** www.ospin.de

Ospin provides solutions for a variety of challenges in the clean meat field, ranging from bioprocess design to automated bioreactor systems. It aims to establish an open bioprocessing platform as the operating system of modern biotech. They offer technology consulting services as well as digitisation and automation services to increase the efficiency of cultured meat companies production. Ospin is a private company and their finances are undisclosed.

## SARTORIUS

**sartorius**

**Main Product:** Biopharmaceuticals, equipment
**Founded:** 1870, Germany
**Website:** www.sartorius.com

Sartorius AG is a biopharmaceutical company designing bioreactors and fermenters for industry and laboratories. They provide a scalable range of single-use or glass and stainless steel bioreactor solutions. They acquired a number of Danaher Group's life sciences businesses in 2020.

Their shares are listed on the Frankfurt Stock Exchange with a market capitalisation of EUR 29.3 billion.

*Mentioned in Chapter 3, p.165.*

## SUNP BIOTECH

**Main Product:** 3D printers
**Founded:** 2014, New Jersey, USA
**Founders:** Wei Sun
**Website:** www.sunpbiotech.com

SunP are creating 3D bioprinting systems, bioinks and *in vitro* biological models for personalised tissue engineering products and cancer study. In 2014 they began designing 3D biofabrication products that include a patented screw-based extrusion technique to eliminate the heavy equipment which often comes with pneumatic systems.

In January 2019 SunP raised US $4.3 million in an early venture capital round.

## THERMO FISHER SCIENTIFIC

**Main Product:** Biopharmaceuticals
**Founded:** 2006, Massachusetts, USA
**Website:** www.thermofisher.com

Thermo Fisher Scientific is an established company in the biopharmaceutical space, which offers a range of bioreactors suited for mammalian cell culture as well as microbial fermentation for large-scale commercial biomanufacturing. Their designs are anywhere from one-litre glass bioreactors to 2,000 litre single-use bioreactors.

Thermo Fischer is publicly traded (NYSE: TMO), and had a market cap, as on close 13 November 2020, of US $193 billion.

*Mentioned in Chapter 3, p.165.*

## VIVAX BIO

| | |
|---|---|
| **Main Product:** | 3D Bioprinting |
| **Founded:** | 2018, New York, USA |
| **Founders:** | Yakov Balahovsky |
| **Website:** | www.vivaxbio.com |

Vivax Bio and its Moscow R&D subsidiary, 3D Bioprinting Solutions, are working on 3D bioprinters based on a range of different technologies, and are consistently rated among the top bioprinters in the world. They are working on bioprinting solutions for cultivated meat and, at the end of 2018, their proprietary 3D bioprinter, OrganAut, was used by Aleph Farms to grow meat in microgravity on the International Space Station. Their experiments on the ISS as of 2019 included biofabrication of protein crystals, biofilms and cultured meat constructs. 3D Bioprinting Solutions are also involved in advancing tissue engineering and conducting research on printed organ transplants in mice, as well as printing organoid models for drug discovery purposes. They have signed a number of framework agreements with several startups in the clean meat field.

KFC recently signed a partnership with 3D Bioprinting Solutions to develop a hybrid plant-based and cell-cultured chicken nugget that will be tested over the course of the latter end of 2020.

The company's financial information is undisclosed.

# FERMENTATION – DAIRY

## BETTER DAIRY

| | |
|---|---|
| **Main Product:** | Cultivated dairy |
| **Founded:** | 2020, London, UK |
| **Founders:** | Jevan Nagarajah, Christopher Reynolds |
| **Website:** | www.betterdairy.co.uk |

Better Dairy aims to create dairy products that are identical to traditional dairy at the molecular level, without involving animals. Instead, they use 'synthetic biology and yeast fermentation', similarly to brewing beer. They have recently achieved their first results in the laboratory by producing casein, an important protein in milk. The company is distinguished by its focus on machine learning – Chris Reynolds used machine learning for drug discovery during his PhD and later spun out an (unsuccessful) company doing similar things. Some elements of their business model remain flexible: they will probably be B2B (selling low-cost protein ingredients) rather than creating consumer products; they will probably use pichia yeast rather than trichoderma fungi (trichoderma has higher protein yield but more processing difficulties e.g. poisonous by-products). By the end of 2021, they foresee lab-scale production of around 3,000 litre bioreactors with yields of five grams per litre – they might scale it up to 10,000 litres for proof of concept on a mass scale, but not on a regular basis.

Following a pre-seed round of £80k from Entrepreneur First, Better Dairy's seed round of £1.6m is now completed, led by CPT Capital. This money will chiefly be used to prove their belief that machine learning can deliver significant improvements to protein yield compared to their competitors (such as Perfect Day, who probably do not use machine learning) and to accumulate IP (patents and proprietary data). If their efforts are successful, they envision seeking further funding in early 2022. They need new lab facilities – they have been working out of shipping containers in West London since Covid-19 forced them out of Imperial College London's labs.

## BIOMILQ

| | |
|---|---|
| **Main Product:** | Cultivated human breast milk |
| **Founded:** | 2020, North Carolina, USA |
| **Founders:** | Michelle Egger |
| **Website:** | www.biomilq.com |

BIOMILQ is a women-owned company focussing its efforts on breast milk. The market they have identified is large – nearly four out of five mothers have to stop breastfeeding before the recommended six months, and turn to dairy-based formula instead. BIOMILQ aims to provide comprehensive and sustainable infant nutrition that adequately caters for the specific requirements babies have for human milk. They are culturing mammary cells outside the body in order to utilise their ability to produce the more the 2,000-plus molecules constituting breast milk, such as human casein and lactose.

It has been estimated that the baby formula global market size will reach US $104 billion by 2026, so this is a vital market to tap.

BIOMILQ raised US $3.5 million in June 2020 from Breakthrough Ventures, Bill Gates' investment firm focused on climate change.

*Further details of the company's activities are featured in Chapter 3, p.111.*

## CALIFIA FARMS

| | |
|---|---|
| **Main Product:** | Plant-based milk |
| **Founded:** | 2010, California, USA |
| **Founders:** | Greg Steltenpohl |
| **Website:** | califiafarms.com |

Califia Farms is a manufacturer of alternative plant-based milks, juices, dairy-free creamers, and ready-to-drink coffees.

The company has raised a total of US $340 million, including a Series D round in 2018 which netted US $225 million with participation from Ambrosia Investments, Temasek, and the Qatar Investment Authority.

*Further details of the company's activities are featured in Chapter 3, p.103.*

## LEGENDAIRY FOODS

| | |
|---|---|
| **Main Product:** | Cheese |
| **Founded:** | 2019, Germany |
| **Founders:** | Raffael Wohlgensinger |
| **Website:** | www.legendairyfoods.de |

Founded in 2019, LegenDairy Foods use precision fermentation to create the milk proteins that go into producing dairy products. The process utilises genetically modified yeast to produce casein and whey and reconstitutes them with plant-based fats to produce cheese. This is the same technology that has been used commercially since the 1980s to produce human insulin and the enzyme chymosin, which is responsible for curdling milk into making cheese.

The products produced today through precision fermentation have a global market value of around US $100 billion. With the cost of this process rapidly falling, it looks to be very close to outcompeting traditional animal agriculture as a source of food production, in both price and efficiency. 'The cost of producing a single molecule by PF has fallen from $1m/kg in 2000 to about $100/kg today. We expect the cost to fall below $10/kg by 2025', according to the RethinkX report *(see bibliography)*.

By beginning with cheese, LegenDairy hopes to be able to make up for the shortfalls of competing vegan dairy products, which are unable to produce the casein and whey proteins responsible for the taste and texture of the cheese. LegenDairy will be able to make dairy products that exhibit all the traits of animal milk-based derivations while eliminating cholesterol for consumers, along with the mass use of hormones and antibiotics associated with the dairy cow industry.

In December 2019, LegenDairy launched a seed funding round co-led by Agronomics and M Ventures, and joined by CPT Capital, an investor in alternative proteins, and raising EUR 4.7 million. There is an enormous market to capture: the global dairy market in 2017 was US $413 billion.

We are very excited about this type of food production for both its scalability and versatility.

*Further details of the company's activities are featured in Chapter 3, p.109.*

## NEW CULTURE

**Main Product:** Cheese
**Founded:** 2018, Bay Area, California, USA
**Founders:** Inja Radman, Matt Gibson
**Website:** www.newculturefood.com

New Culture is working on producing lactose-free cheese without cows. They are specifically focusing on mozzarella; the most consumed type of cheese in the US, with global sales of US $10 billion in 2019 and a compound annual growth rate of roughly five per cent.

In September 2019, they closed a US $3.5 million seed round led by Evolv Ventures (Kraft Heinz Company), Bee Partners, Mayfield, CPT Capital, Boost VC, and SOSV (who are behind the accelerator IndieBio).

## PERFECT DAY

**Perfect Day.**

**Main Product:** Dairy proteins
**Founded:** 2014, Bay Area, California, USA
**Founders:** Perumal Gandhi, Ryan Pandya
**Website:** www.perfectdayfoods.com

Perfect Day produces casein and whey proteins found in dairy milk using their fermentation platform. They have produced ice cream and are planning in 2020 to commercialise their protein on several continents through partnerships in a range of dairy product categories.

Their US $140 million Series C raise in December 2019 – led by Temasek, with Horizons Ventures

– was expanded to US $300 million in July 2020 through a new tranche led by the Canada Pension Plan Investment Board which invested US $50 million. This brings Perfect Day's total funding to US $361.5 million. Bob Iger, the well-regarded executive chairman of Walt Disney, has recently joined the board of Perfect Day.

*Further details of the company's activities are featured in Chapter 3, p.106.*

## TURTLETREE LABS

**Main Product:** Human breast milk
**Founded:** 2019, Singapore
**Founders:** Fengru Lin, Mkulima Britt, Max Rye
**Website:** www.turtletreelabs.com

The global dairy market is worth US $716 billion. TurtleTree Labs use cell-based methods to make 'clean milk' without the pollution, inefficient use of land, water and energy, and pathogen risk associated with traditional dairy farming. Various Singapore government agencies support the company in alignment with Singapore's goal to produce 30 per cent of its nutritional needs by 2030 (30by30), and they can license their tech to local processors to infiltrate new markets. TurtleTree Labs are producing the world's first cultivated human breast milk which represents a significant investment opportunity given that the current infant nutrition market is US $45 billion and expected to grow to US $103 billion by 2026. They can replicate all HMOs, proteins and fats that make up human breast milk.

In June 2020, TurtleTree Labs raised US $3.2 million in seed funding, which included investment from Green Monday Ventures, CPT Capital, Artesian, KBW Ventures, and New Luna Ventures.

*Further details of the company's activities are featured in Chapter 2, p.75, and Chapter 3, p.111.*

# INGREDIENTS

## AFINEUR

**Main Product:** Proteins
**Founded:** 2014, New York, USA
**Founders:** Camille Delebecque, Sophie Deterre
**Website:** www.afineur.com

Afineur uses a proprietary fermentation process to upcycle waste biomass and to enhance the flavours of certain foods. For example, they have produced a bitterless coffee. Afineur uses carefully-selected microbes to create a type of microbiome in which they can induce fermentation to create a variety of different food types, including a type of cultured coffee. The general idea is to improve the taste of plant-based foods by engineering their synthetic microbes to feed on the foods in a fermentation process, thus enhancing nutrition and flavour. They have also created a protein for vegans, Afineur Cultured Protein, which is low in calories and sugar, with no cholesterol.

Camille trained at both Harvard and Paris Descartes Universities and is an agronomic engineer, while Sophie, also a PhD, is a food and flavour expert, having previously worked on developing a new distillery for Grand Marnier.

IndieBio offered the seed funding for their venture in 2014 and Afineur reached its Kickstarter crowdfunding target within six hours in 2015. More recently, in 2016, TechStars invested an undisclosed amount in the company.

## ARZEDA

**Main Product:** Proteins
**Founded:** 2008, Washington, USA
**Founders:** Alexandre Zanghellini, Daniela Grabs, Eric Althoff
**Website:** www.arzeda.com

Arzeda is developing novel enzymes for the efficient production of rare sugars, natural sweeteners and other health-improving oligosaccharides. Their enzymes decrease the cost of manufacturing and enable both biocatalytic and fermentation processes. They also design pesticidal peptides for crops and non-immunogenic therapeutic enzymes. They have raised a total of US $15.2 million.

## BIOSCIENZ

**Main Product:** Egg proteins, pesticide alternatives, ovalbumin
**Founded:** 2011, Netherlands
**Founders:** Wim de Laat
**Website:** www.bioscienz.nl

BioscienZ is developing techniques to use microbial fermentation of sugar beet to produce egg white proteins. These proteins will be distributed B2B as an animal-free food ingredient and binding agent. Among their other projects is a plan to use *Pseudomonad* bacteria to fight certain bacterial diseases in crops without recourse to chemicals/pesticides. Their finances are currently undisclosed.

## CLARA FOODS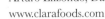

**Main Product:** Eggs
**Founded:** 2014, Bay Area, California, USA
**Founders:** Arturo Elizondo, David Anchel
**Website:** www.clarafoods.com

**Clara Foods**

Clara Foods is another company using precision fermentation to produce proteins. They are currently working on producing egg albumen in order to create egg products, which are very near to commercialisation. The reason they are targeting the egg-white protein is because it is so widely used in the culinary world due to its binding properties.

Their plan is to have their ingredients used in protein drinks and supplements later in 2020 before releasing an ingredient to replace eggs in baked goods and scrambles in 2021.

From their last funding round Clara Foods has raised over US $50 million, with several strategic billion-dollar food companies investing.

*Further details of the company's activities are featured in Chapter 3 p.117.*

## GELTOR

# GELTOR

**Main Product:** Collagen
**Founded:** 2015, California, USA
**Founders:** Alexander Lorestani, Nick Ouzounov
**Website:** www.geltor.com

Geltor has focussed its attention on the production of high-performing, animal-free collagen. Their first protein product, Collume, was launched in 2018 for skincare products, winning the prestigious CEW Beauty Award for Innovation of the Year. They are now expanding their protein portfolio in food and beverage. They recently made a deal with GELITA to commercialise the world's first animal-free biodesigned collagen for dietary supplements. These proteins can be designed to afford unique advantages because they do not need to simply be an exact replacement for pig collagen, leading to more tailored usage.

The proteins are created using precision fermentation and Geltor has a portfolio of over 200. To demonstrate the versatility of its method of production the company has performed stunts like making gummy bear (or elephant) sweets from mastodon DNA, an extinct precursor to elephants.

Geltor has raised total funds of US $114.3 million after a US $91.3 million Series B round.

*Further details of the company's activities are featured in Chapter 3, p.136.*

# MOTIF FOODWORKS
## (PREVIOUSLY MOTIF INGREDIENTS)

**Main Product:**  Specialised proteins, cheese
**Founded:**  2019, Massachusetts, USA
**Founders:**  Jonathan McIntyre
**Website:**  www.madewithmotif.com

Motif Foodworks is a maker of microbially produced functional ingredients for plant-based foods. They read the DNA of specific animal and plant proteins, which are key to a certain flavour or texture and write it into a microorganism, which will then express the target protein during fermentation. These are proteins which constitute only a small part of the formulation of plant-based meats but which have a big impact on the eating experience.

Motif FoodWorks' first proteins will be ready for launch in early 2021.

Their most recent funding round raised US $27.5 million and was led by General Atlantic, with participation from CPT Capital. This brings their total funding up to US $118.3 million.

*Mentioned in Chapter 2, p.58, and Chapter 3, p.118.*

# PURIS

**Main Product:**  Pea protein
**Founded:**  1985, Minnesota, USA
**Founders:**  Jerry Lorenzen
**Website:**  www.purisfoods.com

PURIS produces pea protein which it supplies to some of the largest plant-based food companies, such as Beyond Meat. It uses its patented non-GMO seeds to breed high-yield, disease-resistant crops which contribute to the health of the soil in which they are sown. In 2020, PURIS expects to have produced yellow field peas on 300,000 acres of land across 14 US states. They also grow other pulses in the US.

The company also owns a large soy protein isolate factory in Turtle Lake, Wisconsin, as part of its end-to-end food production system which it has termed its World Food System.

PURIS has raised a total of US $137.5 million. Although Cargill and LIVEKINDLY both hold stakes in PURIS, it remains essentially a family-owned company.

*Further details of this company are outlined in Chapter 3, p.88.*

## RIPPLE FOODS

**ripple**

Dairy-Free. As It Should Be

| | |
|---|---|
| **Main Product:** | Pea-based dairy alternative |
| **Founded:** | 2014, California, USA |
| **Founders:** | Adam Lowry |
| **Website:** | www.ripplefoods.com |

Ripple Foods produces dairy alternatives using pea protein. They claim that their products have health advantages over traditional dairy (twice the calcium and half the sugar, and just as much protein as cow's milk). They are free of lactose, nuts, gluten, and GMOs, and it is suitable for vegans. Ripple Foods has raised a total of US $145.6 million. Most recently, it raised US $15.1 million in June 2020 in a Series D round led by GV, a venture capital fund owned by Alphabet, the parent company of Google.

*Mentioned in Chapter 3, p.104.*

## THE PROTEIN BREWERY

| | |
|---|---|
| **Main Product:** | Fermotein |
| **Founded:** | 2020, Netherlands |
| **Founders:** | Wim de Laat |
| **Website:** | www.theproteinbrewery.nl |

In January 2020, The Protein Brewery was founded to commercialise protein products made by fermentation technologies developed by BioscienZ. Their Fermotein product is a pure ingredient of brewed fibrous protein (brewed with non-allergenic crops and fungi) which the food industry can use to add to their products. It is high in fibre and uniquely contains the highest concentration of essential amino acids in a meat-free protein. They are working on launching Fermotein from 2021 onwards. The company's finances are undisclosed.

*Mentioned in Chapter 3, p.84.*

# AIR FERMENTATION PROTEIN

## AIR PROTEIN

**Main Product:** Air Protein
**Founded:** 2019, Bay Area, California, USA
**Founders:** Lisa Dyson, John Reed
**Websites:** www.kiverdi.com, www.airprotein.com

Air Protein is a spin out from California-based Kiverdi, another carbontech company founded in 2008. Inspired by NASA experiments in the 1960s to create food out of a closed loop carbon cycle in space, co-founder Lisa Dyson sought to apply the same thinking to the carbon cycle on earth. She saw that carbon transformation could reduce carbon-based materials to their fundamental elements to be built up into a range of bio-based materials for the benefit of the planet.

They have developed Air Protein created from air, with an amino acid profile comparable to meat protein and which has the potential to make food in a matter of hours rather than months, immune from the vagaries of the weather. This protein can be reinforced with vitamins and will be used to make meatless burgers and protein-enriched cereals and beverages. This technology looks to be hugely scalable as well, with the advantages of super efficiency – it is estimated that the microorganisms used could produce 10,000 times more food per square kilometre, using 2,000 times less water, than soybeans.

Air Protein is looking to raise US $20 million to fund its production plant.

*Further details of the company's activities are featured in Chapter 3, p.113.*

## DEEP BRANCH BIOTECHNOLOGY

**Main Product:** Proton compound feed
**Founded:** 2018, Nottingham, UK
**Founders:** Peter Rowe, Robert Mansfield
**Website:** www.deepbranchbio.com

Proton is a bulk protein source for compound feed. It is created using recycled carbon dioxide which is converted into sustainable single cell protein (SCP), and it could completely or partially replace soy and fishmeal in feed. The amino acid profile of Proton is tailored to be optimal for both aquaculture and livestock nutrition.

They currently lead a project in Nottingham which recycles the emissions from Drax power station into sustainable feed. Deep Branch Biotechnology lead a consortium, REACT-FIRST, which will receive over £2 million in government funding to convert the power station's emissions into a sustainable alternative to soy and fishmeal. The REACT-FIRST project will work with Sainsbury's and the Scottish Aquaculture Innovation Centre to become a part of the fish and poultry supply chain.

## NOVONUTRIENTS

| | |
|---|---|
| **Main Product:** | Fish feed |
| **Founded:** | 2009, Bay Area, California, USA |
| **Founders:** | Brian Sefton |
| **Website:** | www.novonutrients.com |

NovoNutrients transforms industrial waste carbon dioxide into feed through industrial biotech, initially for the fast-growing aquaculture sector. Fishmeal is the biggest cost of fish farming, constituting a US $232 billion global industry. Brian Sefton has established and led several companies, including in software development and drug discovery. Their product, Novomeal, is made from bacteria proteins fed on carbon dioxide and incubated in bioreactors to create fishmeal.

Their seed funding is undisclosed but involved investors such as IndieBio and SOSV. They also received a US $300k grant from the US Department of Energy in July 2019.

## SOLAR FOODS

**SOLARFOODS**

| | |
|---|---|
| **Main Product:** | Solein |
| **Founded:** | 2017, Finland |
| **Founders:** | Pasi Vainikka, Juha-Pekka Pitkänen |
| **Website:** | www.solarfoods.fi |

Finnish company Solar Foods is using a proprietary organism with renewable electricity to convert the carbon dioxide in air and water into a high protein ingredient. 'Solein' can be used in pasta, yoghurt, bread and ready meals to increase the protein content. It could also help to buttress the plant-based food industry by providing Solein to companies such as Beyond and Impossible to meet their protein demand, which is forecast to increase by orders of magnitude. Further to this, Solar Foods believes it could play a vital role in the cultivated meat space, by developing an alternative for FBS by providing the sugars and amino acids required to grow muscle cells at scale.

It has been estimated to be 10 times more efficient than soy production in terms of land usage and it is hoped that Solein would be able to compete with soy on price within the next five years.

Solar recently closed a EUR 15 million Series A round led by Fazer Group, a Finnish confectionary and food company, with participation from Agronomics, CPT Capital and Lifeline Ventures. This takes its total funds raised to just over EUR 20 million.

*Further details of the company's activities are featured in Chapter 3, p.114.*

# PLANT-BASED COMPANIES AND BRANDS

## ALPHA FOODS

| | |
|---|---|
| **Main Product:** | Cheese, chicken, beef |
| **Founded:** | 2015, California, USA |
| **Founders:** | Cole Orobetz, Loren Wallis |
| **Website:** | www.alphaplantbased.com |

Alpha Foods makes plant-based foods, including pizzas, burritos, chick'n nuggets, and burgers. In February 2020, Alpha Foods successfully completed a US $28 million Series A fundraising round, led by AF Ventures. This takes total funding to US $40.4 million. Blue Horizon Ventures and New Crop Capital also participated in the latest round.

*Mentioned in Chapter 3, p.87.*

## ALCHEMY FOODTECH

ALCHEMY

| | |
|---|---|
| **Main Product:** | Alchemy Fibre |
| **Founded:** | 2015, Singapore |
| **Founders:** | Alan Phua, Verleen Goh |
| **Website:** | www.alchemyfoodtech.com |

Alchemy FoodTech creates everyday staples with Alchemy Fibre, which is a patented blend of plant-based ingredients and is a slowly digestible carbohydrate (SDC) high in dietary fibre. They believe that combating diabetes starts with the food industry and develop their novel active ingredients to fight the disease.

In January 2019, Alchemy Foodtech conducted a seed round which raised US $1.8 million.

## THE BETTER MEAT CO

**Main Product:** Plant protein
**Founded:** 2018, California, USA
**Founders:** Joanna Bromley, Paul Shapiro
**Website:** www.bettermeat.co

Better Meat is a B2B provider of plant protein to manufacturers of 'hybrid' products who are seeking to reduce meat costs by blending in plant protein. In June 2019, they announced a partnership to provide some of the plant protein for Perdue Farms' Chicken Plus range.

Better Meat has raised a total of US $9.7 million. This includes a US $8.1 million seed round, led by American VC funds Greenlight Capital and Green Circle Foodtech Ventures, a division of Green Circle Capital. Other participants in the round were Hong Kong-based Lever VC and American sausage maker Johnsonville.

## BEYOND MEAT

**Main Product:** Beef, Pork, Chicken
**Founded:** 2009, California, USA
**Founders:** Ethan Brown
**Website:** www.beyondmeat.com

Beyond Meat is available widely in restaurants and supermarkets worldwide. As of June 27, 2020, Beyond Meat's portfolio of plant-based meat was available in approximately 112,000 retail and foodservice outlets in 85 countries. Beyond Meat's plant-based products were first made available across the US in 2012 and have since expanded to major global supermarkets. They are made from simple, plant-based ingredients such as peas, mung beans, rice, coconut oil, potatoes and a range of plant-based vitamins and minerals. Beyond Meat is the trailblazer in the alternative protein industry, having set the standard for subsequent companies including Impossible.

Beyond Meat's IPO took place on 2nd May 2019 with an IPO price of $25/share which valued the company at approximately US $1.5 billion. The market cap as of late October 2020 stood at over US$ 10 billion. In September 2020, the company signed a deal to open two production facilities near Shanghai to make the most of the rapidly-growing Chinese market. Shares did plunge as much as 22 per cent in November 2020 after reporting a poor Q3 and with confusion surrounding the extent of Beyond Meat's involvement in McDonald's new McPlant burger.

*Further details of their activities are outlined in Chapter 2, p.46, and Chapter 3, p.77.*

# PERDUE/CHICKEN PLUS

**Main Product:** Chicken
**Founded:** 2019, Maryland, USA
**Website:** www.perdue.com/products/perdue-chicken-plus

Chicken Plus is a Perdue brand selling blended vegetable and chicken products such as nuggets, tenders and patties. Chicken Plus contains cauliflower, chickpeas and other plant protein blended with antibiotic-free chicken meat to encourage children to consume their recommended vegetable content without turning their noses up. Similarly to Raised & Rooted, it is an interesting experiment in trying to capture the flexitarian market.

Perdue is the top seller of fresh chicken in the US, with products focussed on containing zero antibiotics as well as being organically-raised. With their programmes verified by the USDA, they are setting new standards for animal care and antibiotic-free poultry farming.

# CLIMAX FOODS

**CLIMAX FOODS**

**Main Product:** Plant-based cheese
**Founded:** 2019, Bay Area, California, USA
**Founders:** Oliver Zahn
**Website:** www.climaxfoods.com

Dr Zahn's credentials are impressive and include roles as the head of data science at Google, senior data analyst at SpaceX, and lead data scientist at Impossible Foods.

Climax Foods' mission is to reverse engineer foods derived from animal protein and build them back up from plants. They are starting with cheese, in an effort to replace cows. They are using computer modelling to predict which combinations of proteins, carbohydrates, and fats will correspond to specific flavour, scent, and texture profiles. In terms of their business model, they have yet to work out whether they will operate as an ingredients supplier, a consumer-facing company, or whether they will license their technology out to others.

In September 2020 Climax Foods raised a seed round of US $7.5 million from investors including Canaccord Genuity Group and S2G Ventures.

## DARING FOODS

**Main Product:** Chicken
**Founded:** 2019, New York, USA
**Founders:** Eliott Kessas, Ross Mackay
**Website:** www.daringfoods.com

Daring Foods makes plant-based chicken. They launched in January 2019 with products containing only five ingredients, all of which are non-GMO.

In early 2020 Rastelli Foods Group, an American food company supplying hotels, restaurants and retail markets, invested US $10 million in Daring Foods, combining cash with infrastructure and distribution support. Rastelli, with annual global revenues of US $450 million, will be the exclusive national distributor of Daring Foods products.

## IMPOSSIBLE FOODS

**Main Product:** Beef and pork
**Founded:** 2011, Bay Area, California
**Founders:** Pat Brown
**Website:** www.impossiblefoods.com

Impossible Foods is the maker of the Impossible Burger, one of the first 'bleeding' burgers. Having already been sold by the likes of Burger King, the Impossible Burger became available at retail stores in the USA for the first time in October 2019. Their plant-based burger, which contains no cholesterol, received kosher certification in May 2018 and halal certification in December 2018. Following the criticism of both Impossible and Beyond products over their high sodium and saturated fat content, Impossible launched its Impossible Burger 2.0 in January 2019, which contained 30 per cent less sodium and 40 per cent less saturated fat, and was also gluten-free.

They have raised US $687.5 million over 11 funding rounds, including US $300 million from their most recent Series E raise. Impossible has received notable investment from Google Ventures, UBS, Khosla Ventures, Viking Global, Li Ka-shing's Horizons Ventures, and Bill Gates. There has been speculation as to an IPO in 2020 although no official information has been made available.

*Further details of their activities are outlined in Chapter 2, p.46, and Chapter 3, p.79.*

## CONAGRA BRANDS/GARDEIN

**Main Product:** Plant-based food
**Founded:** 2003, Canada
**Founders:** Yves Potvin
**Website:** www.gardein.com

Gardein makes a variety of plant-based meat alternatives. The company was responsible for introducing several major innovations to the field, including twin-screw extrusion to allow plant fibres to be aligned.

In November 2014, Gardein was bought by Pinnacle Foods for $154 million; in October 2018 Pinnacle Foods was bought by Conagra Brands at a valuation of around $10.9 billion.

*Further details of their activities are outlined in Chapter 2, p.48.*

## GOOD CATCH

**Main Product:** Plant-based tuna
**Founded:** 2016, Pennsylvania, USA
**Founders:** Chad Sarno, Eric Schnell
**Website:** goodcatchfoods.com

Good Catch produces tuna alternatives using legumes such as pea, chickpea, soy fava, and lentils, plus seaweed powder for additional protein. Its products are low in fat and high in protein and omega oils. It is a brand of Gathered Foods. It is currently distributed in select supermarkets along the East Coast of the US, but wider expansion is expected through 2021 as a result of a recent JV agreement between Gathered Foods and Bumble Bee Foods, a large seafood company. Good Catch has raised a total of US $50.7 million, including a Series C round in January 2020 that netted US $32 million.

*Further details of their activities are outlined in Chapter 3, p.83.*

## GREEN MONDAY

**Main Product:** Plant-based group
**Founded:** 2012, Hong Kong
**Founders:** David Yeung, Francis Ngai
**Website:** www.greenmonday.org

Green Monday is a hybrid organisation based in Hong Kong and centred around a theme of sustainability and climate change. It has a social venture ('Green Monday Foundation') best known for its campaign to popularise a single plant-based meal on Mondays (hence the name) in order to reduce meat consumption. It also has a venture capital branch with investments in various companies in the green food industry, such as TurtleTree Labs and Perfect Day. Through its subsidiary OmniEat, it has a popular brand called OmniPork which sells plant-based alternatives to pork-based Asian foods, such as dumplings and stir fry.

Green Monday is privately-held and recently announced it had raised US $70 million in a round led by TPG's The Rise Fund and Swire Pacific Limited. Green Monday has recently placed its Omni products into about 400 branches of McDonald's in Hong Kong and Macau.

*Mentioned in Chapter 3, p.82.*

## KELLOGG'S/INCOGMEATO

**Main Product:** Chicken nuggets, sausages, ground beef
**Founded:** 2019, Michigan, USA
**Website:** www.morningstarfarms.com/incogmeato/home.html

Incogmeato is a sub-brand of MorningStar Farms, a division of Kellogg's. They sell 100 per cent plant-based bratwurst, Italian sausage, and frozen chicken nuggets. They have also developed a burger which is meant to 'bleed' like the Impossible Burger but without the GMO haem Impossible use to achieve the effect. They are a new addition to the Kellogg Company's plant-based portfolio. Kellogg's had a market capitalisation of US $ 23.7bn in August 2020.

*Mentioned in Chapter 3, p.97.*

## MAPLE LEAF FOODS/LIGHTLIFE

**Main Product:** Beef, pork, chicken
**Founded:** 1979, Massachusetts, USA
**Website:** www.lightlife.com

Lightlife produces plant-based meat substitutes, such as burgers, hot dogs, mince, and chicken. In August 2018, Lightlife products became available in Canada – the company's first foray outside the USA. In 2017, Lightlife was bought by Maple Leaf Foods for US $140 million. Previously it had been owned by Brynwood Partners (2013-2017), and Conagra Brands (2000-2013).

# THE LIVEKINDLY COLLECTIVE

LIVEKINDLY

**Main Product:** Plant-based brands
**Founded:** 2020, California, USA and Europe
**Founders:** Kees Kruythoff, Roger Lienhard
**Website:** www.livekindly.co/our-company/

The LIVEKINDLY Collective (TLKC) manages a portfolio of geographically dispersed plant-based food brands. In South Africa, LIVEKINDLY operates The Fry Family Food Company; in Germany, LikeMeat; and recently the company acquired five-year old Oumph!, a Swedish company which sells products in the UK and the Nordics. This latest acquisition is part of LIVEKINDLY's strategy of assembling a collection of heritage and startup vegan brands, to create a global yet local ecosystem of plant-based food companies. They also own the lifestyle brand LIVEKINDLY.

In March 2020, LIVEKINDLY disclosed the successful completion of a US $200 million founders' funding round. The round was led by Blue Horizon Ventures, which Roger Lienhard co-founded.

*Further information about the LIVEKINDLY Collective can be found in Chapter 3.*

## THE FRY FAMILY FOOD COMPANY

**Main Product:** Beef, chicken
**Founded:** 1991, South Africa
**Founders:** Wally Fry, Debbie Fry
**Website:** www.fryfamilyfood.com

The Fry Family Food Company makes plant-based meat substitutes such as burgers, nuggets, mince, etc. Its products, unpatented and GMO-free, are sold in over 30 countries. Each year they look at their turnover to evaluate how many animal lives were saved by people choosing their products instead of animal meat. In 2019 that number was 647,737 chickens, 11,354 cows, 10,055 pigs and three million prawns.

The Fry Family Food Company is owned by LIVEKINDLY.

## LIKEMEAT

| | |
|---|---|
| **Main Product:** | Pork, chicken, beef |
| **Founded:** | 2013, Germany |
| **Founders:** | Timo Recker |
| **Website:** | www.likemeat.com |

LikeMeat specialises in vegan meat alternatives such as plant-based bratwursts, escalopes, pulled pork, chicken pieces, and mince. LikeMeat products are distributed around the EU and USA in the retail and service industry market.

LIVEKINDLY have just acquired a majority stake (51 per cent) in LikeMeat, which signifies a big step in LIVEKINDLY assembling a strong portfolio of plant-based meat companies to exploit the growing market.

## OUMPH!

| | |
|---|---|
| **Main Product:** | Pork, beef |
| **Founded:** | 2014, Sweden |
| **Founders:** | Anders Wallerman, Anna-Kajsa Lidell |
| **Website:** | www.oumph.uk |

Oumph! produces plant-based meat substitutes, such as meatballs, mince, sausages. Since 2019, Oumph! has been distributed in the UK (through Asda and Bella Italia), building on its success in Scandinavia.

Oumph! was originally a brand set up by Food for Progress, a Swedish initiative to introduce sustainability to the global food supply. In June 2020, Oumph! was bought by LIVEKINDLY for an undisclosed sum.

## MEATI

| | |
|---|---|
| **Main Product:** | Fungal-based meat alternatives |
| **Founded:** | 2015, Colorado, USA |
| **Founders:** | Tyler Huggins, Justin Whiteley |
| **Website:** | www.meati.com |

Meati makes fungi-based alternatives to meat, particularly steak and chicken substitutes. Mycelium is the main ingredient.

In September 2020, Meati raised US $28.2 million in Series A funding from 44 investors.

*Mentioned in Chapter 3, p.159.*

## THE MEATLESS FARM

**MEATLESS FARM**
~LOVINGLY MADE FROM PLANTS~

| | |
|---|---|
| **Main Product:** | Plant-based food |
| **Founded:** | 2016, Leeds, United Kingdom |
| **Founders:** | Morten Toft Bech |
| **Website:** | www.meatlessfarm.com |

The Meatless Farm produces plant-based meat alternatives such as hamburgers and mince. They primarily operate in the UK, but in June 2019 they announced a deal with Whole Foods to stock their products in shops across the USA.

In September 2020, Meatless Farm announced the successful completion of a US $31 million funding round, following a previous round of US $17 million. The capital for both rounds was largely provided by private and family office investors. In 2019, Channel 4 invested a 'seven-figure' sum through its Commercial Growth Fund, exchanging equity for cash and advertising airtime. Beyond Investing and Stray Dog Capital have also participated.

*Further details of their activities are outlined in Chapter 3, p.80.*

## MONDE NISSIN/QUORN

Monde Nissin

Quorn

| | |
|---|---|
| **Main Product:** | Plant-based food |
| **Founded:** | 1998, Stokesley, United Kingdom |
| **Website:** | www.quorn.co.uk |

Quorn makes vegetarian foods, using mycoprotein as the main ingredient. The company enjoys strong brand recognition, especially in the UK, where its vegan sausage rolls (released through Greggs) became a phenomenon in 2019. The company is believed to be highly profitable and expanding production, although it faces increasingly stiff competition in the plant-based meat alternative market from companies like Impossible Foods and Beyond Meat.

In 2015, Quorn was acquired by Monde Nissin at a valuation of £550 million and further details are outlined in Chapter 2.

## NEW WAVE FOODS

**Main Product:** Shrimp
**Founded:** 2015, Bay Area, California, USA
**Founders:** Dominique Barnes, Michelle Wolf
**Website:** www.newwavefoods.com

New Wave Foods makes plant-based shrimp substitutes, using seaweed and other natural ingredients. They trade in Scotland as Shore Seaweed and sell seaweed crisps, pesto and other snacks, produced at a factory in Wick, Scotland.

They have raised a total of US $2.3 million across eight funding rounds (including four seed rounds from 2015 to 2018). Most recently, in June 2020, they raised £1.7 million from the Scottish Investment Bank. In September 2019, they received an investment from Tyson Foods.

*Mentioned in Chapter 2, p.53.*

## NO EVIL FOODS

# NO EVIL
FOODS

**Main Product:** Pork, chicken
**Founders:** Mike Woliansky, Sadrah Schadel
**Founded:** 2014, North Carolina, USA
**Website:** www.noevilfoods.com

No Evil Foods sells plant-based meat substitutes, such as 'El Capitan' chorizo, 'Comrade Cluck' chicken, and 'Pit Boss' BBQ pulled pork. They operate in 25 states in the US. Their financial data is undisclosed.

## NOVAMEAT

# NOVA
MEAT

**Main Product:** Beef, pork, chicken
**Founded:** 2018, Spain
**Founders:** Giuseppe Scionti
**Website:** www.novameat.com

Novameat claims to be able to replicate the texture of meat through 3D printing. They will provide the machinery to other food-manufacturers under licensing agreements. As of January 2020, their final product has not yet been publicly tasted.

Novameat raised a seed round of undisclosed size in September 2019, with New Crop Capital participating.

# NOQUO

**Main Product:** Plant-based cheese
**Founded:** 2019, Sweden
**Founders:** Anja Leissner, Sorosh Tavakoli
**Website:** www.noquofoods.com

Noquo is developing cheese from plant derived ingredients. They are beginning with cheese because they have not seen any good plant-based alternatives on the market and believe they understand the structure of casein and how best to mimic it. Their Holy Grail is to produce a cheese that melts just like the conventional alternative.

Noquo has raised a seed of US $3.6 million from Northzone and Inventure.

*Further details of their activities are outlined in Chapter 3, p.109.*

# NOTCO

**Main Product:** Plant-based food
**Founded:** 2015, Chile
**Founders:** Karim Pichara, Matías Muchnick, Pablo Zamora
**Website:** www.notco.com

NotCo creates plant-based alternatives to animal-based food. Their three main ranges are Not Milk, Not Mayo, and Not Icecream [*sic*]. They use an AI platform called 'Giuseppe' to determine combinations of plant ingredients that give products that resemble the organoleptic characteristics of the animal-based equivalent. They operate primarily in Latin America.

In September 2020, they successfully raised US $85 million in Series C funds for a US expansion. This valued the company at US $300 million.

*Further details of their activities are outlined in Chapter 3, p.104.*

## OATLY

**Main Product:** Oat-based milk products
**Founded:** 1990, Sweden
**Founders:** Rickard Öste, Bjorn Öste
**Website:** www.oatly.com

Oatly uses oats to make a vegetarian substitute for milk and other dairy products (yoghurt, chocolate milk, etc). They sold over US $200 million worth of their products in 2019, which has been forecast to double for 2020.

In July 2020, Oatly raised US $200 million in new funds, taking their estimated total fundraising to US $241 million. Blackstone led the latest financing round, which valued the company at around US $2 billion. This round also attracted a host of celebrities such as Jay-Z, Oprah Winfrey, and Natalie Portman. The cash raised will be used to build more factories in the US and the UK where sales growth has been strongest. There are rumours that Oatly will seek a listing, mostly likely in Europe, and that its value on IPO could be close to EUR 5 billion.

*Further details of their activities are outlined in Chapter 3, p.106.*

## PARABEL

**Main Product:** Water lentil-based drinks
**Founded:** 2010, Florida, USA
**Founders:** Anthony Tiarks, Peter Sherlock
**Website:** www.parabel.com

Parabel uses water lentils to make Lentein (high-protein powder) and derivative products, such as an electrolyte drink, a milk substitute, and a 'superfood' protein shake. Water lentils are one of the few plants to contain vitamin B12.

Parabel's financial data is not readily available.

*Mentioned in Chapter 2, p.55.*

## PLANTED

# planted.

**Main Product:** Chicken
**Founded:** 2019, Switzerland
**Founders:** Christoph Jenny, Pascal Bieri, Eric Stirnemann, Lukas Boni
**Website:** www.planted.ch

Planted creates plant-based meats made from pea protein for food service in central Europe. Their debut product is *planted.chicken*, which is developed to be gluten and soy-free and low in cholesterol and carbohydrates while containing all the best plant protein and dietary fibres.

Planted has raised 7 million Swiss francs (around US $7.64 million) to scale up production from investors including Blue Horizon Corporation, Good Seed Ventures, Hiltl AG, Mica Ventures, Joyance Partners, and the ETH Foundation.

## TYSON FOODS/RAISED & ROOTED

**Main Product:** Chicken
**Founded:** 2019, Arkansas, USA
**Founders:** John Tyson
**Website:** www.raisedandrooted.com

Raised & Rooted, a Tyson Foods brand, sells plant-based chicken nuggets and plant-based beef burgers in over 7,000 stores in the US. They are also experimenting with blended meat, which is replacing part of the beef with plant protein as a way to cut down on animal products within foods such as burgers. In comparison to Beyond and Impossible products, Tyson's blended patties have 40 per cent fewer calories and contain 60 per cent less saturated fat. This will be an interesting experiment to see what appeals most to the increasing numbers of flexitarians in the consumer market.

Tyson Foods is the second-largest processor and distributor of meat products in the world. It has invested in a number of cultured meat companies, including Memphis Meat and Future Meat Technologies, while also acquiring a meaningful stake in Beyond Meat. That large traditional meat companies like Tyson are moving into this space to diversify and capitalise on these new opportunities, shows the general direction of travel for global meat production towards cultivated products.

*Mentioned in Chapter 3, p.98.*

# MOO'S LAW

## REBBL

**Main Product:** Herbal drinks
**Founded:**     2012, Bay Area, California, USA
**Founders:**    David Batstone
**Website:**     www.rebbl.co

REBBL (acronym: roots, extracts, berries, bark, and leaves) sells boxes of 'elixirs' containing drinks bottles with herbs and proteins. Most elixirs are vegan, but some contain honey. Their marketing centres on health benefits ('balancing, revitalizing, vitality, energizing').

The company has raised a total of US $34 million. Most recently CAVU Venture Partners led a US $20 million round in May 2018.

*Mentioned in Chapter 3, p.104.*

## REBELLYOUS FOODS

**Main Product:** Chicken nuggets
**Founded:**     2017, Washington, USA
**Founders:**    Christie Lagally
**Website:**     www.rebellyous.com

Rebellyous Foods are developing low cost plant-based meat, starting with a chicken nugget for K-12 schools as well as patties and chicken strips. Christie Lagally chose chicken meat because it constitutes almost half of the US meat industry by volume and has thus far received less attention than beef alternatives in the sector.

Uniquely, Rebellyous Foods is determined to increase efficiency and scale by designing their own equipment rather than using the off-the-shelf equipment of their competitors, which Christie believes is often ill-adapted from the conventional meat industry. Instead of using extruders they use a faster, more energy efficient 'mix and form' production method.

In early 2020 Rebellyous closed a US $6 million Series A funding round co-led by Clear Current Capital, Fifty Years and Liquid 2 Ventures. Around US $3 million of this money raised will go towards R&D on equipment to increase the speed and efficiency and reduce costs of plant-based meat production. Agronomics is also an investor in this company.

*Further details of their activities are outlined in Chapter 3, p.91.*

# REBEL KITCHEN

**Main Product:** Plant-based drinks
**Founded:** 2014, London, UK
**Founders:** Ben Arbib, Tamara Arbib
**Websites:** www.rebel-kitchen.com, www.nurturebrands.com

Rebel Kitchen makes plant-based drinks. Its three product ranges are: Mylk (dairy-free milk), Mylkshake (Mylk plus flavouring, e.g. chocolate), and Coconut Water. Its products are distributed online through Amazon and Ocado and through supermarkets such as Waitrose and Whole Foods.

In 2019, the company merged with Nurture Brands, which has two other plant-based snack companies. Their financial data is undisclosed.

*Mentioned in Chapter 3, p.104.*

# REDEFINE MEAT

**Min Product:** Steak
**Founded:** 2018, Israel
**Founders:** Eshchar Ben-Shitrit
**Website:** www.redefinemeat.com

Redefine Meat combines proprietary 3D modelling with plant-based food formulations to produce vegan meat. Their 3D printer can create a complex matrix meat efficiently and at scale. They are hoping to have their alternative-meat 3D printer tested at select restaurants this year and on the market in 2021.

Redefine has raised over US $6 Million including recent support from CPT Capital, PHW Group, and Hanaco Ventures.

*Mentioned in Chapter 3, p.99.*

# SIMULATE

**Main Product:** Chicken
**Founded:** 2018, New York, USA
**Founders:** Ben Pasternak
**Website:** www.eatnuggs.com

# MOO'S LAW

SIMULATE is the parent company of NUGGS, which makes plant-based chicken nuggets from texturised pea protein. The company claims their product contains twice the protein with 20 per cent fewer calories compared to conventional chicken, as well containing zero cholesterol. At 15, its founder, Ben Pasternak, was the youngest person to receive backing from Silicon Valley venture capitalists, after creating the Monkey app, which he sold in late 2017. Pasternak, now 21, has moved into the plant-based meat sector to exploit its rapid growth.

McCain Foods, an industry giant, led a US $7 million funding round for NUGGS in 2019. Other notable investors include Rainfall Ventures, Greylock Discovery Fund, Maven Ventures and NOMO Ventures, as well as Bob Pittman, the founder of MTV, and John Maloney, the former president of Tumblr. They are currently supplying directly to the consumer under the tagline 'kills you slower', promoting the healthier profile of their product.

SIMULATE raised another US $4.1 million in a round led by Lerer Hippeau in July 2020. They intend to launch a DOGGs line of hot dog replacements and chicken patties before the end of the year.

*Mentioned in Chapter 3, p.93.*

## THIS 🥩 🥩 🥩

**Main Product:** Chicken and pork
**Founded:** 2018, London, UK
**Founders:** Andy Shovel, Pete Sharman
**Website:** www.this.co

THIS is a startup making plant-based substitutes for chicken and pork, drawing their protein mostly from pea and soy. PETA awarded THIS prizes for 'Best Vegan Bacon' and 'Best Vegan Chicken' in 2019. They had an annualised revenue of £3 million within six months of launching and their products appear in over 1200 stores and chains around the UK.

They have raised US $13.2 million to date. They raised £4.7 million in a January 2020 seed round from Backed, Five Seasons Ventures, Idinvest Partners, Seedcamp and Manta Ray Ventures, with a further £4 million raised in August 2020 via equity crowdfunding. THIS's campaign on the crowdfunding platform Seedrs was the fastest ever to reach £1.5 million: the campaign raised over £3.6 million in total.

# VEESTRO

**Main Product:** Delivering prepared vegan meals
**Founded:** 2012, California, USA
**Founders:** Mark Fachler, Monica Klausner
**Website:** www.veestro.com

LA-based Veestro offers ready-to-eat vegan food delivered to customers' doorsteps. Their 100 per cent plant-based meals cost between US $9.90 and US $11.70 per meal depending on whether customers order in a package of 10 or 20 meals. They saw a 30 per cent increase in sales in March 2020, when the Covid-19 pandemic lockdown was announced.

Veestro have raised US $3.6 million over three funding rounds, the latest being led by Blue Horizon Ventures in April 2020, which raised US $1.7 million.

*Mentioned in Chapter 3, p.87.*

# THE VEGETARIAN BUTCHER

**Main Product:** Pork, beef
**Founded:** 2010, Netherlands
**Founders:** Jaap Korteweg
**Website:** www.thevegetarianbutcher.com

The Vegetarian Butcher produces various plant-based alternatives to meat including chicken, meatballs, beef burgers and tuna. In November 2019, the company was contracted by Burger King to provide vegetarian burgers to its European outlets.

The Vegetarian Butcher was acquired by Unilever in December 2018 for an undisclosed amount.

*Further details of their activities are outlined in Chapter 2, p.98.*

# ZHENMEAT

**Main Product:** Pork, beef
**Founded:** 2017, China
**Founders:** Vince Lu Zhongming
**Website:** www.zhenmeat.com

Marketing itself as 'the Chinese answer to Impossible Foods', Zhenmeat aims to popularise plant- and fungus-based alternatives to Chinese dishes that contain meat. It is the only mainland alternative meat manufacturer to use haem and therefore has an advantage in taste. They sell their products online and target restaurants and supermarkets. Their main competitors in Asian-style meat substitutes are Hero Protein and Green Monday's OmniPork, both from Hong Kong, and Phuture Foods from Malaysia.

By September 2019, it had raised RMB 5 million (*c. £572k*) from mainland investors. In July 2020, Zhenmeat raised US $140k in seed funding from Big Idea Ventures, an American VC.

*Mentioned in Chapter 3, p.82.*

# OTHER

## ALIFE FOODS

**Main Product:** Refining and branding
**Founded:** 2019, Germany
**Founders:** Steffen Sonnenberg, Dat Tran, Joe Natoli, Bernd Boeck
**Website:** www.alifefoods.de

Alife Foods are working on refining and branding cultivated meat. They cover the second part of the supply chain, as a middleman between producers of cultivated meat, industry organisations and food and retail consumers, with the aim of offering slaughter-free meat options to all consumers. The company's financial information is undisclosed.

## GLYCOSYN

**Main Product:** Human milk oligosaccharides
**Founded:** 2003, Massachusetts, USA
**Founders:** David Newburg, Ardythe Morrow, Guillermo Ruiz-Palacios
**Website:** www.glycosyn.com

GlycoSyn specialises in contract discovery, development and GMP manufacture of complex pharmaceutical ingredients. In 2018 they partnered with Ginkgo Bioworks in a US $14 million deal to produce human milk oligosaccharides (hMOS) for products that will promote a healthy gut.

GlycoSyn's financial data is undisclosed.

# TROPIC BIOSCIENCES

**Main Product:** Tropical crops
**Founded:** 2016, Norwich, UK
**Founders:** Eyal Maori, Gilad Gershon, Ofir Meir
**Website:** www.tropicbioscience.com

Tropic Biosciences is developing enhanced-performance crops, mostly grown in the tropics. It has a technology platform, GEiGS (Gene Editing induced Gene Silencing) which is used to promote disease resistance in key crops such as rice, the staple food for about half of the world's population, and bananas, the most commonly eaten fruit worldwide. Tropic is using CRISPR gene editing techniques to combat the Panama Disease fungus threatening the global supply of the Cavendish banana, which accounts for 99 per cent of all bananas exported worldwide. Tropic is also working on genetically combating 'rice blast', a serious disease affecting one of the world's main staple foods.

In 2020, Tropic Biosciences raised US $28.5 million in a Series B round led by Temasek, bringing the company's total funding to US $40 million. Other investors in the company include Agronomics, Skyviews Life Science, Sumitomo Corporation, and Five Seasons Ventures.

*Details of the company's activities are featured in Chapter 3, p.160.*

# CHICKPEA PROTEIN

## CHICKP

**CHiCK.P**

**Main Product:** Chickpea protein
**Founded:** 2016, Israel
**Founders:** Ram Reifen
**Website:** www.chickp-protein.com

ChickP are developing plant proteins derived from chickpea isolates, namely S930 and G910, which can be used in plant-based meats and dairy at an industrial scale. They are able to extract 90 per cent pure protein from a chickpea seed. They have turned their attention to the alternative dairy industry due to the fact that plant-based milk alternatives containing ChickP have been demonstrated to better mimic cow's milk and yoghurt in taste, texture, and nutritional value. In addition, co-products generated during the protein's production process are the ChickP Starch and Fibers, which are currently in R&D stages.

Ram Reifen, ChickP's founder, is a gastroenterologist and professor of human nutrition at Hebrew University in Jerusalem and has studied the use of chickpea in fighting malnutrition in children and mothers.

ChickP received its Series A funding from a group of investors in Singapore, and is now working to expand its business development and increase sales.

*Mentioned in Chapter 2, p.54.*

## INNOVOPRO

**Main Product:** Chickpea protein
**Founded:** 2013, Israel
**Founders:** Dr. Ascher Shmulewitz
**Website:** www.innovopro.com

Innovopro is using chickpeas to produce a non-allergenic protein for 'free from' foods. In mid-2020 Migros, a Swiss retailer, launched a line of dairy-free yoghurts made with InnovoPro's chickpea protein CP Pro 70, offering a gluten- and lactose-free alternative to dairy yoghurts with no compromise on taste. InnovoPro claims to be the first company in the world to produce a 70 per cent chickpea protein concentrate that is available to consumers.

They have conducted a US $15 million Series B with investors including Jerusalem Venture Partners, Custos Privatstiftung, Wolfgang Leitner, CEO of Andritz AG, and CPT Capital. In total, Innovopro has raised US $20.8 million.

*Mentioned in Chapter 2, p.54.*

# PLANT TISSUE CULTURE/OTHER

## CHI BOTANIC

**Main Product:** Plant tissue culture
**Founded:** 2017, Florida, USA
**Founders:** Jonathan Meuser, Robert Jinkerson
**Website:** www.chibotanic.com

Chi Botanic grows plant cultures to supply industries which require small portions of a plant or chemicals derived from them. They call it 'nanoponics' as they are able to grow their plant cell cultures efficiently under controlled conditions and independent of geography, reducing the cost to the environment and, ultimately, the consumer.

Chi Botanic has raised a total of US $1.2 million in funding over two rounds. Their latest funding of US $950k was raised in March 2020 via convertible notes from SOSV and Better Ventures.

# MICHROMA

| | |
|---|---|
| **Main Product:** | Dyes |
| **Founded:** | 2019, Bay Area, California, USA |
| **Founders:** | Ricky Cassini, Mauricio Braia |
| **Website:** | www.michroma.co |

Michroma uses fermentation to create a range of natural colourings for a variety of industries, with a goal to disrupt the entire food industry by replacing all food colourants, particularly cochineal red 80. They already have a way to produce red, orange, and yellow and are now looking to scale up their process while developing methods to create blue and green. This has applications in colouration for plant-based foods.

The company moved from Argentina to San Francisco in September 2019 and secured two investments from GridX and IndieBio totalling US $500k.

# SHIRU

| | |
|---|---|
| **Main Product:** | Proteins |
| **Founded:** | 2019, Bay Area California, USA |
| **Founders:** | Jasmin Hume |
| **Website:** | www.shiru.com |

Shiru uses machine learning and precision biology to identify and create ideal food proteins. Jasmin Hume was formerly the director of food chemistry at JUST before moving to focus on creating proteins for the food industry which exhibit specific qualities, such as solubility, emulsification and binding, and foam stability. As such they are not creating replacements for foods, but rather ingredients with specific applications due to their functionality. They will own the IP for their catalogue of proprietary ingredients.

Shiru completed a US $3.5 million seed round in 2019 led by venture capital firm Lux Capital. They are planning to use this to further build up their technical team.

## UPM BIOMEDICALS

**Main Product:** Wood-based scaffolding
**Founded:** 1996, Finland
**Website:** www.upmbiomedicals.com

UPM Biomedicals sell innovative and sustainable wood-based solutions for biomedical applications. They use renewable wood from sustainably managed forests to create their products such as GrowDex, which is a nanofibrillar cellulose hydrogel for 3D cell culturing, free from any animal-derived material. Their latest innovation, FibDex, is an advanced one-time application wound dressing designed for efficient healing and patient comfort, which provides improved vascularity and skin comfort.

In January 2020 UPM announced that it will invest EUR 550 million in a biorefinery with an annual capacity of 220 kilotonnes, to convert solid wood into biochemicals bio-monoethylene glycol (BioMEG), bio-monopropylene glycol (BioMPG), and lignin-based renewable functional fillers. The facility is to be up and running by the end of 2022.

UPM Biomedicals is part of UPM, a public company with a market cap of around EUR 14 billion.

# CELL CULTURED PET FOOD

## BOND PET FOODS

**Main Product:** Chicken
**Founded:** 2015, Colorado, USA
**Founders:** Rich Kelleman, Pernilla Turner Audibert
**Website:** www.bondpets.com

Bond Pet Foods develops vegan dog treat bars and produces animal protein through precision fermentation for cruelty-free pet food. They are aiming for an initial production launch of 20,000 dog treat bars in Q2 2020 and are anticipating a demonstration of cultured chicken dog food in Q3 2020. They have no direct competitors working on cultured chicken proteins for dog food.

The US pet food market is expected to reach US $30 billion in 2022 of which dog food accounts for 70 per cent.

At the end of 2019, Bond announced completion of its seed funding round, raising a fairly small US $1.2 million. This was led by Lever VC, a leader in investment in alternative proteins, and joined by Agronomics, KBW Ventures and Andante Asset Management.

*Mentioned in Chapter 3, p.157.*

## BECAUSE ANIMALS

| | |
|---|---|
| **Main Product:** | Mouse |
| **Founded:** | 2016, Pennsylvania, USA |
| **Founders:** | Shannon Falconer, Joshua Errett |
| **Website:** | www.becauseanimals.com |

Because Animals is a startup working on cultivated meat pet food. They are hoping to bring cultured meat products to market by 2021. Because Animals also have some supplements and dog treats.

In November 2019 they completed a US $2.5 million seed from backers including Keen Growth Capital, Draper Associates and SOSV.

## HOWND

| | |
|---|---|
| **Main Product:** | Pet care, dog treats |
| **Founded:** | 2013, Borehamwood, UK |
| **Founders:** | Jo Amit, Mark Hirschel |
| **Website:** | www.dogslovehownd.com |

HOWND creates ethical, vegan pet products, including hemp treats for dogs and grooming products, such as shampoo and styling spray. They have received certifications from the Ethical Company Organisation, the NatureWatch Organisation, and Cruelty-Free International. The company was founded as Butch and Bess in 2013, and rebranded to HOWND in 2015.

HOWND has raised £192k through a single round of crowdfunding (329 investors) at a pre-money valuation of £2.2 million.

*Mentioned in Chapter 3, p.157.*

## WILD EARTH

**Main Product:** Dog food
**Founded:** 2017, Bay Area, California, USA
**Founders:** Abril Estrada, Kristin Wuhrman,
Ron Shigeta, Ryan Bethencourt
**Website:** www.wildearth.com

Wild Earth is beginning with Koji-based protein to create dog food which can be selectively fermented to exhibit high levels of vitamin A and is then baked into dog biscuits. They are also looking to cultivate mouse meat to be sold in cat food. The global pet food market in 2018 was worth US $91 billion and Wild Earth has attracted a number of high-profile investors. Their most recent funding round was led by VegInvest, raising US $11 million. Combined with other investors, including Mars Petcare, Felicis Ventures, and Peter Thiel's Founders Fund, they have raised a total of US $16 million thus far.

*Further details of the company's activities are featured in Chapter 3, p.156.*

# BIOFABRICS

## ANANAS ANAM
## (PIÑATEX)

**Main Product:** Plant-based leather alternative
**Founded:** 2013, London, UK
**Founders:** Carmen Hijosa
**Website:** www.ananas-anam.com

Ananas Anam collects waste pineapple leaves from the harvest in the Philippines, extracts the fibres, and processes them to form a leather-like material called Piñatex. The material has been used by several well known brands, including H&M and Hugo Boss.

Their total fundraising data is not available, but they most recently received US $1.49 million from a single angel investor in October 2019. Their total annual revenue for 2019 was US $1.57 million.

*Mentioned in Chapter 2, p.53.*

# BOLT THREADS

**Main Product:** Mycelium materials
**Founded:** 2009, Bay Area, California, USA
**Founders:** Dan Widmaier, David Breslauer, Ethan Mirsky
**Website:** www.boltthreads.com

Bolt Threads is a material solutions company. It invests in and scales advanced, credible materials that are nature-derived and sustainable. Their products include Mylo, a mycelium-based material derived from mushroom cells; Microsilk, which is spun from the same protein as spider's web; and B-Silk, which is a biomaterial made with sugar, water, and yeast for use in beauty, solids, and biomedicine.

They are a large company in the materials space, with their Series D raise bringing in US $123 million to constitute their total raise of US $213 million. This round was led by Baillie Gifford, Fidelity Investments, and Temasek. They have recently partnered with Stella McCartney and Patagonia.

*Mentioned in Chapter 3, p.151.*

# ECOVATIVE DESIGN

**Main Product:** Mycelium replacement for plastic
**Founded:** 2007, New York, USA
**Founders:** Eben Bayer, Gavin McIntyre
**Website:** www.ecovativedesign.com

Ecovative Design are seeking to reduce the amount of plastic in consumer products by using mycelium to produce a number of materials such as MycoFlex, a high performance foam, and MycoComposite, which uses mycelium to bind together organic agricultural by-products such as wood chips to produce durable, biodegradable materials. Their cultivated meat spin-off, Atlast Food Co., was discussed on page 214 of this chapter.

Ecovative has raised US $30.1 million total in over 11 rounds, the latest in October 2019.

## FUROID

# FUROID™

**Main Product:** Cell-based fur, wool
**Founded:** 2019, Netherlands
**Founders:** Heinrich Kunz, Maria Zakurnaeva and Dr. Sergej Leonov
**Website:** www.furoid.com

Furoid's goal is to manufacture bioengineered pelts and wool for the textile and pelt/wool industry. They are working on the replication of wool fibres, (Cashmere and Merino) by adapting their technology for the production of animal and human hair fibres, meaning that their technology is already ready to be scaled. Furoid technology has the added benefit of making obsolete the process of tanning and colouration, because these can be engineered into the product at the cellular level. The company is building a stem cell database from iPSCs for endangered species and the team is hoping to launch their MAGICCAVIAR project, focussed on creating cell cultured caviar soon.

## GALY

# GALY

**Main Product:** Cotton
**Founded:** 2019, Bay Area, California, USA
**Founders:** Luciano Bueno
**Website:** www.galy.co

GALY is developing cultivated cotton using cell culture. It recently won the H&M Global Change Award – a prize of EUR 300k – out of 5,893 entries from 175 different countries. GALY's technology removes all the steps of traditional cotton farming and the decreased land requirement and water usage offers potential for a local angle to cotton production, without needing any pesticides, herbicides or insecticides.

Founder Luciano Bueno has previous experience building companies within the textile industry and was included in Brazil's Forbes 30 under 30 list in 2019.

In March 2020 Galy received a US $500k investment from Agronomics.

*Further details of the company's activities are featured in Chapter 3, p.152.*

# MODERN MEADOW

**Main Product:** Leather
**Founded:** 2011, New York, USA
**Founders:** Andras Forgacs, Francoise Marga, Gabor Forgacs, Karoly Jakab
**Website:** www.modernmeadow.com

Modern Meadow is an exciting biofabrication company with a great team behind it. They design engineered cells to create tailored micro-organisms that produce essential proteins. Fermentation is then used to multiply billions of collagen-producing cell factories. These collagen proteins form the building blocks of materials which can exhibit a range of structural properties.

Founders Andras and Gabor Forgacs are notable for being both Director and CSO of the cultivated meat company Fork & Goode, as well as the founders of the biomedical company Organovo, which I have recognised as a potential Juvenescence investment.

Modern Meadow has raised approximately US $54 million and is hoping to become a key source of materials for a global fashion industry valued at US $3 trillion.

*Further details of the company's activities are featured in Chapter 3, p.148.*

# MYCOWORKS

⬥ MYCOWORKS

**Main Product:** Mycelium leather
**Founded:** 2013, Bay Area, California, USA
**Founders:** Philip Ross, Sophia Wang
**Website:** www.mycoworks.com

Mycoworks has developed Reishi, a material made of fine mycelium, a proprietary woven cellular microstructure which imitates the collagen structure of animal leather. Co-founder Phil Ross began using mycelium in the 1990s as a medium for sculpture. It is now being developed for use in the fashion industry, offering new opportunities for customised product design not possible with traditional leather hides.

MycoWorks has received US $62 million total funding.

## PROVENANCE BIOFABRICS   PROVENANCE

**Main Product:** Collagen for biofabrics
**Founded:** 2016, Bay Area, California, USA
**Founders:** Christian Ewton
**Website:** www.provenance.bio/fabrics

Provenance Biofabrics, a division of Provenance Bio, produces advanced non-animal proteins for manufacturers of consumer goods. They produce an advanced, complex form of collagen (normally found in mammals) which gives structure to cultivated meats and biofabrics, and in future will give support to bioinks and shape fidelity for cutting-edge 4D-printed products. They will be able to create exotic hides such as crocodile and ostrich.

## SPIBER

**Main Product:** Synthetic protein materials
**Founded:** 2007, Japan
**Founders:** Kazuhide Sekiyama, Junichi Sugahara
**Website:** www.spiber.jp

In 2015, Spiber unveiled the 'Moon Parka' prototype, made from cultivated spider silk. In 2019, they released 50 of them in collaboration with North Face - the first commercially available jacket from this material. They call the fabric QMONOS - *kumonosu* means 'spiderweb' in Japanese. They claim that it is stronger than steel and more flexible than nylon, and that a piece of fabric 1cm thick could stop a jumbo jet in mid-air. Synthetic structural proteins have the advantage of being biological, biodegradable, and adaptable to a wide range of functions – the company sees a future role in car manufacturing as well as apparel. In 2017, they revealed a prototype 'Kinetic Car Seat' in collaboration with Lexus. They have accumulated strong IP, including a database of 800 gene models of spider silk, seven patents granted and 15 pending.

Mass production costs remain their biggest problem, but they are approaching a level that is competitive with traditional materials: in 2017, costs had been reduced to Y10,000/kg (£74/kg, similar to cashmere).

In April 2019, the company announced a new funding round of JPY 6.5 billion (*c.* £48 million), of which JPY 5 billion was provided as a loan by a banking syndicate, and JPY 1.5 billion was secured through a lease contract with Mitsubishi to upgrade its facilities in Tsuruoka, Yamagata. This takes its total fundraising to JPY 28.94 billion (c. £213 million).

*Further details of the company's activities are outlined in Chapter 3, p.152.*

# VITROLABS

| | |
|---|---|
| **Main Product:** | Leather |
| **Founded:** | 2016, Bay Area, California, USA |
| **Founders:** | Ingvar Helgason, Dusko Ilic |
| **Website:** | www.vitrolabsinc.com |

VitroLabs is creating leather by seeding proliferated cells onto a scaffold in their proprietary scalable bioreactor platform, which enables them to grow sheets of leather on vertically stacked palettes. While they are currently using a polyester scaffolding, they are looking to replace this with a sustainable cellulose scaffold.

Their business model targets the luxury goods and fashion industry and they have drawn interest from major fashion labels, one of which is planning a capsule range using VitroLabs' leather.

VitroLabs is expected to commence a Series A funding round soon after the publication of this book. The company has raised US $9 million in seed funding to date, including support from Agronomics, Firstminute Capital, Fifty Years and Khosla Ventures.

*Further details of the company's activities are featured in Chapter 3, p.148.*

## GLOSSARY

**Adenosine triphosphate (ATP):** an organic compound fundamental to all life which stores and releases energy for many cellular processes, including muscle contraction, nerve impulse propagation, and chemical synthesis.

**Adipocytes** (aka **lipocytes and fat cells**): the cells that primarily compose adipose tissue, specialised in storing energy as fat and providing insulation. They are derived from mesenchymal stem cells which give rise to adipocytes through adipogenesis.

**Adipose tissues:** fat, the loose connective tissue composed mostly of adipocytes. Adipose tissue stores energy and insulates the body.

**Adult (somatic) cells:** any cells of a living organism other than the reproductive cells.

**Adventurous periphery:** the edges of the clean foods industry. Companies in this space are producing novel plant strains and are employing innovative agricultural technologies such as vertical farming or new irrigation systems.

**Agro-Luddites:** the Luddites were bands of English workers in the 19th Century who, believing that their jobs were threatened, destroyed machinery in cotton and wool mills. The new Agro-Luddites are opposed to advancements in the agricultural industry.

**Amino acids:** the organic compounds that form the building blocks of proteins and contain amine and carboxyl functional groups.

**Anoikis:** a form of programmed cell death (apoptosis) that occurs in anchorage-dependent cells when they detach from the surrounding Extra Cellular Matrix (ECM).

**Annular slit die:** the rounded opening which shapes the substance exiting an extruder.

**Apoptosis:** a form of programmed cell death that is genetically regulated. It is different from necrosis, in which cells die due to injury. Apoptosis is an orderly process in which the cell's contents are packaged into small packets of membrane for "garbage collection" by immune cells.

**Assay:** an investigative procedure in the laboratory for qualitatively assessing or quantitatively measuring the presence, amount, or functional activity of a target entity.

**Basal medium:** a minimal medium which promotes the growth of cells. It contains amino acids, sugar, salts, and vitamins, but is not supplemented by growth factors.

**Bay Area:** the San Francisco Bay Area in California, USA, where many of the cultivated meats startups have based themselves.

**Biomass:** the total quantity of organic material in a given area or volume.

**Biopsy:** a small sample of tissue taken for examination or to extract certain cells.

**Bioreactor:** a container used to create the optimal conditions for facilitating biological processes. In industry they can be used for fermentation or to grow cell cultures.

**Botulism:** a rare but life-threatening condition caused by toxins produced by *Clostridium botulinum* bacteria. The bacteria themselves are not harmful but, when deprived of oxygen, poisonous toxins are formed. When foods are incorrectly canned, preserved or cooked, food-borne botulism can occur. Symptoms begin with weakness, fatigue and vision problems, and can escalate to vomiting, constipation, and respiratory compromise.

**Cardiomyocyte stem cells:** cells that make up the heart muscle/cardiac muscle. As the chief cell type of the heart, cardiac cells are primarily involved in the contractile function of the heart that enables the pumping of blood around the body.

**Casein:** a protein found in mammalian milk which gives it a unique flavour and contributes towards the texture of cheese. They comprise around 80 per cent of the proteins found in cow's milk and between 20-45 per cent of the proteins found in human milk.

**Cell-based:** referred to in this book in the context of food, is an animal product grown directly from cells, *in vitro*, without the need for the whole animal. Also known as cultured, clean or cultivated meat.

**Cell lineage:** the developmental history of a tissue or organ from a zygote (fertilised embryo). For example, a simplified cell lineage of a human biliary epithelial cell (which lines the bile tract) would lead back to the hepatoblast (the foetal precursor of the main liver mass), then to the foregut, then to the endoderm (the innermost primary germ layer of the embryo), and finally to the zygote.

**Cellular reprogramming:** the process of reverting mature, specialised cells back into an unspecialised, embryonic-like state forming induced pluripotent stem cells (iPSCs).

**Chondrocytes:** cells found in cartilage connective tissue. They are the only cells located in cartilage. They produce and maintain the cartilage matrix.

**Clean meat** (aka **cultivated, cultured, lab-grown, or cell-based meat**): genuine meat products derived from growing animal cells *in vitro*, without the need for the whole animal.

**Coronavirus:** Coronaviruses are a large family of viruses causing a variety of symptoms from the common cold to diseases such as MERS-CoV. In 2019 a novel strain of coronavirus, SARS-CoV-2, was discovered in Wuhan, China leading to a global shutdown of trade and movement in 2020 due to its causing Covid-19.

**Covid-19:** the Coronavirus disease which was first identified in Wuhan, China in December 2019 and has caused more than one million deaths to date and a wide shut down of the global economy in 2020.

**Creutzfeldt-Jakob Disease (CJD):** a rare and fatal condition affecting the brain. Variant CJD (vCJD) is caused by consuming meat from a cow that had Mad Cow Disease (BSE). After the link between BSE and CJD was discovered in 1996, strict and effective controls were introduced to prevent infected cattle meat from entering the food chain.

**CRISPR (clustered regularly interspaced short palindromic repeats):** a family of DNA sequences found in the genomes of prokaryotic organisms such as bacteria and archaea. These sequences are derived from DNA fragments of bacteriophages that had previously infected the prokaryote. Researchers can use them to easily alter DNA sequences and modify gene function. CRISPR is commonly used to refer to this type of gene editing technology.

**Cultured:** cells or tissue grown *in vitro*, without the need for the whole animal. In the context of this book, cultured usually refers to genuine meat or seafood products derived from *in vitro* animal cell growth.

**Differentiation:** the process by which cells acquire particular features, turning from one cell type into another usually more specialised cell type.

**Dulbecco's Modified Eagle Medium (DMEM):** The basal medium DMEM is a modified version of Eagle's Medium, containing a higher concentration of amino acids and vitamins. The original DMEM formula contains 1000 mg/L of glucose and was first reported for culturing embryonic mouse cells.

**Electrolysis:** the process by which direct electric current is used to cause a chemical reaction that would not happen spontaneously. One example of electrolysis is the decomposition of water into hydrogen and oxygen using electricity.

**Embryonic stem cells (ESCs):** pluripotent stem cells derived from the undifferentiated inner mass cells of a human embryo.

**Endothelium:** a single layer of cells that lines the interior surface of organs and body cavities, particularly blood vessels and lymphatic vessels. They control the flow of substances and fluids between vessels and tissue.

**Engineered protein:** a protein that has been produced by scientists through deliberate design and alteration of the protein sequence, so that the protein has a particular use or value.

# MOO'S LAW

***Escherichia coli (E. coli):*** a bacterium commonly found in foods, animals and the intestines of humans. Most E. coli strains are harmless and actually keep the gut healthy but some can produce toxins that cause illness.

**Extra Cellular Matrix (ECM):** a three-dimensional network of macromolecules, such as collagen, enzymes, and glycoproteins, located outside of the cell membrane that provides structural and biochemical support to surrounding cells.

**Extrusion:** a manufacturing process that enables the continuous production of homogeneous and finely-structured products. The twin-screw extrusion process is widely used in the production of plastics and in the food industry. It consists of two co-rotating screws in a closed barrel which compress, mix, and heat the raw materials (solids, liquids or slurries) to extrude the desired product.

**Faecal contamination:** occurs when faecal coliforms (a type of intestinal bacterium) from humans or other animals contaminate water, food, or other surfaces due to the presence of faecal waste.

**Fermentation:** a biological process carried out by bacteria, yeasts, or other microorganisms that creates a chemical change in an organic substance. This process can create products for use in industry.

**Fibroblasts:** cells that synthesise the Extra Cellular Matrix (ECM) and collagen, produce the structural framework (stroma) for animal tissues, and play a critical role in wound healing. Fibroblasts are the most common cells of connective tissue in animals.

**Fluorescence activated cell sorting (FACS):** a method of separating and sorting a mixture of cells one cell at a time using the light-scattering and fluorescence characteristics of each cell.

**Genetic drift:** the change in the frequency of an existing gene variant (allele) in a population due to chance.

**Germ layer:** a group of cells in an embryo that interact with each other as the embryo develops, and contribute to the formation of all organs and tissues. All animals, except perhaps sponges, form two or three germ layers. In vertebrates these are the ectoderm, mesoderm and endoderm.

**Greenhouse gas emissions** (aka **polluting emissions**): primarily include carbon dioxide, methane, nitrous oxides and fluorinated gases. These gases are responsible for trapping heat and raising the earth's surface temperature. Common sources of these pollutants include burning fossil fuels, deforestation and cattle farming.

**Griddle Parity™:** the point at which cultivated- or plant-based products reach equal or lower cost than existing conventional meats. It is a key step towards the successful commercialisation of alternative meats.

**Growth factors:** substances capable of stimulating or inhibiting various cellular processes or behaviours, such as metabolism, proliferation, and differentiation.

**Haem:** an iron-containing compound of the porphyrin class which forms the non-protein part of haemoglobin and some other biological molecules. It lends the red pigment to blood.

**Haematopoietic stem cells (HSCs):** the stem cells that give rise to other blood cells in the red bone marrow in a process called haematopoiesis.

**Hayflick Limit:** an explanation of the mechanisms behind cellular aging. The concept states that a normal human cell can only replicate and divide around 50 times before the telomeres (caps on the end of chromosomes) wear down. At this point, the cell enters senescence, can no longer divide, and will eventually undergo programmed cell death or apoptosis. Pluripotent stem cells (such as iPSCs and ESCs) can bypass the Hayflick Limit and achieve cell immortality.

**Human milk oligosaccharides (HMOs):** carbohydrates formed of a chain of sugar molecules found exclusively in human breast milk, where they exist in high concentrations.

**Hydrocolloids:** usually polysaccharides (complex polymers) and sometimes proteins of high molecular weight produced by microbial synthesis or extracted from plants and seaweed. They are often called gums and are used in foods to change the viscosity or texture.

# Glossary

**Hydrogel:** a 3D network of hydrophilic polymers that can hold a large amount of water without compromising its structure, due to chemical or physical cross-linking of individual polymer chains.

**Hydrogenotrophs:** organisms that are able to metabolise molecular hydrogen as a source of energy. Carbon-reducing hydrogenotrophs produce hydrocarbons and water from carbon dioxide and hydrogen.

**Hydroponic farming** (aka **hydroponics**): the process of growing plants with mineral nutrients provided through a water solvent instead of soil.

**Induced Pluripotent Stem Cells (iPSCs):** mature adult cells that have been reprogrammed back into an embryonic, pluripotent-like state that enables them to then differentiate into any cell type.

**Integrin:** transmembrane receptor proteins which attach cells to the Extra Cellular Matrix (ECM).

**Juvenescence:** the movement in pharmaceuticals and therapeutics aiming to extend healthy lifespan by treating ageing itself as a disease. Jim Mellon's previous book — also called 'Juvenescence' — explained these advances and described the investment opportunities they present.

**Ketosis:** a metabolic state in which fat provides most of the fuel for the body. It occurs when there is limited access to glucose (blood sugar), which is the preferred fuel source for many cells in the body. Ketosis is most often associated with ketogenic (high fat and very low-carbohydrate) diets.

**Leghaemoglobin:** an oxygen carrying haemoprotein found in the nitrogen-fixing root nodules of leguminous plants such as alfalfa or soybeans.

**Liming:** a stage of the leather-production process in which hides are treated with an alkaline solution to remove various fats and proteins to produce a soft and durable leather.

**Mad Cow Disease** (aka **bovine spongiform encephalopathy or BSE**): a transmissible, degenerative and fatal disease affecting the central nervous system of adult cattle.

**Mammary gland cells:** cells in humans and other mammals which produce milk to feed young offspring. Mammals get their name from the Latin word mamma ('breast').

**Mechanotransduction:** any of the mechanisms by which cells convert external mechanical stimuli into internal electrochemical activity (such as activating electrochemical pathways and regulating genetic transcription).

**Medium** (aka **growth medium or culture medium**): a solid, semi-solid, or liquid designed to support the growth of cells or microorganisms.

**Meristem:** a type of tissue found in plants, consisting of undifferentiated cells that are capable of cell division. Cells in the meristem can develop into all the other tissues and organs that occur in plants.

**Mesenchymal stem cells:** multipotent adult stem cells present in multiple tissues, including umbilical cord, bone marrow, and fat tissue. They can self-renew by dividing and can differentiate into multiple tissues including bone, cartilage, muscle and fat cells, and connective tissue.

**Middle East Respiratory Syndrome (MERS):** a viral respiratory illness which was first reported in Saudi Arabia in 2012 and subsequently spread to several other countries, including the United States. Most people infected with MERS-CoV developed severe respiratory illness, including fever, cough, and shortness of breath. Many of them have died.

**Microbiome:** all the communities of microorganisms that reside inside and on the outside of human tissues and fluids.

**Minimum Essential Medium:** a growth medium developed by the American physician Harry Eagle in the 1950s, containing the 13 amino acids required in sera for cell survival and viability. It also consisted of glucose, inorganic salts and vitamins, as well as dialyzed serum.

**Mycoprotein:** a protein derived from fungi. Currently Quorn products are made using mycoprotein from *Fusarium venenatum*.

**Myofibrils:** components of skeletal muscle. Long filaments that run in parallel to one another, forming muscle myofibres.

**Myosatellites** (aka **satellite cells or muscle stem cells**): small multipotent cells, found in mature muscle, with little cytoplasm.

**New Agrarian Revolution:** an ongoing technological revolution involving the production of food from alternative sources. This follows the previous agrarian revolutions: firstly, our transition from nomadic hunter-gatherer lifestyles to farming settlements about 10,000 years ago; and, secondly, the rise in agricultural productivity from the mid-17th to 19th Centuries that began in Great Britain as a result of the introduction of mechanisation and other techniques.

**Pangolin:** a mammal found in Asia and Sub-Saharan Africa. Their meat and scales are highly sought after for Chinese medicine, making them both endangered and a possible vector for disease.

**Perfusion:** the passage of fluid through the circulatory system or lymphatic system to an organ or a tissue, usually referring to the delivery of blood to a capillary bed in tissue.

**Phytoestrogens:** plant-based compounds that mimic oestrogen in the body. They have been found to be beneficial in combatting symptoms and conditions caused by oestrogen deficiency.

**Plastic pollution:** the accumulation of plastic objects and particles in the environment. Plastic objects damage wildlife and microplastics can enter the food chain through the oceans.

**Polluting emissions:** (see **Greenhouse gas emissions**) contaminating and harmful gases and particles that are released into the atmosphere as a consequence of human activities. These include the greenhouse gases (carbon dioxide, methane and nitrous oxides). Common sources of these pollutants include burning fossil fuels, deforestation and cattle farming.

**Pluripotent:** relating to a stem cell that is capable of differentiating into multiple specialised cell types.

**PTSD:** Post Traumatic Stress Disorder is a mental health condition caused by a traumatic experience.

**RNAi (Ribonucleic acid interference):** the biological process in which RNA molecules inhibit gene expression or translation, by neutralising the targeted messenger RNA (mRNA) molecules that would usually transfer genetic information from the cell nucleus to the cytoplasm (where proteins are made).

**SARS (Severe Acute Respiratory Syndrome):** a condition arising from a coronavirus first identified in 2003. SARS-CoV is thought to have spread from its natural reservoir (perhaps bats) to other animals (civet cats) and ultimately to humans in the southern Chinese province of Guangdong in 2002.

**Scaffold:** materials engineered to give cells the ability to grow into structured three-dimensional tissue. Cells are often 'seeded' into these structures, which inform the shape of the tissue as it grows.

**Seed train:** the process by which a small number of cells are allowed to replicate and transferred into larger and larger culture volumes until an adequate number of cells for the inoculation of a bioreactor is generated.

**Senescence:** the gradual deterioration of cells with age. Cellular senescence is the process whereby cells irreversibly stop dividing as a result of unrepaired DNA damage or other cellular stresses. Organismal senescence refers to the gradual deterioration of an entire organism and the loss of functional characteristics over time.

**Shear-cell technology:** a technology, developed at the University of Wageningen in the Netherlands, that transforms vegetable proteins such as soy, pea, rapeseed, or wheat into a layered fibrous structure that mimics the texture and appearance of meat.

**Single-cell protein** (aka **microbial protein**): protein derived from edible, unicellular microorganisms which may be used as an ingredient or a substitute for protein-rich foods. Depending on the source, it may be suitable for human consumption or as animal feed.

# Glossary

**Spanish Flu:** the Spanish Flu lasted from 1918-20 when an influenza A (H1N1) virus strain infected 500 million people, around a third of the world's population at the time. Around 50 million people died.

**Specialised:** a descriptor of cells that have developed certain characteristics to perform a particular function. For instance, red blood cells do not have a nucleus to maximise their haemoglobin-carrying capacity, to transport oxygen around the body.

**Superbug:** an informal term for a bacterium that has become resistant to the antibiotics usually used to treat it, such as methicillin-resistant Staphylococcus aureus (MRSA) or any multidrug-resistant bacterium.

**Swine fever:** a highly contagious viral disease affecting pigs which causes them to have fever, lesions, necrosis and, typically, death within 15 days.

**Swine flu** (aka **H1N1**): a disease caused by an influenza A virus strain (H1N1pdm09). The virus became pandemic in 2009 and 2010, killing an estimated 284,000 people worldwide.

**Totipotent:** the characteristic of an immature cell or stem cell capable of giving rise to any cell type. When used to refer to a blastomere, this characteristic describes its ability to develop into a complete embryo.

**Transcription activator-like effector nucleases (TALEN):** restriction enzymes that can be engineered to cut specific sequences of DNA.

**Transcription factors:** proteins involved in gene expression that help to turn genes "on" or "off" by binding to a specific DNA sequence.

**Transdifferentiation:** the conversion of one mature somatic cell type to another. It is also known as lineage reprogramming and involves transforming one mature somatic cell into another without undergoing an intermediate pluripotent state or progenitor cell type.

**Vegan mafia:** an unofficial collection of early stage investors in the clean foods space who include CPT Capital (Jeremy Coller's group), Stray Dog Capital, New Crop Capital and Blue Horizon Ventures.

**Vertical farming:** the practice of growing plants in vertically stacked layers in a carefully controlled indoor environment, to maximise efficiency of crop growth.

**Wet market:** a marketplace selling fresh meat, poultry, seafood and other perishable items. Some wet markets, such as Huanan Seafood Wholesale Market in Wuhan, China, also sell live wildlife that is often slaughtered on site.

**Yamanaka factors:** four key transcription factors (proteins controlling the transfer of genetic information from DNA to messenger RNA), highly expressed in embryonic stem cells, that induce pluripotency when overexpressed. The factors' names are Oct4, Sox2, Klf4, and c-Myc. Shinya Yamanaka won a Nobel Prize in 2012 for his discovery of how these factors could be used to transform any adult cell into a pluripotent state.

**Zoonotic:** any disease or infection that is transmissible from animals to humans.

# BIBLIOGRAPHY

**Books**

Alberts B, *et al.*, *Essential Cell Biology*, (5th edn, W. W. Norton & Co. 2019).

Bekoff, M, *The Emotional Lives of Animals* (1st edn, New World Library 2007).

Benson G J, and B E Rollin, eds, *The Well-Being of Farm Animals: Challenges and Solutions* (1st edn, Blackwell Publishing, 2004).

Bhat, Z F, *et al.*, 'Chapter 73 - Cultured meat - a humane meat production system' in R Lanza, R Langer, J P Vacanti, and A Atala, eds, *Principles of Tissue Engineering* (5th edn, Academic Press 2020).

Donaldson, B, and C Carter, eds, *The Future of Meat without Animals* (1st edn, Rowman & Littlefield, 2016).

Drexler, Madeline, *Secret Agents: The Menace of Emerging Infections* (1st edn, Joseph Henry Press 2002).

Eisnitz, G A, *Slaughterhouse: The Shocking Story of Greed, Neglect, and Inhumane Treatment inside the U.S. Meat Industry* (1st edn, Prometheus Books, 2006).

Francione, G L, and Charlton A, *Eat Like You Care: An Examination of the Morality of Eating Animals* (1st edn, Exempla Press 2013).

Freston, K, and B Friedrich, *Clean Protein: The Revolution that will Reshape Your Body, Boost Your Energy - and Save Our Planet* (1st edn, Hachette 2018).

Harari, Y N, *Sapiens: A Brief History of Humankind* (1st edn, Harper, 2015).

Harari, Y N, *Homo Deus: A Brief History of Tomorrow* (1st edn, Harvill Secker, 2016).

Khan, A, *An Introduction to Cellular Agriculture* (e-book, 1st edn, CellAgri, 2019).

Kleeman, J, *Sex Robots & Vegan Meat: Adventures at the Frontier of Birth, Food, Sex & Death* (1st edn, Picador 2020).

Pollan, M, *The Omnivore's Dilemma: A Natural History of Four Meals* (1st edn, Penguin 2006).

Post, M J, and J-F Hocquette, 'New Sources of Animal Proteins: Cultured Meat' in P P Purslow, ed., *New Aspects of Meat Quality: From Genes to Ethics* (1st edn, Woodhead Publishing 2017).

Purdy C, *Billion Dollar Burger: Inside Big Tech's Race for the Future of Food* (1st edn, Little, Brown Book Group 2020).

Reese J, *The End of Animal Farming: How Scientists, Entrepreneurs, and Activists Are Building an Animal-Free Food System* (1st edn, Beacon Press 2018).

Rogers, L J, *Minds of Their Own: Thinking and Awareness in Animals* (1st edn, Westview Press 1997).

Safran Foer J, *We Are the Weather: Saving the Planet Begins at Breakfast* (1st edn, Penguin 2019).

Safran Foer, J, *Eating Animals: Should We Stop?* (2nd edn, Penguin 2018).

Shapiro, P, *Clean Meat: How Growing Meat without Animals Will Revolutionize Dinner and the World* (1st edn, Gallery Books, 2018).

Stull, D D, and M J Broadway, *Slaughterhouse Blues: The Meat and Poultry Industry in North America* (2nd edn, Wadsworth Publishing 2012).

Ward, O, A Oven, and R Bethencourt, *The Clean Pet Food Revolution: How Better Pet Food Will Change the World* (1st edn, Lantern Books 2020).

Wurgaft, B A, *Meat Planet: Artificial Flesh and the Future of Food* (1st edn, University of California Press 2019

# Bibliography

## Journal Articles

Alexander, P, *et al.*, 'Could consumption of insects, cultured meat or imitation meat reduce global agricultural land use?' (2017) 15 *Global Food Security* 22.

Alvaro, C, 'Lab-Grown Meat and Veganism: A Virtue-Oriented Perspective' (2019) 32 *Journal of Agricultural and Environmental Ethics* 127.

Ashley, P J, 'Fish welfare: Current issues in aquaculture' (2007) 104:3-4 *Applied Animal Behaviour Science* 199.

Bekker, G A, *et al.*, 'Explicit and implicit attitude toward an emerging food technology: The case of cultured meat' (2017) 108 *Appetite* 245.

Benjaminson, M A, *et al.*, 'In vitro edible muscle protein production system (mpps): stage 1, fish' (2002) 51:12 *Acta Astronautica* 879.

Bianco, P, *et al.*, 'Mesenchymal Stem Cells: Revisiting History, Concepts, and Assays' (2008) 2:4 *Cell Stem Cell* 313.

Boyd, W, 'Making Meat: Science, Technology, and American Poultry Production' (2001) 42:4 *Technology and Culture* 631.

Bryant, C J, and J C Barnett, 'What's in a name? Consumer perception of in vitro meat under different names' (2019) 137 *Appetite* 104.

Bryant, C J, 'Culture, meat, and cultured meat' (2020) 98:8 *Journal of Animal Science* e1

Bryant, C J, *et al.*, 'Strategies for overcoming aversion to unnaturalness: The case of clean meat' (2019) 154 *Meat Science* 37.

Choudhury, D, *et al.*, 'The Business of Cultured Meat' (2020) 38:6 *Trends in Biotechnology* 573.

Choudhury, D, *et al.*, 'Commercialization of Plant-Based Meat Alternatives' (2020) *Trends in Plant Science* e1.

Chriki, S, and J-F Hocquette, 'The Myth of Cultured Meat: A Review' (2020) 7:7 *Frontiers in Nutrition* e1.

Dekkers, B L, *et al.*, 'Structuring processes for meat analogues' (2018) 81 *Trends in Food Science & Technology* 25.

Despommier, D, 'Vertical farms, building a viable indoor farming model for cities' (2019) Special Issue 20 *Field Actions Science Reports* 68.

Espinosa, R, *et al.*, 'Infectious Diseases and Meat Production' (2020) 76 *Environmental and Resource Economics* 1019.

Faustman, C, *et al.*, 'Cell-based meat: the need to assess holistically' (2020) 98:8 *Journal of Animal Science* e1.

Fernandes, A M, *et al.*, 'Conceptual evolution and scientific approaches about synthetic meat' (2019) 57 *Journal of Food Science & Technology* 1991.

Galanakis, C M, 'The Food Systems in the Era of the Coronavirus (COVID-19) Pandemic Crisis' (2020) 9:4 *Foods* 523.

Gaydhane, M K, *et al.*, 'Cultured meat: state of the art and future' (2018) 3:1 *Biomanufacturing Reviews* e1.

Fish, K D, *et al.*, 'Prospects and challenges for cell-cultured fat as a novel food ingredient' (2020) 98 *Trends in Food Science & Technology* 53.

Gasteratos, K, '90 Reasons to Consider Cellular Agriculture' (2019) student paper published by Harvard University

Gomez-Luciano, C A, *et al.*, 'Consumers' willingness to purchase three alternatives to meat proteins in the United Kingdom, Spain, Brazil, and the Dominican Republic' (2019) 78 *Food Quality and Preference* e1.

Graf, T, 'Historical Origins of Transdifferentiation and Reprogramming' (2011) 9:6 *Cell Stem Cell* 517.

Grasso, A C, *et al.*, 'Older Consumers' Readiness to Accept Alternative, More Sustainable Protein Sources in the European Union' (2019) 11:8 *Nutrients* e1.

Grossi G, *et al.*, 'Livestock and climate change: impact of live-stock on climate and mitigation strategies' (2019) 9:1 *Animal Frontiers* 69.

Hamdan M N, *et al.*, 'Cultured Meat in Islamic Perspective' (2018) 57 *Journal of Religion and Health* 2193.

Heidemann, M S, *et al.*, 'Uncoupling Meat from Animal Slaughter and Its Impacts on Human-Animal Relationships' (2020) *Frontiers in Psychology* e1.

Ilea, R C, 'Intensive Livestock Farming: Global Trends, Increased Environmental Concerns, and Ethical Solutions' (2009) 22:2 *Journal of Agricultural and Environmental Ethics* 153.

Kadim, I T, *et al.*, 'Cultured meat from muscle stem cells: A review of challenges and prospects' (2015) 14:2 *Journal of Integrative Agriculture* 222.

Knowles, T G, *et al.*, 'Leg Disorders in Broiler Chickens: Prevalence, Risk Factors and Prevention' (2008) 3:2 *PLOS One* e1545.

Kolkmann, A M, *et al.*, 'Serum-free media for the growth of primary bovine myoblasts' (2020) 72 *Cytotechnology* 111.

Landers, T F, *et al.*, 'A Review of Antibiotic Use in Food Animals: Perspective, Policy, and Potential' (2012) 127:1 *Public Health Reports* 4.

Lee, H J, *et al.*, 'Status of meat alternatives and their potential role in the future meat market — A review' (2020) 33:10 *Asian-Australasian Journal of Animal Sciences* 1533.

Lynch, J, and R Pierrehumbert, 'Climate Impacts of Cultured Meat and Beef Cattle' (2019) *Frontiers in Sustainable Food Systems* e1.

May, A, '*In vitro* meat: protein for twelve billion?' (2012) MSc thesis submitted to the University of Otago.

Melzener, L, *et al.*, 'Cultured beef: from small biopsy to substantial quantity' (2020) *Journal of the Science of Food and Agriculture* e1.

Miller, J, 'In Vitro Meat: Power, Authenticity and Vegetarianism' (2012) 10:4 *Journal for Critical Animal Studies* 41.

Miller, D J, 'Sydney Ringer; physiology saline, calcium and the contraction of the heart' (2004) 555:3 *The Journal of Physiology* 585.

Mohorcich, J, and J Reese, 'Cell-cultured meat: Lessons from GMO adoption and resistance' (2019) 143 *Appetite* e1.

Mok, W K, *et al.*, 'Technology innovations for food security in Singapore: A case study of future food systems for an increasingly resource-scarce world' (2020) 102 *Trends in Food Science & Technology* 155.

Moritz M S M, *et al.*, 'Alternatives for large-scale production of cultured meat: A review' (2015) 14:2 *Journal of Integrative Agriculture* 208.

Ong, S, *et al.*, 'Cell-based meat: Current ambiguities with nomenclature' (2020) 102 *Trends in Food Science & Technology* 223.

Orzechowski, A, 'Artificial meat? Feasible approach based on the experience from cell culture studies' (2015) 14:2 *Journal of Integrative Agriculture* 217.

Osen, R, and U Schweiggert-Weisz, 'High-Moisture Extrusion: Meat Analogues' (2016) *Reference Module in Food Sciences* e1.

Painter, J, *et al.*, 'The coverage of cultivated meat in the US and UK traditional media, 2013-2019: drivers, sources, and competing narratives' (2020) 162 *Climatic Change* e1.

Pimental, D, *et al.*, 'Reducing Energy Inputs in the US Food System' (2008) 36:4 *Human Ecology* 459.

# Bibliography

Rolland, N C M, *et al.*, 'The effect of information content on acceptance of cultured meat in a tasting context' (2020) 15:4 *PLOS One* e1.

Sachs, A, and S Kettenmann, 'A Burger by Any Other Name: Regulatory Challenges and Opportunities for Cell-Cultured Meat' (2019) 15:2 *SciTech Lawyer* 18.

Salter, A M, 'Improving the sustainability of global meat and milk production' (2017) 76:1 *Proceedings of the Nutrition Society* 22.

Siegrist, M, *et al.*, 'Perceived naturalness and evoked disgust influence acceptance of cultured meat' (2018) 139 *Meat Science* 213.

Stephens N, and Ellis M, 'Cellular agriculture in the UK: a review' (2020) 5:12 *Wellcome Open Research* e1.

Stephens N, *et al.*, 'Bringing cultured meat to market: Technical, socio-political, and regulatory challenges in cellular agriculture' (2018) 78 *Trends in Food Science & Technology* 155.

Tiberius V, *et al.*, 'Setting the table for meat consumers: an international Delphi study on in vitro meat' (2019) 3:10 npj *Science of Food* e1.

Tomiyama, A J, *et al.*, 'Bridging the gap between the science of cultured meat and public perceptions' (2020) 104 *Trends in Food Science & Technology* 144.

Tuomisto, H L, and M J T D Mattos, 'Environmental impacts of cultured meat production' (2011) 45:14 *Environmental Science & Technology* 6117.

Valente, J d P S, *et al.*, 'First glimpse on attitudes of highly educated consumers towards cell-based meat and related issues in Brazil' (2019) 14:8 *PLOS One* e1.

Van Boeckel T P, *et al.*, 'Global trends in antimicrobial resistance in animals in low- and middle-income countries' (2019) 365:6459 *Science* 1266.

Van der Valk, J, *et al.*, 'Optimization of chemically defined cell culture media – Replacing fetal bovine serum in mammalian in vitro methods' (2010) 24:4 *Toxicology In Vitro* 1053.

Van der Weele, C, and J Tramper, 'Cultured meat: every village its own factory?' (2014) 32:6 *Trends in Biotechnology* 294.

Verbeke, W, *et al.*, 'Challenges and prospects for consumer acceptance of cultured meat' (2015) 14:2 *Journal of Integrative Agriculture* 285.

Warner, R D, 'Review: Analysis of the process and drivers for cellular meat production' (2019) 13:12 *Animal* 3041.

Weinrich, R, *et al.*, 'Consumer acceptance of cultured meat in Germany' (2020) 162 *Meat Science* e1.

Wild, F, 'Manufacture of Meat Analogues through High Moisture Extrusion' (2016) *Reference Module in Food Science* e1.

Wilks, M, *et al.*, 'Testing potential psychological predictors of attitudes towards cultured meat' (2019) 136 *Appetite* 137.

Wilks, M, and C J C Phillips, 'Attitudes to in vitro meat: A survey of potential consumers in the United States' (2017) 12:2 *PLOS One* e1.

Zuidhof, M J, *et al.*, 'Growth, efficiency, and yield of commercial broilers from 1957, 1978, and 2005' (2014) 93:12 *Poultry Science* 2970.

**Policy Papers and Reports**

Compassion in World Farming Trust, 'The Welfare of Broiler Chickens in the European Union' (2005).

Council for Agricultural Science and Technology (CAST), 'Global Risks of Infectious Animal Diseases' (2005) 28 CAST Issue Paper.

Food and Agriculture Organization of the United Nations, 'Livestock's Long Shadow: Environmental Issues and Options' (2006).

Food and Agriculture Organization of the United Nations, 'The State of World Fisheries and Aquaculture: Meeting the Sustainable Development Goals' (2018).

Froggart, A, and L Wellesley, 'Meat Analogues: Considerations for the EU' (2019) research paper by Chatham House.

Greene, J L, and S Angadjivand, 'Regulation of Cell-Cultured Meat' (2018) *Congressional Research Service*

Humane Society of the United States, 'An HSUS Report: Human Health Implications of Non-Therapeutic Antibiotic Use in Animal Agriculture' (2009).

Institute of Mechanical Engineers, 'Global Food: Waste Not Want Not' (2013).

Jagow, R B, ed., 'Study of Life Support Systems for Space Missions Exceeding One Year in Duration. Phasa IA. Final Report. Volume I: Analysis of New Concepts' (1967), report prepared for NASA.

PATH, 'Cultured Proteins: An Analysis of the Policy and Regulatory Environment in Selected Geographies' (2019).

*RethinkX* report by C Tubb, and T Seba, 'Rethinking Food and Agriculture 2020-2030: The Second Domestication of Plants and Animals, the Disruption of the Cow, and the Collapse of Industrial Livestock Farming' (2019).

Rorheim, A, *et al.*, 'Cultured Meat: An Ethical Alternative to Industrial Animal Farming' (2016) policy paper by *Sentience Politics*.

United States Government Accountability Office, 'Food Safety: FDA and USDA Could Strengthen Existing Efforts to Prepare for Oversight of Cell-Cultured Meat' (2020) report to the Chairwoman, Subcommittee on Labor, Health and Human Services, Education, and Related Agencies, Committee on Appropriations, House of Representatives.

World Health Organization, *et al.*, 'Report of the WHO/FAO/OIE joint consultation on emerging zoonotic diseases, in collaboration with the Health Council of the Netherlands' (2004).

World Health Organization, *et al.*, 'The Control of Neglected Zoonotic Diseases: From Advocacy to Action' (2014).

**Websites – Chapter 1**

Woodward, Aylin, 'Both the new coronavirus and SARS outbreaks likely started in Chinese 'wet markets.' New photos show what the markets looked like.' *Business Insider* (26 February 2020).

Centers for Disease Control and Prevention, 'Zoonotic Diseases' (14 July 2017).

Garrett, Laurie, 'The Next Pandemic?' *Foreign Affairs* (July/August 2005).

Richburg, Keith B, 'Bird Flu. SARS. China coronavirus. Is history repeating itself?' *Stat* (27 January 2020).

Live Science, '11 (sometimes) deadly diseases that hopped across species' (6 March 2020).

National Health Service, 'Creutzfeldt-Jakob disease (CJD)' (14 June 2018).

Mackenzie, Debora, 'Many more people could still die from mad cow disease in the UK' *New Scientist* (18 January 2017).

# Bibliography

Doucleff, Michaeleen, 'For the Love of Pork: Antibiotic Use on Farms Skyrockets Worldwide' *NPR* (20 March 2015).

Larsen, Janet, 'Meat Consumption in China Now Double That in the United States' *Earth Policy Institute* (24 April 2012).

McKenna, Maryn, 'Farm Animals Are the Next Big Antibiotic Resistance Threat' *Wired* (19 September 2019).

World Health Organization, 'Antimicrobial resistance in the food chain' (November 2017).

Dall, Chris, 'FDA: Antibiotic use in food animals continues to rise' *Center for Infectious Disease Research and Policy* (22 December 2016).

Vegconomist, 'Cell-Based Pioneers Aleph Farms Opens Visitor Centre and Gen-Z Program in Bid to Foster Transparency in Cultured Meat' (4 February 2020).

Everington, Keoni, 'Last serpent shop shutters in Taipei's Snake Alley' *Taiwan News* (21 May 2018).

Carrington, Damian, 'Deadly diseases from wildlife thrive when nature is destroyed, study finds' *The Guardian* (5 August 2020).

Tollefson, Jeff, 'Why deforestations and extinctions make pandemics more likely' *Nature* (7 August 2020).

Poinski, Megan, 'Is coronavirus accelerating the growth of plant-based meat?' *Food Dive* (13 October 2020).

**Websites – Chapter 2**

Good Food Institute, 'Plant-Based Market Overview' (2020).

MarketsandMarkets, 'Plant-based Meat Market by Source (Soy, Wheat, Pea, Quinoa, Oats, Beans, Nuts), Product (Burger Patties, Sausages, Strips & Nuggets, Meatballs), Type (Pork, Beef, Chicken, Fish), Process, and Region - Global Forecast to 2025' (May 2019).

Food and Agriculture Organization of the United Nations, 'Meat and Meat Products' (15 March 2019)

Justia, 'Patents Assigned to Impossible Foods Inc' (23 June 2020).

Chartier, K, and Rabobank, 'The European market for Meat Substitutes: Challenges and Opportunities', presentation from the Plant Protein Conference (2019).

Deloitte, 'Plant-based alternatives: Driving industry M&A' (2019).

The Vegan Society, 'Statistics' (2020).

Smithers, Rebecca, 'Quorn to be the first major brand to introduce carbon labelling' *The Guardian* (9th January 2020).

DiMaio, Tara, 'Is Red Seaweed the Next Big Thing in Plant-Based Protein?' *The Good Food Institute* (4 July 2019).

Watson, Elaine, 'N'ice cream… minus the cows? Smitten teams with Perfect Day to make next-generation vegan ice cream' *FoodNavigator-USA* (8 May 2020).

PR Newswire, 'Infant Formula Market Size to Reach USD 103.75 Billion by 2026' (2 October 2019).

Kaiserman, Beth, 'Plant-based Labeling: Tofurkey's Lawsuit, PBFA Standards', *Nosh* (12 December 2019).

Eagle, Jenny, '"Clean meat" sees rapid growth as start-ups compete to bring first cultured meat product to market' Food Navigator (26 November 2019).

Purdy, Chase, 'The idea for lab-grown market was born in a prisoner-of-war camp' *Quartz* (24 September 2017).

Swartz, Elliot, 'Shared Folder: Cultivated Meat' (2020).

Verzijden, Karin, 'Regulatory pathways for clean meat in the EU and the US - differences & analogies' *Axon Lawyers* (15 March 2019).

Wasley, Andrew, Madlen Davies, Callum Adams, and Josh Robbins, 'Dirty Business: The Livestock Farms Polluting the UK' *The Bureau of Investigative Journalism* (21 August 2017).

Cox, David, 'The planet's prodigious poo problem' *The Guardian* (25 March 2019).

Roser, Max, and Hannah Ritchie, 'Food Supply' *Our World in Data* (2013).

Friedrich, Bruce, 'Dietary change may help us avert future pandemics' *New Scientist* (15 July 2020).

Carrington, Damian, 'Microplastic particles now discoverable in human organs' *The Guardian* (17 August 2020).

Fortune Business Insights, 'Infant Formula Market Size, Share & COVID-19 Impact Analysis, By Type (Infant Milk, Follow-on-Milk, and Others), Distribution Channel (Hypermarkets/ Supermarkets, Pharmacy/Medical Stores, Specialty Stores, and Others), and Regional Forecast, 2020-2027' (August 2020).

Fountain, Henry, 'A Lab-Grown Burger Gets a Taste Test' *The New York Times* (5 August 2013).

**Websites – Chapter 3**

Churchill, Winston, 'Fifty Years Hence' originally published in *Strand Magazine* (December 1931).

Bashi, Zafer, Ryan McCullough, Liane Ong, and Miguel Ramirez, 'Alternative proteins: the race for market share is on' *McKinsey & Company* (16 August 2019).

Kindy, Kimberly, 'More than 200 meat plant workers in the U.S. have died of covid-19. Federal regulators just issued two modest fines." *Washington Post* (13 September 2020).

Good Food Institute, 'Record $824 million invested in alternative protein companies in 2019, $930 million already invested in Q1 2020' (13 May 2020).

Grand View Research, 'Pet Food Market Size Worth $113.08 Billion by 2025' (September 2019).

Grand View Research, 'Pet Food Market Size, Share & Trends Analysis Report by Product (Dry Food, Wet/Canned Food, Nutritious Food, Snacks/Treats, Others), By Application (Dog, Cat, Others).

**Media (Lectures, Films, Podcasts)**

Anthis, Jacy Reese, 'The End of Animal Farming | TEDxUniversityofMississippi' (14 March 2018).

BBC Newsnight, 'Would you eat meat grown in a lab? - BBC Newsnight' (4 April 2018).

*Cowspiracy: The Sustainability Secret*. Directed by Kip Andersen. Netflix, 2014. Film.

Daszak, Peter, 'Peter Daszak at TEDMED 2010' (13 January 2011).

*Earthlings*. Directed by Shaun Monson. Nation Earth, 2005. Film.

*Eating Animals*. Directed by Christopher Dillon Quinn. Big Star Pictures, 2017. Film.

*Food, Inc.* Directed by Robert Kenner. Magnolia Pictures, 2008. Film.

Forgacs, Andras, 'The bio-printing of leather and meat: Andras Forgacs at TEDxMarin 2013' (7 November 2013).

Friedrich, Bruce, 'The next global agricultural revolution' (19 June 2019).

Friedrich, Bruce, 'Meat Without Animals: The Future of Food | TEDxGateway' (12 June 2020).

# Bibliography

Lagally, Christie, 'The Manufacturing Challenges of Plant-Based Meat' (6 October 2020), presentation at the Food Innovation Summit 2020.

*Live and Let Live*. Directed by Marc Pierschel. Syndicado, 2013. Film.

Mutter, Alex, 'Why lab-cultured meat might save the world | TEDxLFHS' (20 May 2020).

*Okja*. Directed by Bong Joon Ho. Netflix, 2017. Film.

Our Changing Climate, 'Are plant-based meats actually sustainable? (Impossible Burger and Beyond Meat)' (8 November 2019).

Petrillo, Erica, 'In vitro meat — the ethics, technology and politics behind it | TEDxUniMannheim' (29 October 2019).

Post, Mark, 'Cultured Meat as a step towards Plant-Based Diets - Dr Mark Post' (26 June 2018).

Post, Mark, 'Cultured beef for food-security and the environment: Mark Post at TEDxMaastricht' (11 May 2014).

Post, Mark, 'Meet the new meat | TEDxHaarlem' (20 June 2013).

Quartz News, 'Is cell-cultured meat ready for the mainstream?' (1 November 2019).

Saragosa, Manuela, BBC Business Daily, 'Wet markets and the coronavirus' *BBC Business Daily* (13 March 2020).

Sekiyama, Kazuhide, 'Changing the world with spider webs: Kazuhide Sekiyama at TEDxTokyo' (12 May 2013).

Shapiro, Paul, 'Clean Meat: The Clean Energy of Food | TEDxSouthLakeTahoe' (3 January 2018).

Shirazi, Alex, *Cultured Meat and Future Food Podcast*.

Specht, Liz, 'Liz Specht on The Future of Food, Alternative Meats, and Many Materials - What's Now: San Francisco' (21 February 2020).

'The New Agrarian Revolution: Bruce Friedrich, Jim Mellon, and Michael Corcoran', The Longevity Forum (12 November 2020)

*The Game Changers*. Directed by Louie Psyhoyos. Refuel Productions, 2018. Film.

Wall Street Journal, 'Tasting the World's First Test-Tube Steak' (11 December 2018).

## Useful Organisations

California Plant Based Alliance**www.cpba.org**

Cultivate **www.cultivate-uk.org**

Elliot Swartz **http://elliotswartz.com/**

Food and Agriculture Organisation of the UN **www.fao.org/home/en/**

Food Navigator **www.foodnavigator.com**

Good Food Institute **www.gfi.org**

Green Queen **https://www.greenqueen.com.hk/**

New Harvest **www.new-harvest.org**

PETA **www.peta.org**

Plant Based News **plantbasednews.org**

The Humane Society of the US **www.humanesociety.org**

The Vegan Society **www.vegansociety.com**

The Vegetarian Society **vegsoc.org**

World Health Organisation **www.who.int**

World Wildlife Fund **www.wwf.org.uk**

# OTHER BOOKS BY JIM MELLON

## JUVENESCENCE
### INVESTING IN THE AGE OF LONGEVITY (2017)

**By Jim Mellon & Al Chalabi**

Who wouldn't want an ultra-long and healthy life? Well, scientific advances will soon allow just that. Based on dozens on interviews and extensive travels across the USA and Europe, Jim and Al forecast that average life expectancy in the developed world will rise to 110-120 within two decades – and much higher after that. The old life paradigm of born, learn, earn, retire and expire is about to be radically changed. The entirety of our lives will be upended; we will learn continuously, start families later, enjoy multiple careers, and have more time for leisure and self-development. Jim and Al use their deep understanding of the underlying science to alert investors to ways in which we can prosper in this new era of longevity, identifying the most exciting investment opportunities that will hopefully provide readers with ultra-long-lived portfolios to accompany their ultra-long lives! Juvenescence isn't just a book or phenomenon, it's about to be a fact.

## AVAILABLE TO BUY AT HARRIMAN HOUSE AND ON AMAZON

# FAST FORWARD
## THE TECHNOLOGIES & COMPANIES SHAPING OUR FUTURE (2014)

### By Jim Mellon & Al Chalabi

As the pace of technological progress intensifies, agile businesses and entrepreneurs are discovering new applications that take advantage of faster and cheaper computer processing power. The status quo is being upended across all industries, and in some cases totally new industries are being created. Fast Forward is a book that filters this chaotic landscape and identifies the areas that will have the greatest impact on our lives, highlighting investment opportunities along the way. These disruptive technologies span the fields of robotics, transportation, the changing internet, life sciences, 3D printing and energy, all of which are experiencing tremendous growth.

## AVAILABLE TO BUY ON AMAZON

# CRACKING THE CODE
## UNDERSTAND AND PROFIT FROM THE BIOTECH REVOLUTION THAT WILL TRANSFORM OUR LIVES AND GENERATE FORTUNES (2012)

### By Jim Mellon & Al Chalabi

Within most people's lifetimes, the developments in the biotechnology sector will allow us to live increasingly long and healthy lives, as well as provide us with technological innovations that will transform the way we live. But these innovations offer more than just hope for a better life, they offer hope for better returns too. Financial returns of incredible magnitude await savvy investors and businesspeople who can see the massive changes on the horizon. This book details these fast-moving trends and innovations and offers extensive advice on how to profit from them in business and investing.

## AVAILABLE TO BUY ON AMAZON

# WAKE UP!
## SURVIVE AND PROSPER IN THE COMING
## ECONOMIC TURMOIL (2005)

By Jim Mellon & Al Chalabi

In their first book together in 2005, Jim and Al cemented their reputation as economic forecasters by warning of a coming financial crisis provoked by a housing crisis that was fuelled by debt and advising readers to be prepared by adopting a defensive position, such as accumulating gold. Time has vindicated their other predictions too, from a rise in global terrorism, to an ageing Western population, to a restructuring of the global balance of power as a result of the relentless Chinese boom. This is not just a cyclical change, it is far more radical and far-reaching than anything experienced in living memory. Worried? You should be.

## AVAILABLE TO BUY ON AMAZON

# INDEX